BOHEMIAN

Lawrence Wells
BOHEMIAN
PAINTINGS 2011–2014

Introductory Essays
by
Lisa Howorth
and
Branislava Kuburović

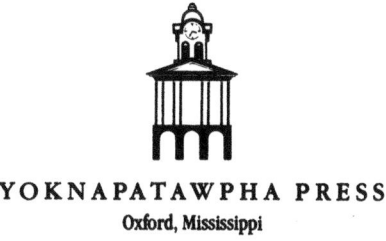

YOKNAPATAWPHA PRESS
Oxford, Mississippi

Lawrence Wells:

Bohemian

Copyright © 2015 Lawrence Wells

Text © 2015 Lisa Howorth, Branislava Kuburović,

Lawrence Wells

Cover Art: Lawrence Wells
Graphic Design: Ken Nash

ISBN-978-0-916242-78-7

Yoknapatawpha Press
P.O. Box 248, Oxford, MS 38655
Email: faulkner@watervalley.net
wells@volny.cz

Printed in the USA

CONTENTS

Lisa Howorth lives in Oxford, Mississippi, where she is a writer and taught art history at the University of Mississippi. Her novel, Flying Shoes, was published in 2014 by Bloomsbury.

LAWRENCE WELLS

by **Lisa Howorth**

I AM LUCKY enough to own two works by Lawrence Wells. I see them every day; they are part of my housescape. Unlike many of the artifacts that I "see" in my home, I rarely fail to notice Wells' paintings—that is to say, they register with me, and cause me to wonder. There's the large self portrait in pastels—it's Lawrence, a guy I have known since he was a kid. The portrait, from 1990, is very disturbing; rich with dissonant color and sexual ambiguity but also an honest, primal innocence. Here is the artist posed pensively with a piece of chalk, poised to make his mark: Who am I? Who do I want the viewer to think I am? Stylistically it is nothing like Rembrandt, who created close to one hundred self-portraits, but plainly the influence is there—the obsessive introspection, the shape-shifting, and maybe the trickery.

The other piece I own is a very small, unframed oil on canvas of a factory leaning threateningly, spewing nastiness and flames—obviously a comment on industry vs nature—a warning? It is so pleasingly composed and so beautiful, though, that I wonder about it, and the artist's intention here, too. I think that this is the real hallmark of Wells' work, beyond his prevalent themes—it asks more questions than it answers, and it challenges in not always pleasing or comfortable ways. This is the heavy lifting that meaningful, successful art does, and that Wells has accomplished.

Lawrence Wells was born in Tuscaloosa, Alabama in 1965, and bounced around as a child between parents in Kentucky and Oxford, Mississippi, and summer school at Phillips Academy in Andover, Massachusetts. Eventually he landed at Indiana University, where he planned to study computer science. This rootlessness set the pattern for a vagabond life, not just logistically, but philosophically. He was always grubbing around, searching for all the usual things young people search for and, after deciding that art was his true vocation, also seeking the intellectual and aesthetic themes and impulses that would excite him, for an original way to express them, and for his place in the art world. Restless, fueled by testosterone, rebelliousness, and a love of music, he began studying painting at the University of Mississippi with Jere Allen in 1989, receiving an MFA in 1992. He also assisted Ke Francis in his studio outside Tupelo, and worked at legendary hotspots—the Hoka Theater and Proud Larry's—becoming a player in the exploding boho scene in Oxford. Wells says that this heady environment "was one of community and support" for artists, musicians and writers, although his enthusiastic participation in all that was going on distracted him. He struggled academically, perhaps the result of escapades like disappearing on tour with The Hilltops, an Oxford band that included his friends Cary Hudson and Laurie Stirratt, later of Blue Mountain, and John Stirratt of Wilco.

Laurie Stirratt remembers: "It was hard to miss Lawrence in Oxford, and it was fun to have a true eccentric in our midst. He was a great artist and dancer! He created two Hilltops album covers that are my favorites. I still follow his work on social media and love how he's grown as an artist since the 80s."

Wells' time at Ole Miss was also when he became deeply interested in the history of art, writing, as I've heard, intense and exuberant papers on images of industry and peasantry in the paintings of Millet, Emil Nolde and Primitivism, on the Frankfurt School and Marcuse. Strongly drawn to political theories and rebellion and how some of these ideas played out in the history of Mississippi, Wells was, as he says, "pushing buttons" and creating in-your-face work that he recalls as "somewhat grotesque" and caused his stepmother, Dean Faulkner Wells, to quip that it made her "stomach churn." This is the Lawrence I remember most vividly: aggressive, altered, sometimes annoying, always intriguing, way smart, often charming, dead serious about his art, and insistent on saying what he thought needed to be said. A flammable and excitable young man.

Wells' ongoing preoccupation with social and political issues and his desire to be on the edge, and in the center of happening creative scenes led him to Prague in 1992, after the revolution of 1989. As he describes it, "There was a whole first wave of Americans there for an adventure. We were seizing the reins of history. Or at least drinking a lot of great beer. I taught English, I read at poetry readings, I lived with old Czech people I could barely communicate with. I had a studio with an older painter, Přemysl Janíček. I painted and drew about Czechs and rock stars and gypsies and beer. I wrote a story, 'Godzilla vs Stalin,' which should have been turned into animation for MTV. It was later included in an anthology of expat writing: The Return of Kral Majales."

Following this first foray to Prague, Wells briefly settled in New Orleans where he worked as a video store clerk—perhaps a vocation quintessentially associated with slackerness. But the job allowed him to watch a huge number of iconic foreign films, and this sparked an interest in the technical possibilities of cinema— art as a narrative of serial images. At the same time he was drawn to Japanese sumi-e drawings and he began to draw in ink. He had a few New Orleans shows, but perhaps the Big Easy was a little too that, and he decamped for the bigger, badder world of Brooklyn. There he bought a 16mm camera, took film classes, began making experimental films, and "lost a lot of time chasing after a number of women."

After going broke, he worked as a web designer, his facility with technology being another facet of his brilliance, though one he finds untrustworthy. After four years, Wells began to feel too small and anonymous in New York and missed the romanticism of being an expat; likening his infatuation with Czechoslovakia to that of Paul Bowles' with Morocco: "The rushing to the edge of the world." Wells returned to Prague in 2001.

It was this homecoming to the Czech Republic that seems to have brought Wells' personal life, artistic ideals, and stylistic achievements to maturity. In 2006 at the age of 40, he married his wife, Magda, and in 2007 their son, Dominik, was born. There is a focus in his work from these years, and more recently—bolder imagery, a subtler delicacy in style, concentration on specific themes that compel him, a confidence in what actually is important, and a paring-down of what may have been random, youthful kvetching. Maybe there is a little bemused sadness and resignation as well—a time to put away childish things and be a father and mate. The work does feature what might be considered, at a superficial glance, kids' stuff: monkeys, spacemen, Indians, skulls and roses, big ships, and computer screens. But the monkeys of 2012 are nightmarish and menacing—do some actually resemble Lawrence? "We are like monkeys staring at the flame in the darkness of our souls." The spacemen of 2011–2013 are astronauts, who, like their partners in American pop stereotypes, the Plains Indians, stand forlorn, forgotten, obsolete—Major Tom and Tonto. The skulls and roses memento mori are suggestive of human extinction, the shortness of life, and the shallow way we often confuse prettiness with beauty in art. 2013's big ships turn out to be the ghostly, doomed Titanic, one of the most grandiose technological follies in history, brought down by nature. 2014's computer screens and TVs are reduced to simple squares—idiot boxes—with primitively rendered automatons stiffly trying to extract something meaningful or true from them. This most recent work is hardly for kids. Garish, gloomy, sexual, prophetic, darkly amusing and sardonic—adults only.

It has been so fascinating to watch Lawrence Wells all these years. Not only is he singular in having known what he wanted to do at an early age and remained committed, he has not compromised his philosophy and artistic values, to which this book is testament. I think there will always be something of excitable youth in Wells and his work no matter how old he is—the question-asker, the jokester, the finger-pointer, the self-mocker, the bullshit-shoveler, the Mephistophelian dancer. For all this he deserves a hearty toast—Na zdraví!

Branislava Kuburović was born in Prijepolje, former Yugoslavia. She studied theatre directing at the Belgrade Academy of Dramatic Arts before emigrating and resettling in Prague in the mid-1990s. She is a writer and researcher in the interdisciplinary fields of performance and visual culture, has a PhD from the University of Roehampton in London, and has published in both academic context and in a number of artist's books. She taught as visiting lecturer at several higher education institutions in the UK including Goldsmiths College and Chelsea School of Art. She currently works and teaches at the School of Art and Design at Prague College.

A BOHEMIAN ARTIST

by Branislava Kuburović

Who is Bohemian?

THE PLAYFUL AMBIGUITY of the title of this book promises a portrait of the artist as unconventional, a free spirit defying social convention in pursuit of his art, at the same time as locating him geographically in the western part of the Czech Republic with its capital Prague, a city loaded with equally romantic connotations. Lawrence Wells has indeed spent a good portion of his active time as a painter in Prague, having first arrived here as part of a wave of thousands of young Americans who came to live in the city in the early 1990s, and returning to it once again in the early 2000s. He has now been residing in Prague for over 13 years, has a young family here and, as the book's title suggests, already belongs in the city, has become Bohemian himself.

Of course the reality of both life and art making is much more complicated than that. The non-conformist lifestyles of the 19th and early 20th centuries' bohemians exemplified by artists active at the time in Paris, London or Berlin, and the many different guises and transformations of global mass youth subcultures since the 1960s, have in the early 21st century lost a great deal of their romantic appeal and revolutionary connotations. The idea of an artistic lifestyle as poverty by choice has also long become obsolete, and has most recently given way to the notion of precarious labour, as artists join an increasingly large proportion of workers losing job security and becoming pauperised once again after the relative security of the post-WWII years in most of the developed parts of the world across the East-West divide.

Being Bohemian, belonging in Bohemia, is equally complex in this relatively small European country where belonging is measured in generations and has since the founding of independent Czechoslovakia in 1918, and even more so after the dissolution of the country into the Czech Republic and Slovakia at the end of 1992, been defined primarily through language and through being part of the Czech nation. As Lawrence Wells has himself noted in an interview, as a foreigner he will always be defined by his nationality, and is in effect and paradoxically somehow more American here than he would ever be in the US, and that fact is unlikely to change any time soon.

Americana

Wells' work presented in this book, which brings together paintings created in a relatively short period between 2011 and 2014, starts exactly with such reckonings. Ape and Essence, the earliest series in the book, gathers together several of the most archetypal American themes and places them together in variants of strange and disturbing gatherings: the Apollo 11 Moon landing, the still unrepentant stance towards the deaths and segregation of Native Americans, and the theory of evolution that is even now still being officially challenged in some of the deeply conservative US states.

Wells does not explain or create any objective, historical or openly political stance towards these themes, and they are indeed never presented in quite such definite terms in the work. Astronauts, Indians, skeletons, monkeys, and the Moon, all of them portrayed in these paintings, are never placed in any easily recognisable context. Instead, they became both painful and playful variations on the question of identity, the limit cases of what it means to be American for someone who is observing both himself and his country from a distance, and whose identity has been challenged by the move to a place which does not share either his language or his most intimate sense of history and belonging.

It is also interesting to note that the same figures of monkeys, astronauts, Indians, and the moon, sometimes joined by a nude female figure, become proxies for the family, that the artist's questioning of what it means to have a family in this situation, the representations of key familial relations, and even the simplest every day, joyful scenes of family life, are continually re-imagined through these same archetypes.

Still Lifes

The background and context of scenes depicted in the Ape and Essence series have gradually moved from what appear like surfaces of a planet, bare and Moon-like itself, to the flat delimited spaces of table tops, the traditional stages for still life painting. These more recent works return repeatedly to depictions of inanimate objects, of a skull, of candles (already present in the Ape and Essence series as certain markers of the passage of time, but also as phallic symbols, or rather as markers of a certain vanitas of virility), and of the reflective surfaces of old computer monitors and spacesuit helmets – the latter two perhaps as variants of hourglasses for the age of space exploration and accelerated pace of advanced technological innovation.

Through this choice of objects of memento mori, the works mark a move from an idiosyncratic personal form of Americana to openly citing and engaging the tradition of still life as one of the principle independent painting genres of a recognisably (Western) European painting tradition. Despite of, and perhaps especially in the light of Wells' references to the crowning achievements of modern technological civilisation in the repertoire of objects, these works still function as allegories of mortality. Indeed, it is only with the inclusion of such contemporary objects that the seemingly traditional symbolic objects of still life painting no longer function simply as memento mori, as reminders of death as the great leveller of all human achievement, but literally as nature morte, as intimations of the possible death of nature, a notion that no longer functions simply as a metaphor in our time with the looming possibility of a global ecological catastrophe.

And yet the artist's perspective is never unambiguously pessimistic. Still lifes, as the artist has concluded, "can contain the whole world", and indeed what allows these works to not be seen simply as contemporary citations of a traditional painterly genre or an expression of desperation are exactly other "stuffs" of the world that bring forth inconsistencies, that are incongruous additions to the repertoire and logic of still life painting.

(Bona) Naturalia

Objects of memento mori are most often joined by another admittedly traditional still life object, a flower or flowers, most often a single cut rose kept well watered in a glass vase which in the artist's words symbolises "the (dying) hope for the future", but also by potted plants that Wells has written about as regional cultures, as self-contained and incommunicable scenes divided up and sustained on absurdly limited and hopelessly separate artificially created "turfs" which make it especially difficult to survive and communicate for those of us who are foreigners, for immigrants who become in Wells' words "like uprooted plants, trying to send a tap root down to find new water. The wind blows us around like dust." But potted plants feel just as much like an homage to the artist's adoptive country and are well known to anyone who has lived in the Czech Republic for any amount of time. They are an ubiquitous decoration in all Czech socialist public institution interiors and can still be seen today, perhaps as remnants and symbols of specifically female labour inside the labyrinths of public institutions which still often employ a predominantly female workforce.

The symbolic presence of nature as a female, as a nude, as a plant, a flower, is another consistent element throughout the series of works presented in the book. There is no landscape present in these works, their exteriors are always sparse, abstract, and brightly and dramatically coloured, and all of the fecundity of nature contained and mostly moved into an interior, where it complicates and animates the space either as ghost-like outlines of naked female bodies, blooming roses, or lush beautiful plants, the latter two always kept in pots and vases.

(Self-)Portraits

Whereas ghostly female outlines mostly remain in the background of the more recent still lifes, in the Cultural Event series the tabletops with man-made and natural objects are literally invaded by miniature human beings,, a childish and child-like remnant of a certain promise of revolutionary communal spirit and the only overt reflection on art as a social process alongside several images of a "Rock Band" in the Imaginary Friends series, which speaks more of friendship than of art. Monkeys are another striking and incongruous addition. Menacing at times, gentle and curious at others, they always stare directly at the viewer and disturb yet another premise of still life painting in which animals are by definition usually depicted as food and thus as already dead. These monkeys are very much alive, animate and animated, their gaze communicating clear and unbridled emotion, unlike anything we can sense in the portraits of the majority of the people depicted in Wells' work.

Even the gazes of people portrayed in the Imaginary Friends series, itself a deeply emotional and careful meditation on the role of friendship and memory, escape us. As the artist writes, the faces of these imaginary friends suggest a back story or unseen events, yet their emotional world remains unavailable even as they look right at us, and we can only sense its intensity from the fine details of the lines, and the expressive yet delicate palette of these works.

The presence of the monkeys is inexplicable and remains unexplained, like that of most of the strongest elements in the work. It is indeed the puzzling aspect of their presence, above and beyond the simple human-ape dichotomy, that grant these beautiful animals a strong effect. Rather than some clear purpose, it is the insistence with which they return in painting after painting that begins to intrigue us. Like the faceless astronauts hidden behind the dark reflective surfaces of their helmets, and the uncomfortable presence of the vulnerable, almost naked bodies of the Native Americans with their simple loincloths and headdresses, often coupled with skeletons and in certain works interchangeable with the astronauts, these portraits of monkeys may be the most direct expression of the artist's own emotions and of the affective force of his own status as a foreigner, of one no longer fitting that once familiar face that could constitute any simple self-portrait.

Ghosts

Ghosts is the title of one of the most recent series of Wells' works, and the transition from female nudes to ghostly outlines of naked bodies of either a single one or a group of five women is another intriguing aspect of his paintings. In the new series, these distinctly feminine, busty shapes are coupled with another kind of ghost, the ghost in the machine in the form of old CRT monitors, as well as the by now familiar skull, potted plants and glass vases with always a single rose in bloom. Social theorist Avery Gordon writes in her Ghostly Matters that "the ghost always registers the actual 'degraded present' [...] in which we are inextricably and historically entangled and the longing for the arrival of a future, entangled certainly, but ripe in the plenitude of non-sacrificial freedoms and exuberant unforeseen pleasures. The ghost registers and it incites [...]". [1]

The presence of these ghosts of the feminine, and the lush, rich colours of these works, embody such exuberance and promise in which the dualism of the mind and the body, exemplified by the monitors and the notion of the ghost in the machine, is dissolved through the sheer power and plenitude of colours and the inciting presence of the feminine. In the best of these works, the outlines of bodies and objects are no longer clearly delineated, their edges have softened and become almost transparent, and the "stupid" machine which now occupies a central position in our daily lives and has earned itself the main role in an entire cycle of Wells' works entitled Stupid Computer, shows itself for what it really is, as (still) but one of the many elements that constitute our shared existence.

Wells has spoken of these works in terms of a certain "retro nostalgia," but once again, it is interesting that for example in the Greek language the notion of nostalghía does not foreclose the past in the way that nostalgia is commonly understood among English-speakers; nostalghía "evokes the transformative impact of the past as unreconciled historical experience. [... It] speaks to the sensory reception of history. [Nostalghía is] the desire or longing with burning pain to journey. It also evokes the sensory dimension of memory in exile and estrangement [...]". [2]

1   Avery F. Gordon, Ghostly Matters: Haunting and the Sociological Imagination, Minneapolis: University of Minnesota Press, 1997, p. 207.
2   C Nadia Seremetakis, in: Idem (ed.), The Senses Still: Memory and Perception as Material Culture

In light of such a living, active notion of nostalgia, and especially considering the explicit link that the notion has to travel and to exile, the expressive, sensuous palette and haunting content of these works can be argued to embody just such a transformative potential of engaging with the ghosts of our past, with both technology and material objects that constitute our everyday existence, and with our unstable and always shifting identities.

The End

It is quite telling that the series of works titled "The End" is not the final cycle in this book. The cycle indeed does not conclude anything but rather marks another transition and points out the seasonal nature of the artist's work. Czech winters tend to be long and grey and the artist sees these works as meditations on travel and emigration, and on a looming disaster of technical civilization embodied by the association with the Titanic of the large ships that appear on the horizon and form the background of most of these works. These ships are just as much a vision of an escape route at a time when one often feels trapped in unending cycles of grey in Prague, and when its extreme distance from the sea is experienced most acutely.

These works also come closest to landscape painting of any of the works in the book, especially in the few images where instead of still lifes the foreground of the painting becomes filled with wild flowers that obviously belong to an exterior and playfully fuse with the sea and the ships in their background, promising a change of season and a happier mood that comes with spring.

This acknowledgement of painters' dependence on light, even if not necessarily a conscious choice, comes across quite strongly in Wells' work, in which colours play such a major role. The representational and symbolic nature of most of his work sometimes distracts the viewer from that fact, but it is ultimately their complex, bold palettes and increasingly physical presence of extremely thick layers of paint that communicate most strongly their not-necessarily clearly defined meanings, and tell an intimate story of persistent, unfolding cycles of life, and of our human emotion that dramatically colours them.

---

in Modernity, Chicago: The University of Chicago Press, 1996 (Boulder, Westview Press, 1994), p. 4.

A Minor Art Practice

In their short but highly influential book entitled Kafka: Towards a Minor Literature (1975), Gilles Deleuze and Félix Guattari introduce the concept of "minority" and "becoming-minor," not as definitions of any stable identities that may be small in number but are inevitably linked to a majority culture, but as forms of resistance to that very unification implicated in the logic of prevalence in our majoritarian cultures and societies, regardless of whether they are defined as state- or business-oriented.

Deleuze and Guattari develop their concept tracing the highly particular quality of Kafka's language, that is, a specific, "impoverished" form of German developing outside the mainstream of the German culture at the time, mixed with Czech influences and with his complex relation to his Jewish identity. This "estranged" relationship to language foregrounds its asignifying aspects, its intensities, it cannot do otherwise but differ and question and is as such intrinsically political, as well as transformational. Such incongruity is more readily understood when it comes to language, whereas we somehow understand vision to be more direct, and thus more universal. But the concept of a "minor art practice", developed among others by Simon O'Sullivan, an artist and scholar teaching at Goldsmiths in London, has been highly useful to me in trying to understand and experience the idiosyncratic, highly emotional, sometimes indecipherable, almost mute yet somehow still extremely raw and open, expressive visual language of these most recent works by Lawrence Wells. This is a minor art practice both in the actual solitude in which the artist is forced to work and develop as a foreigner in a relatively small and extremely self-contained culture, but more interestingly also exactly in this sense of the minor as intrinsically political and transformational, as an active resistance and an ethical position in relation both to prevalent forces in the creation of art and in society.

APE AND ESSENCE

The belief in superiority based on differences in technologies between the modern West and so-called "primitive" tribal peoples is a cultural construct. Many people find a satisfaction in believing that they are somehow better than other groups, but xenophobia is ultimately built on hate and fear of difference. No matter what, we all inhabit the Earth together. If the great Enlightenment project has led to genocide and environmental/social collapse, then one has to question notions of progress and man's feelings of superiority, especially over his fellow man. Technology is tied to righteous self-belief, and science creates fictions that reveal our desires and fears. We are living at a moment when these fictions are becoming exhausted, the world itself is tired

These paintings play with American symbols, the Native American and the Astronaut as an alpha and omega of the American experience. American empire is built on the foundations of the genocide of the native peoples, and this colonialist oppression is a keystone in the development of our modern technological world. The trip to the Moon reveals the escapist fantasy at the heart of the American dream. Science fiction is replete with masculinist fantasies of dominating space. But we are still nothing more than apes with shiny devices, apes in rockets on imaginary journeys to distant stars. We arose from monkeys and walked upright to dominate our planet. Yet even the astronauts are endangered today. Notions of space travel become foolish in our era of resource depletion. The irony is that the monkeys themselves still understand the world better than we do. They are arboreal, they live in the trees, they sleep beneath the moon. What other sciences and fictions could they develop?

"But man, proud man,
Drest in a little brief authority,
Most ignorant of what he's most assured,
His glassy essence, like an angry ape,
Plays such fantastic tricks before high heaven
As make the angels weep ..."

William Shakespeare
Measure for Measure
Act II, Scene 2

Friends, 2011
acrylic on paper,
100 x 70 cm (39" x 27 1/2")

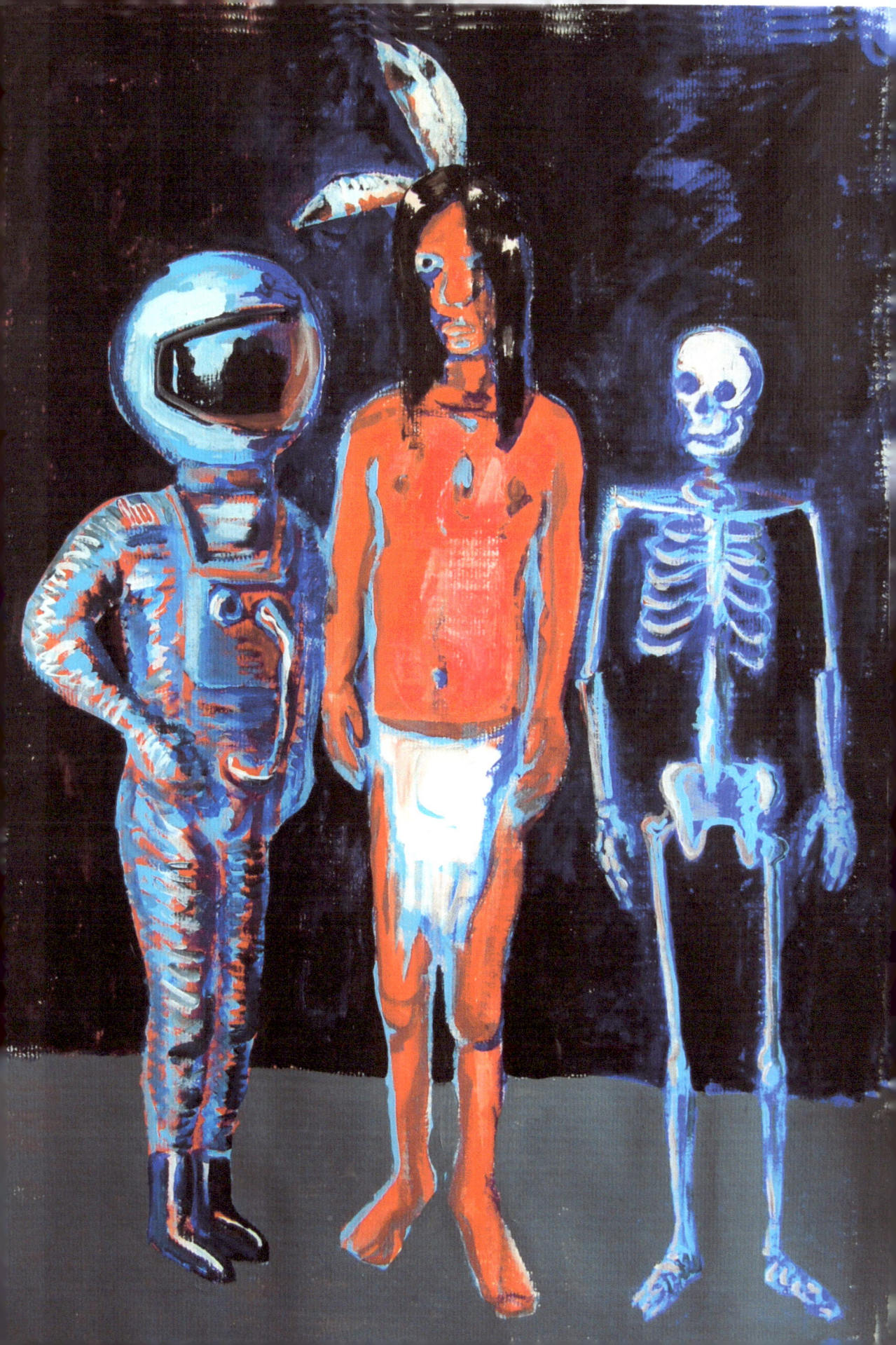

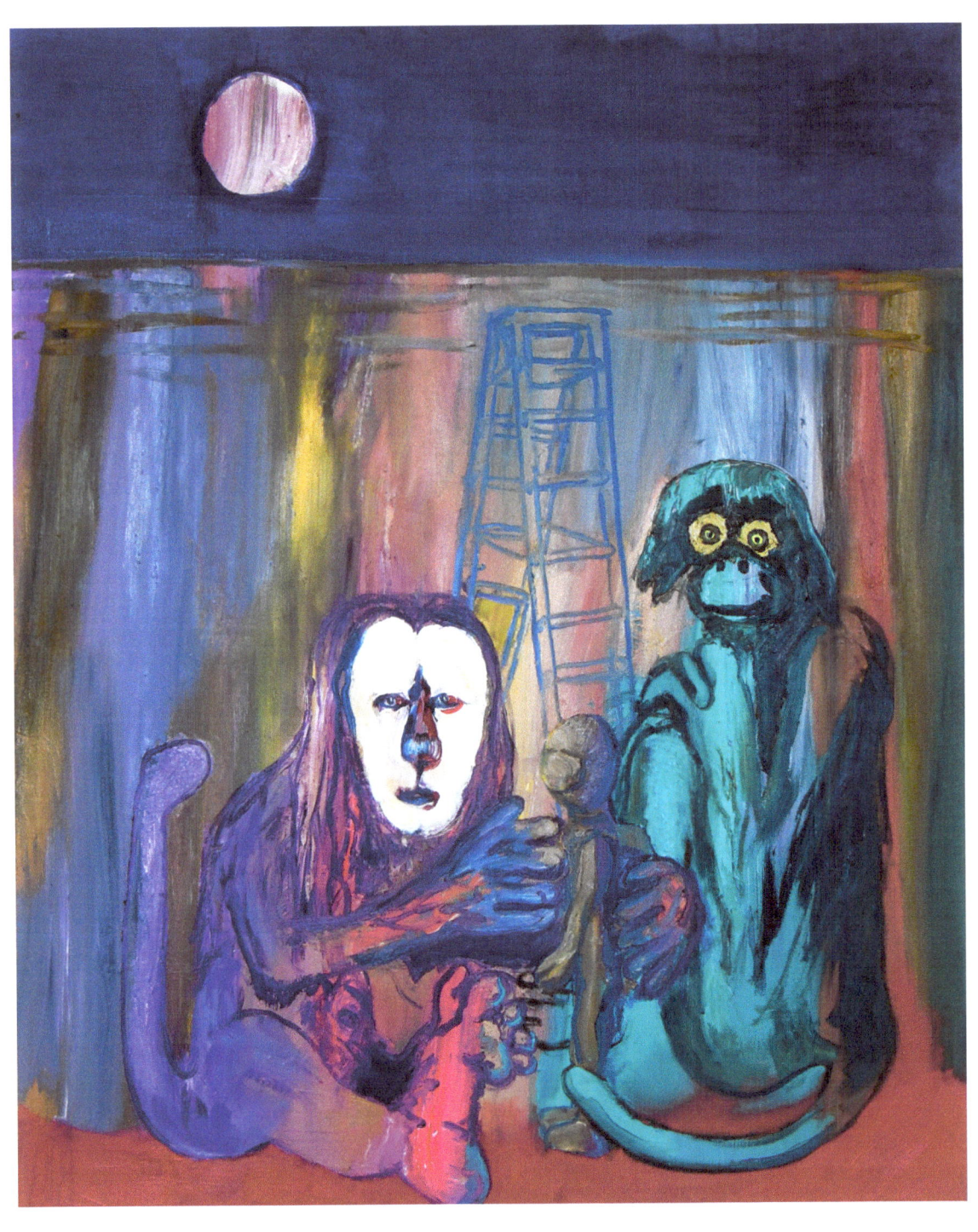

Moon, Monkeys, Ladder, 2012
oil on canvas, 120 x 100 cm (47" x 39")

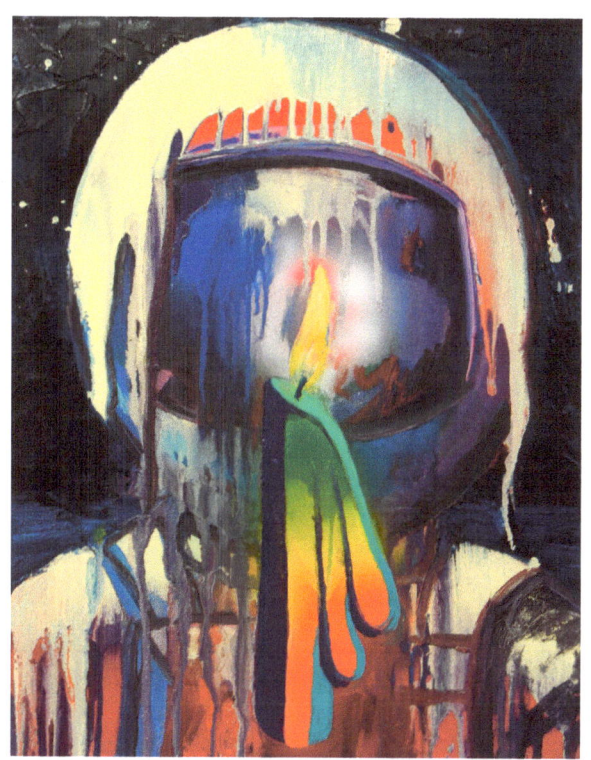

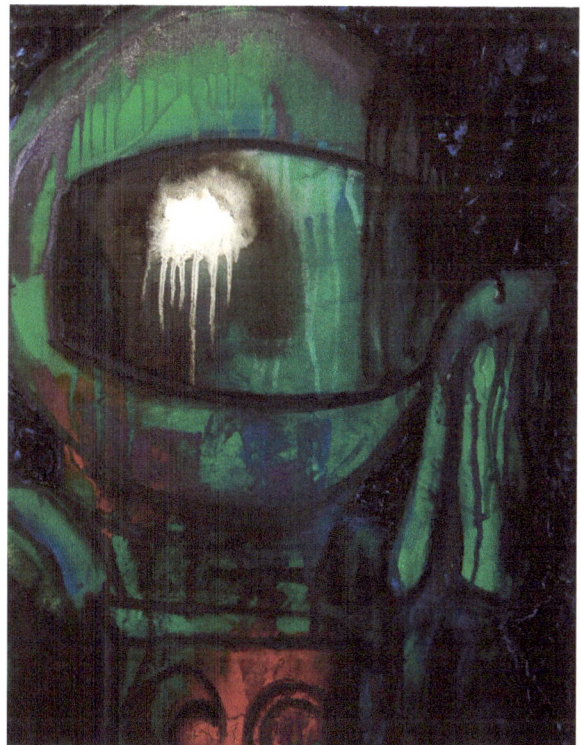

Astronaut and Candle I, 2011
oil on canvas, 60 x 45 cm (23 ½" x 18")

Astronaut and Candle II, 2011
oil on canvas, 60 x 45 cm (23 ½" x 18")

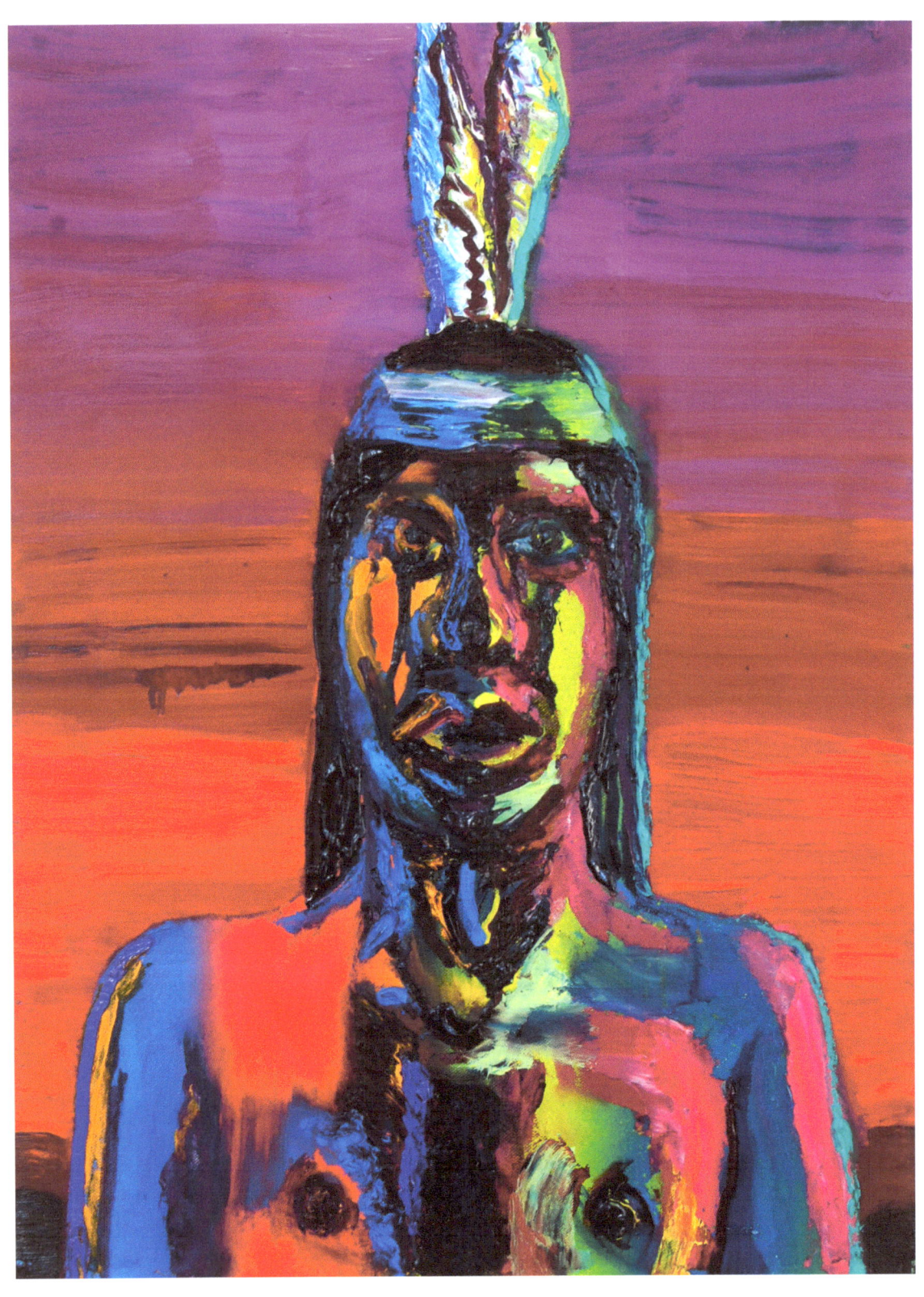

Indian, 2012
oil on canvas, 65 x 45 cm (25 ½" x 18")

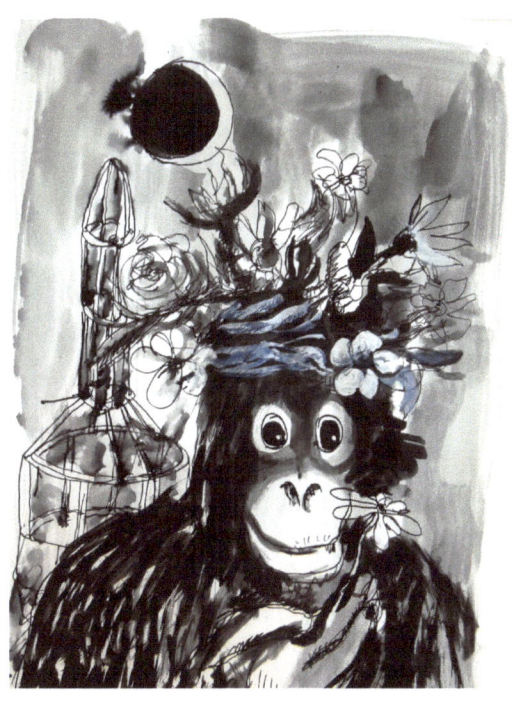

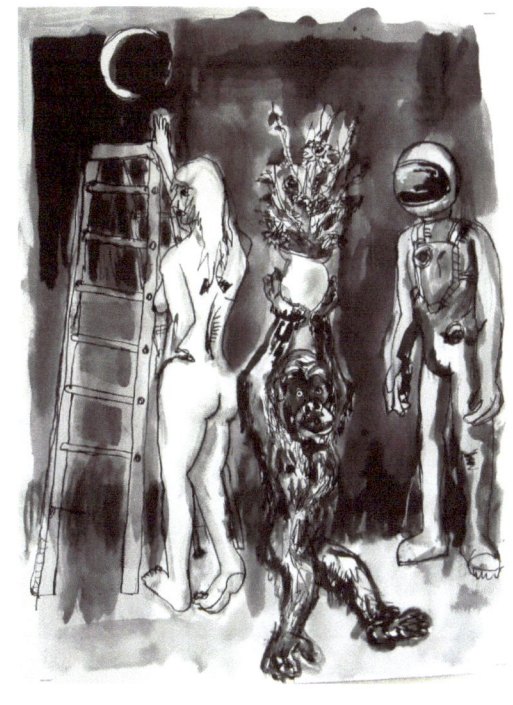

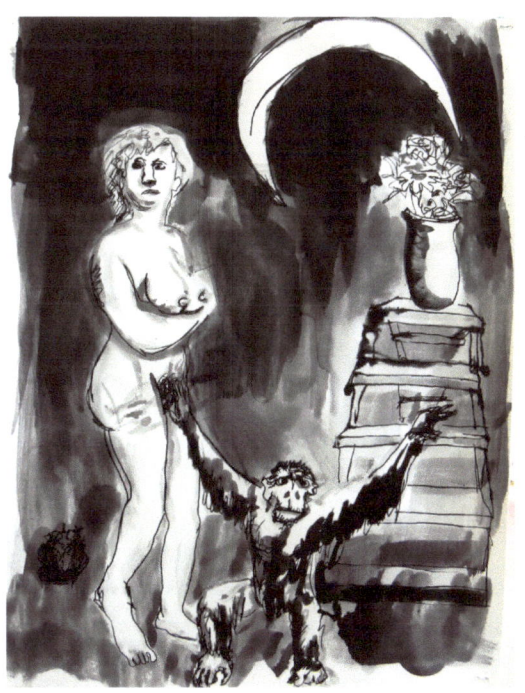

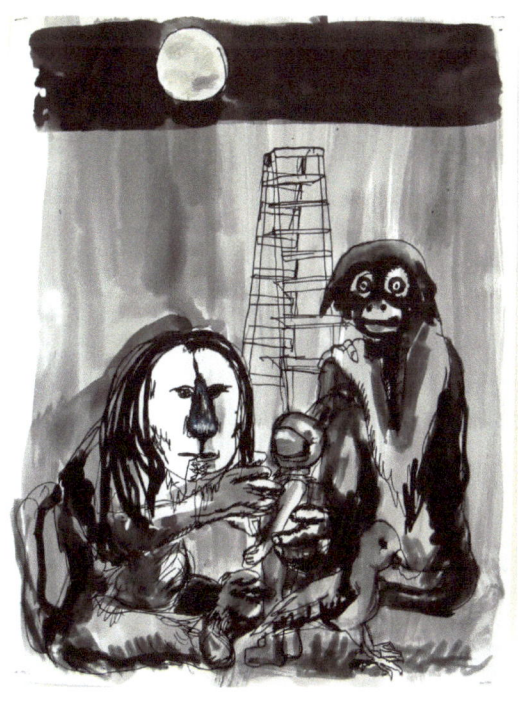

Moon Monkey IV (Orangutan and Flowers),
pen and ink, 65 x 50 cm (25 ½" x 19 ½")

Moon, Monkey, Woman and Ladder, 2012
pen and ink, 65 x 50 cm (25 ½" x 19 ½")

Nude, Ladder, Chimp and Astronaut, 2012
pen and ink, 65 x 50 cm (25 ½" x 19 ½")

Moon, Monkeys, Ladder, 2012
pen and ink, 65 x 50 cm (25 ½" x 19 ½")

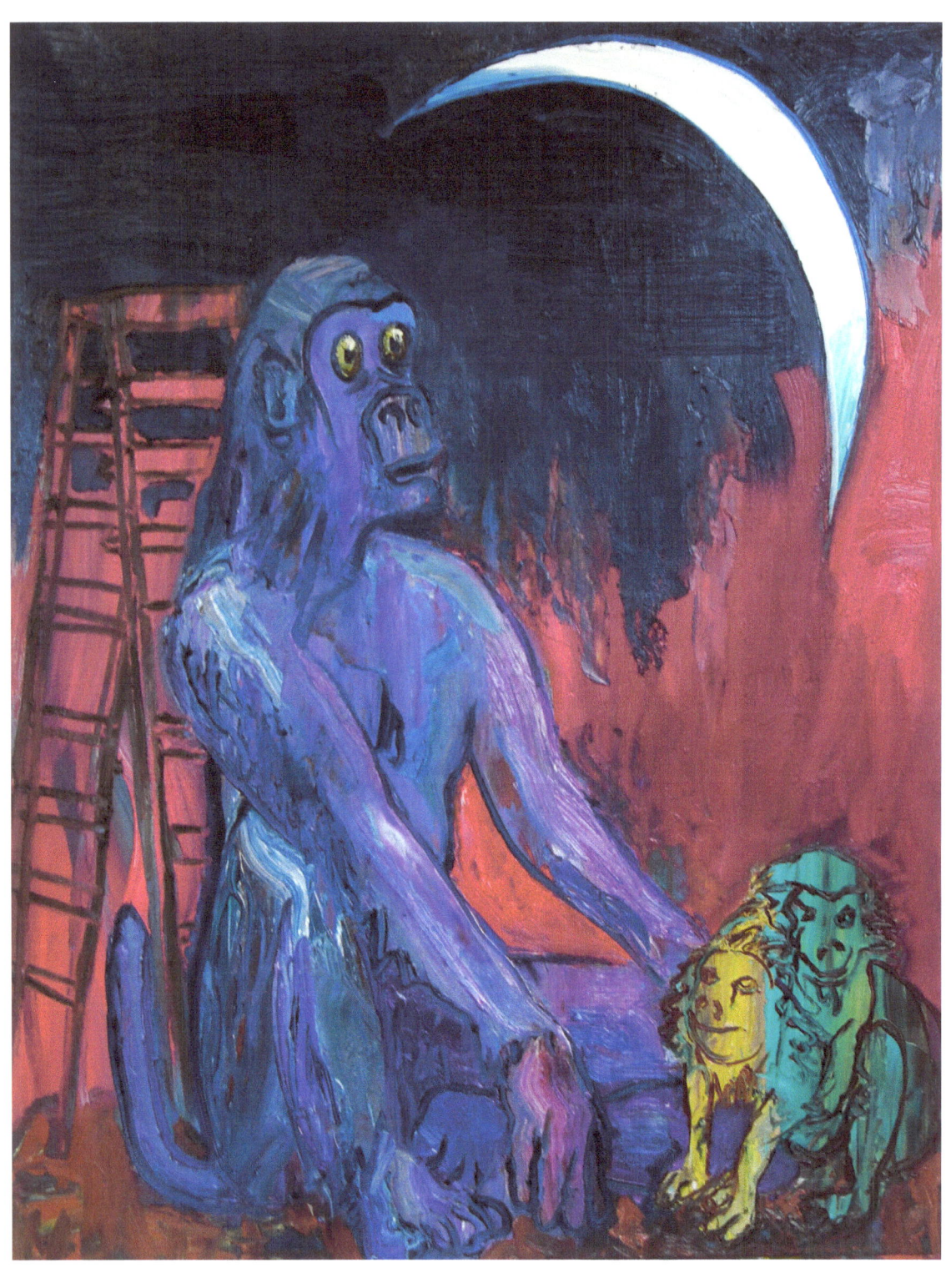

The Moon Came Down, 2012
oil on canvas, 80 x 65 cm (31 ½" x 25 ½")

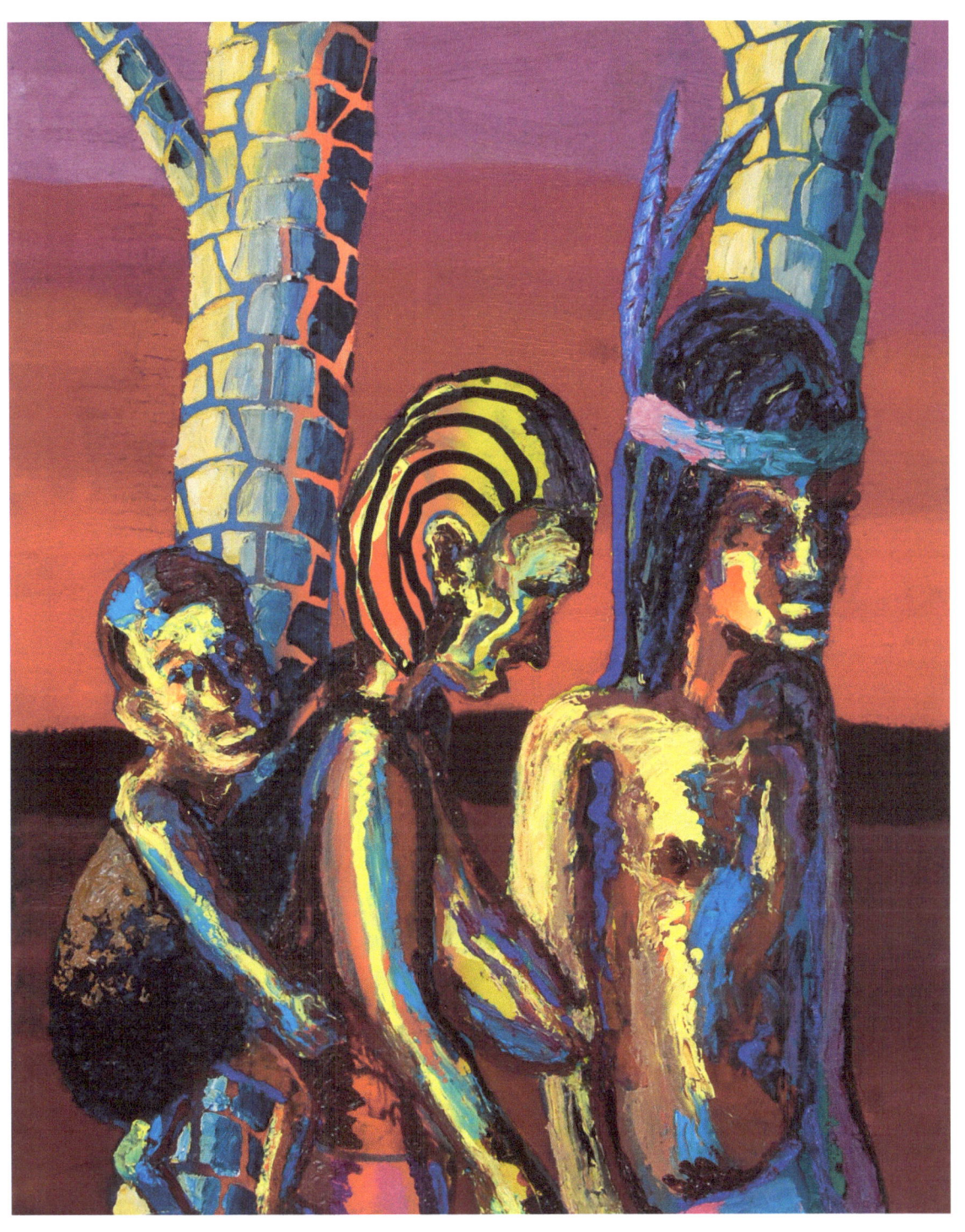

Family, 2012
oil on canvas, 80 x 65 cm (31 ½" x 25 ½")

9

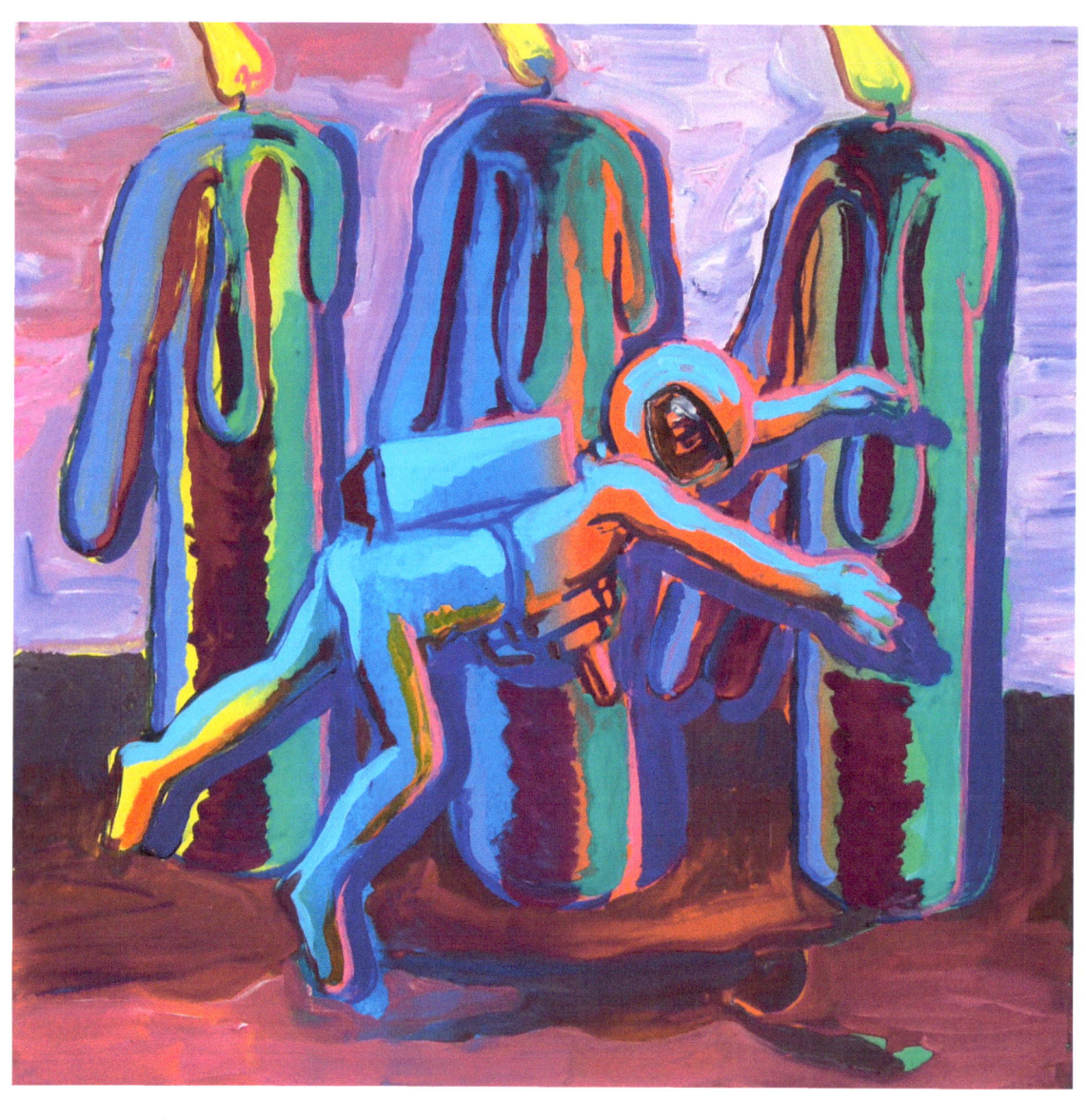

Falling (study), 2011
gouache on paper, 50 x 50 cm (19 ½" x 19 ½")

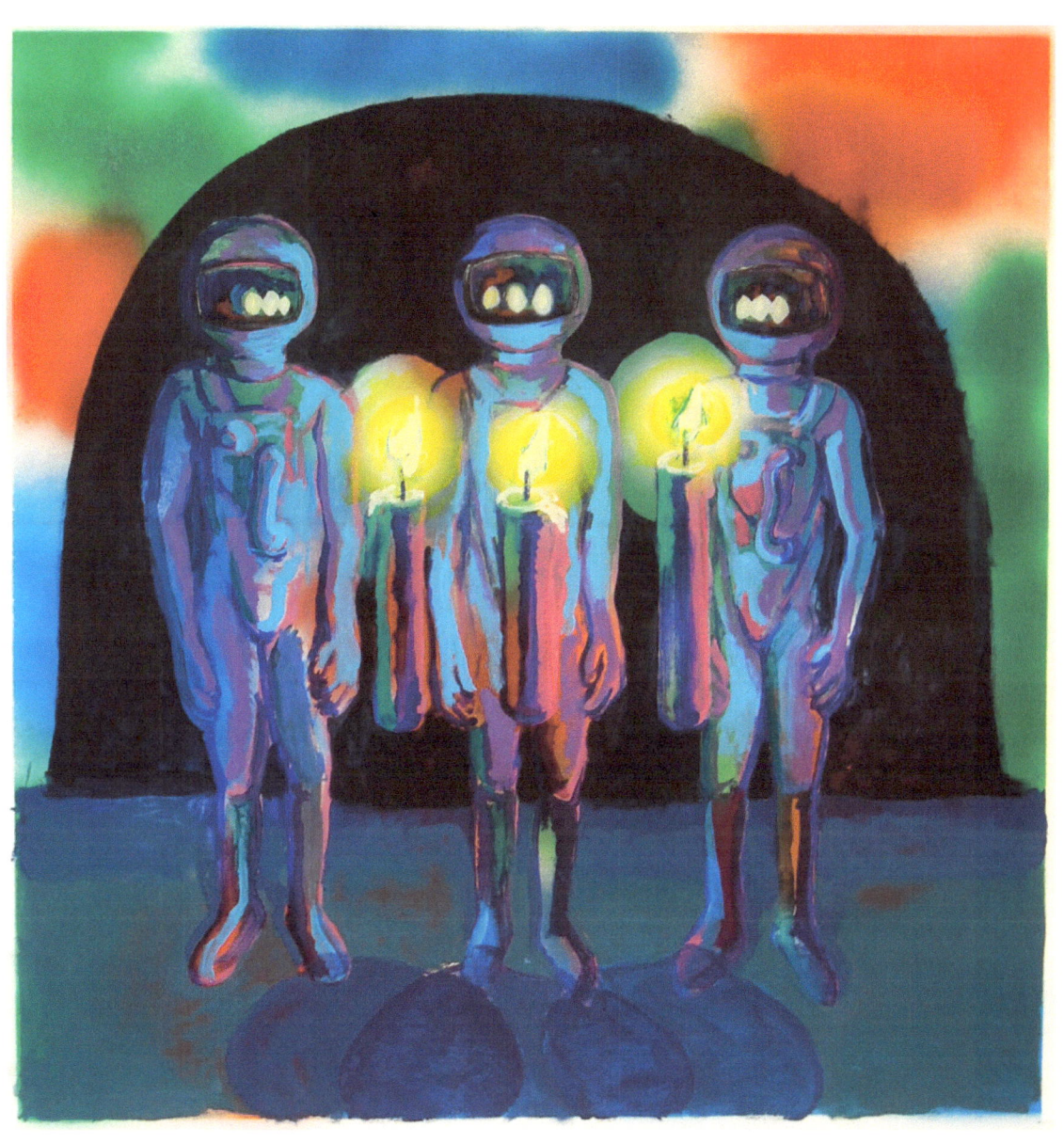

Three Candles, 2011
acrylic on paper, 70 x 70 cm (27 ½" x 27 ½")

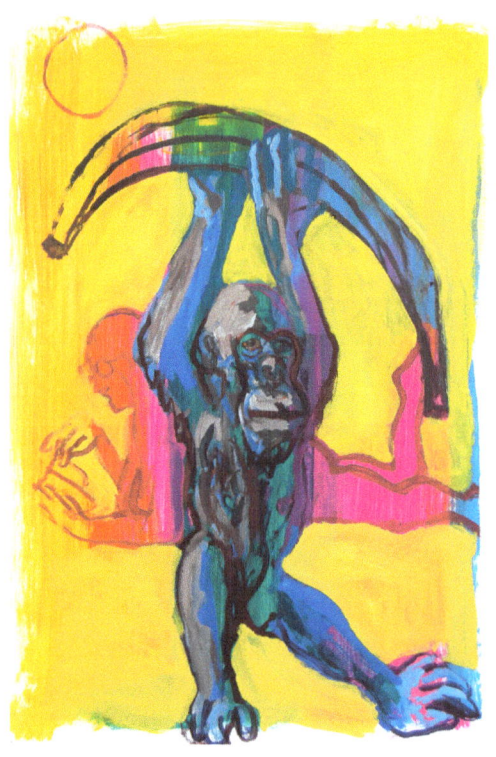

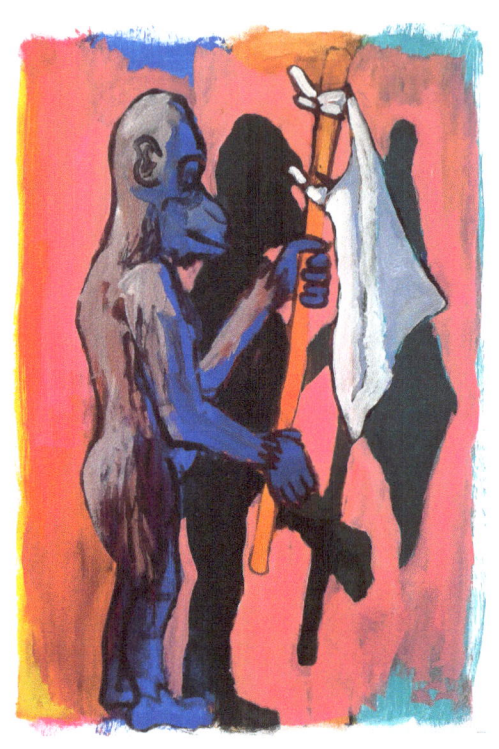

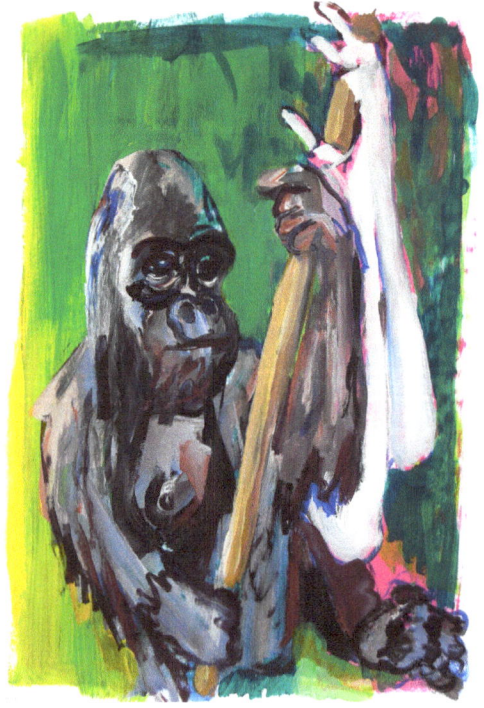

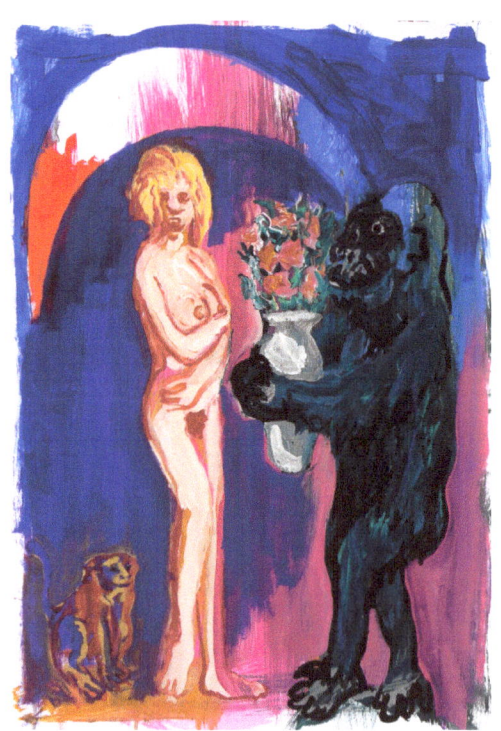

Big Banana, 2012
acrylic on paper, 70 x 50 cm (27 ½" x 19 ½")

White Flag, 2012
acrylic on paper, 70 x 50 cm (27 ½" x 19 ½")

White Flag, 2012
acrylic on paper, 70 x 50 cm (27 ½" x 19 ½")

Nude with Gorilla (I Love You), 2012
acrylic on paper, 70 x 50 cm (27 ½" x 19 ½")

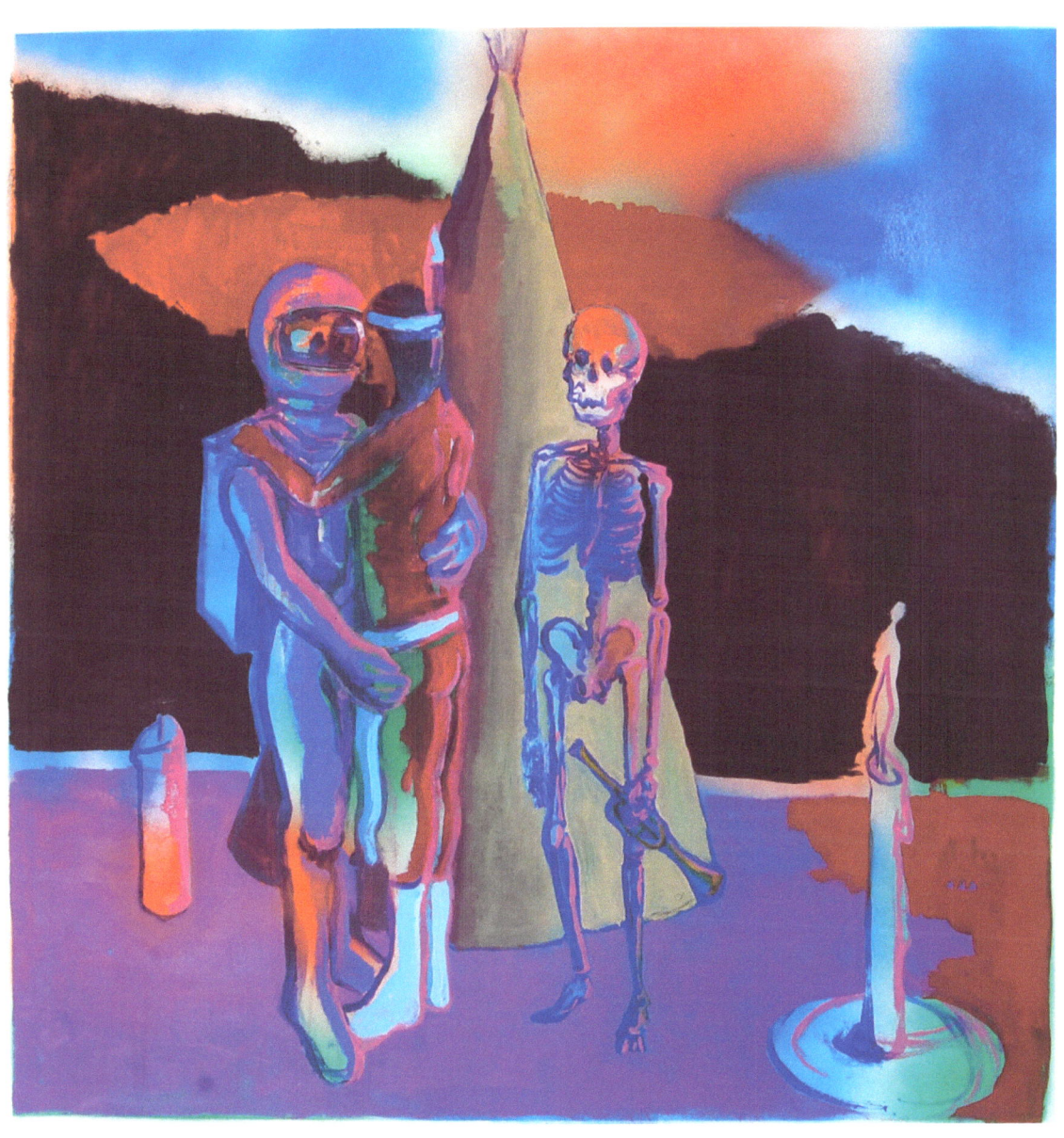

Red Cloud (Two Candles), 2011
acrylic on paper, 70 x 70 cm (27 ½" x 27 ½"

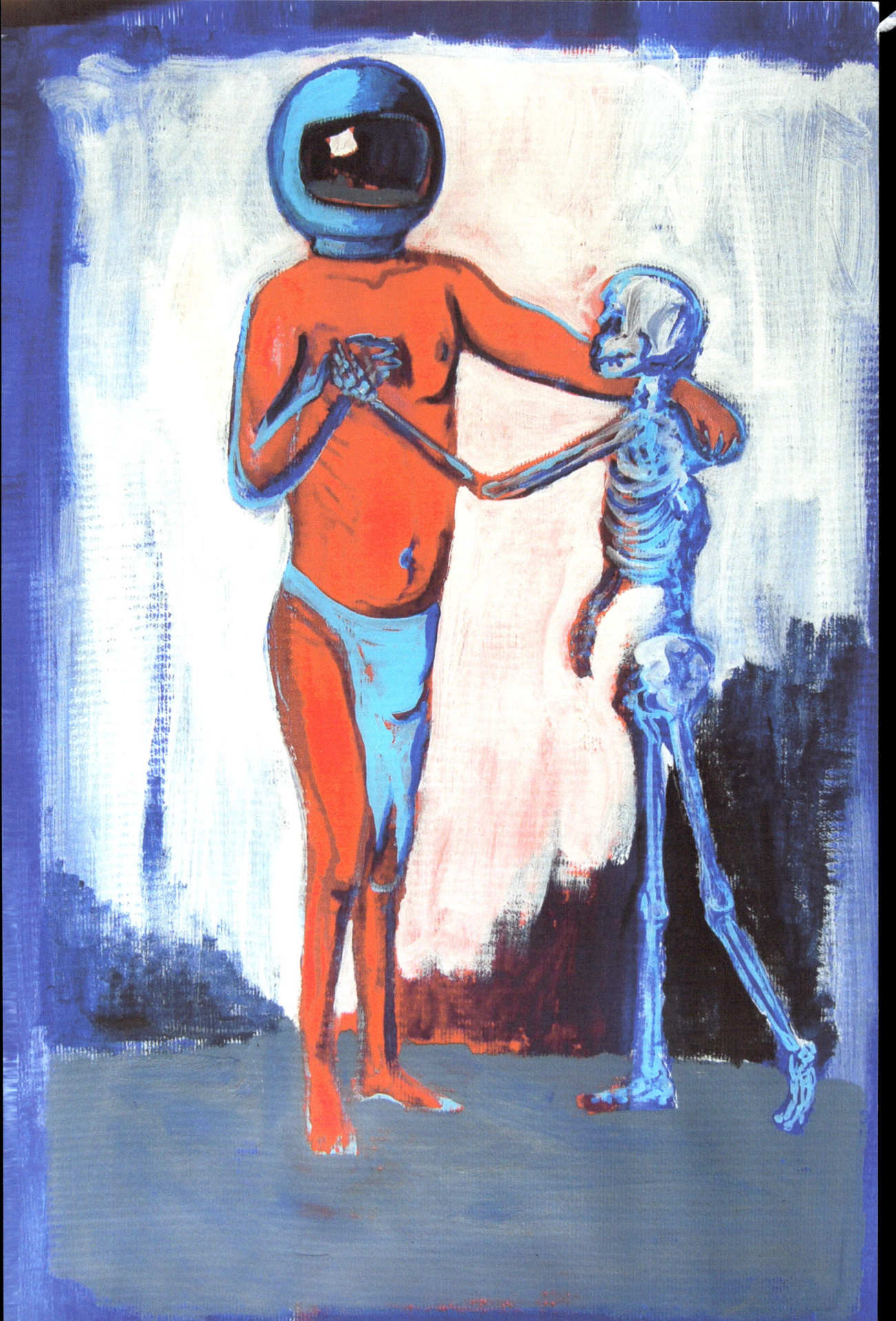

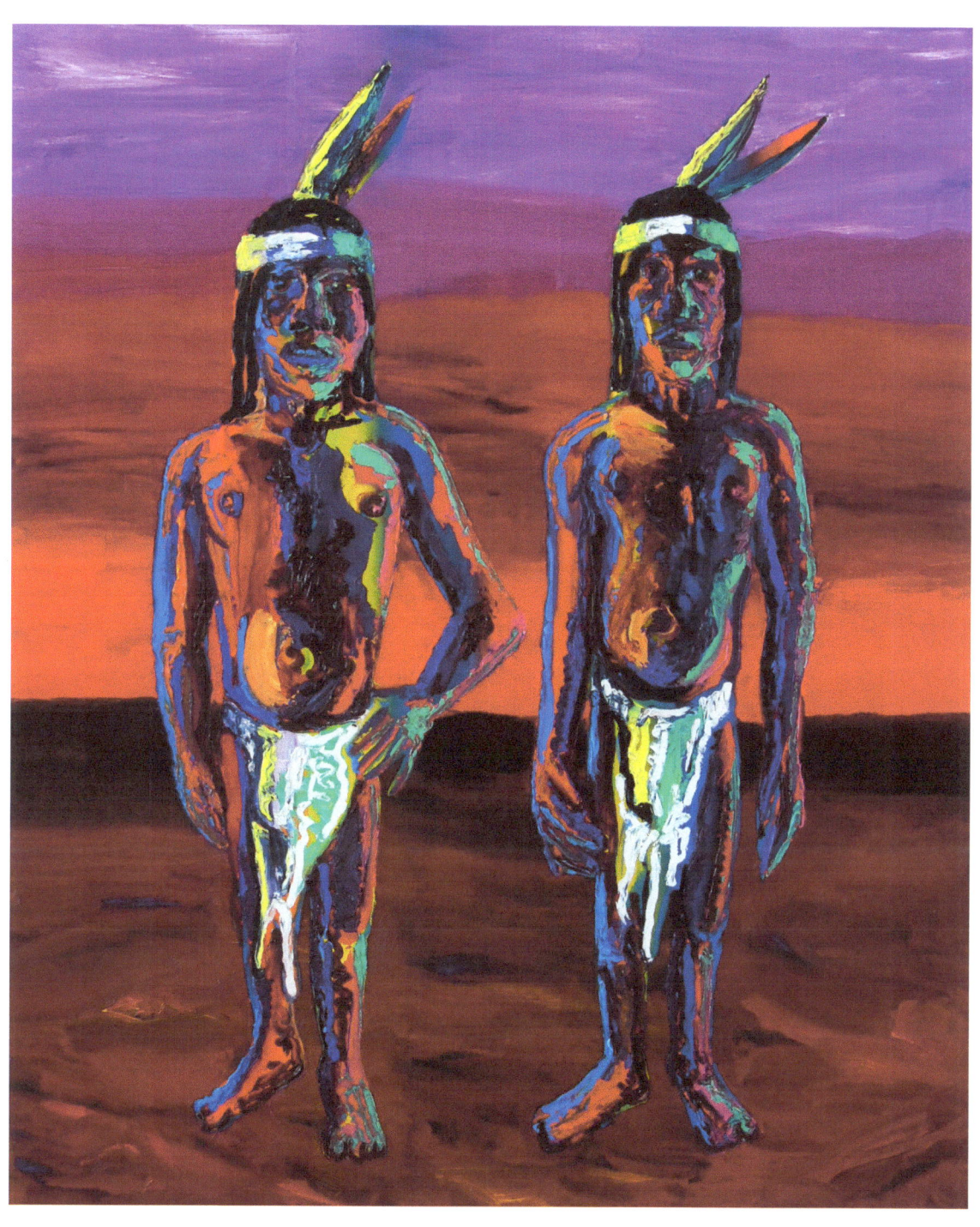

Friends (Dance), 2011
acrylic on paper, 100 x 70 cm (39" x 27 ½")

Two Indians, 2012
oil on canvas, 120 x 100 cm (47" x 39"

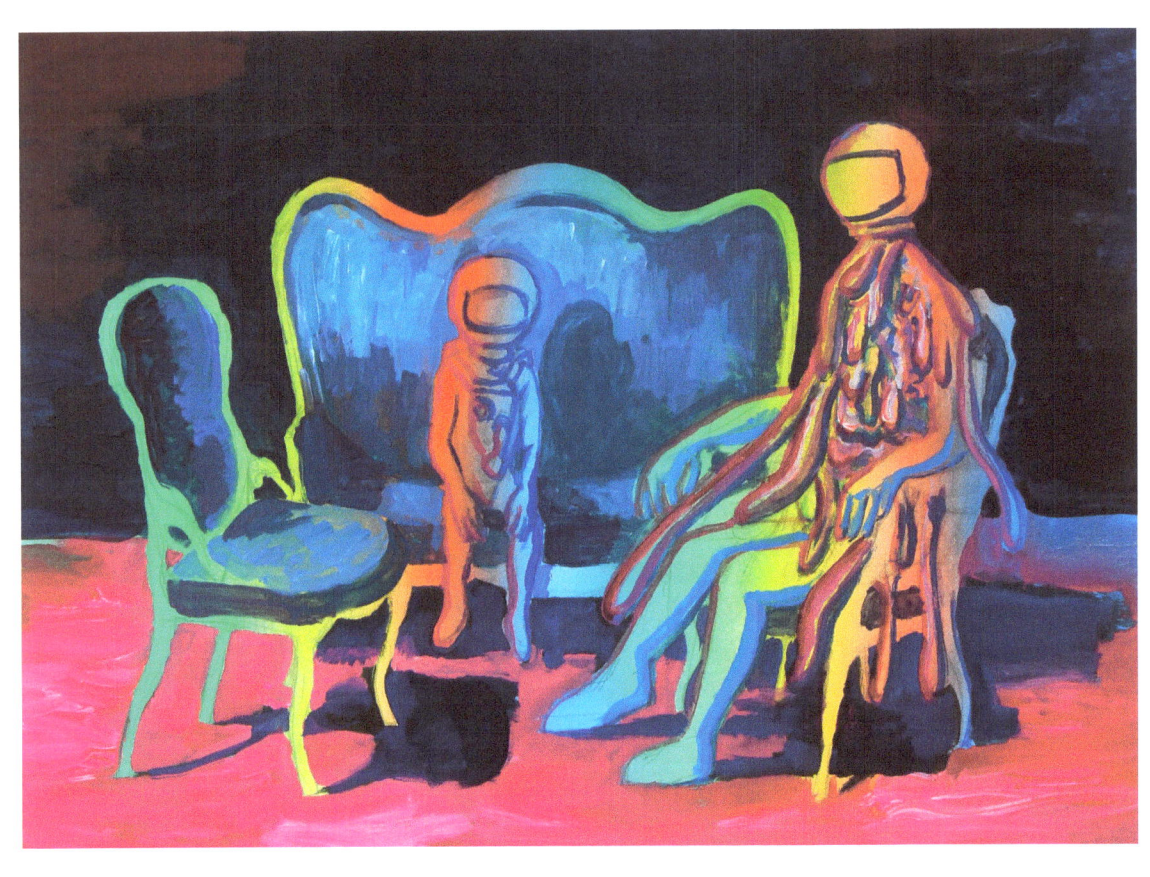

Father and Son, 2011
acrylic on paper, 50 x 70 cm (19 ½" x 27 ½")

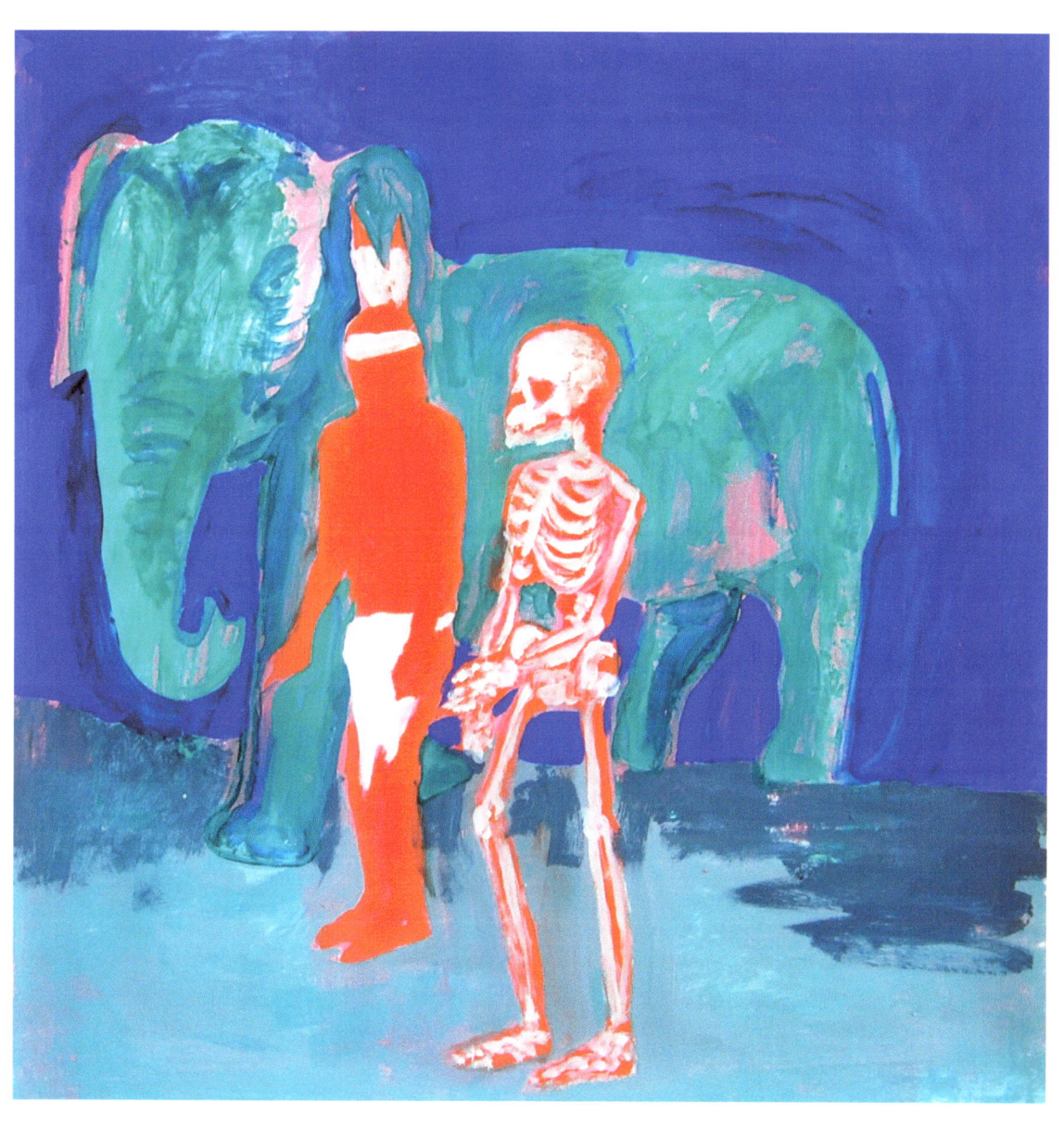

Conversation, 2011
acrylic on paper, 50 x 50 cm (19 ½" x 19 ½")

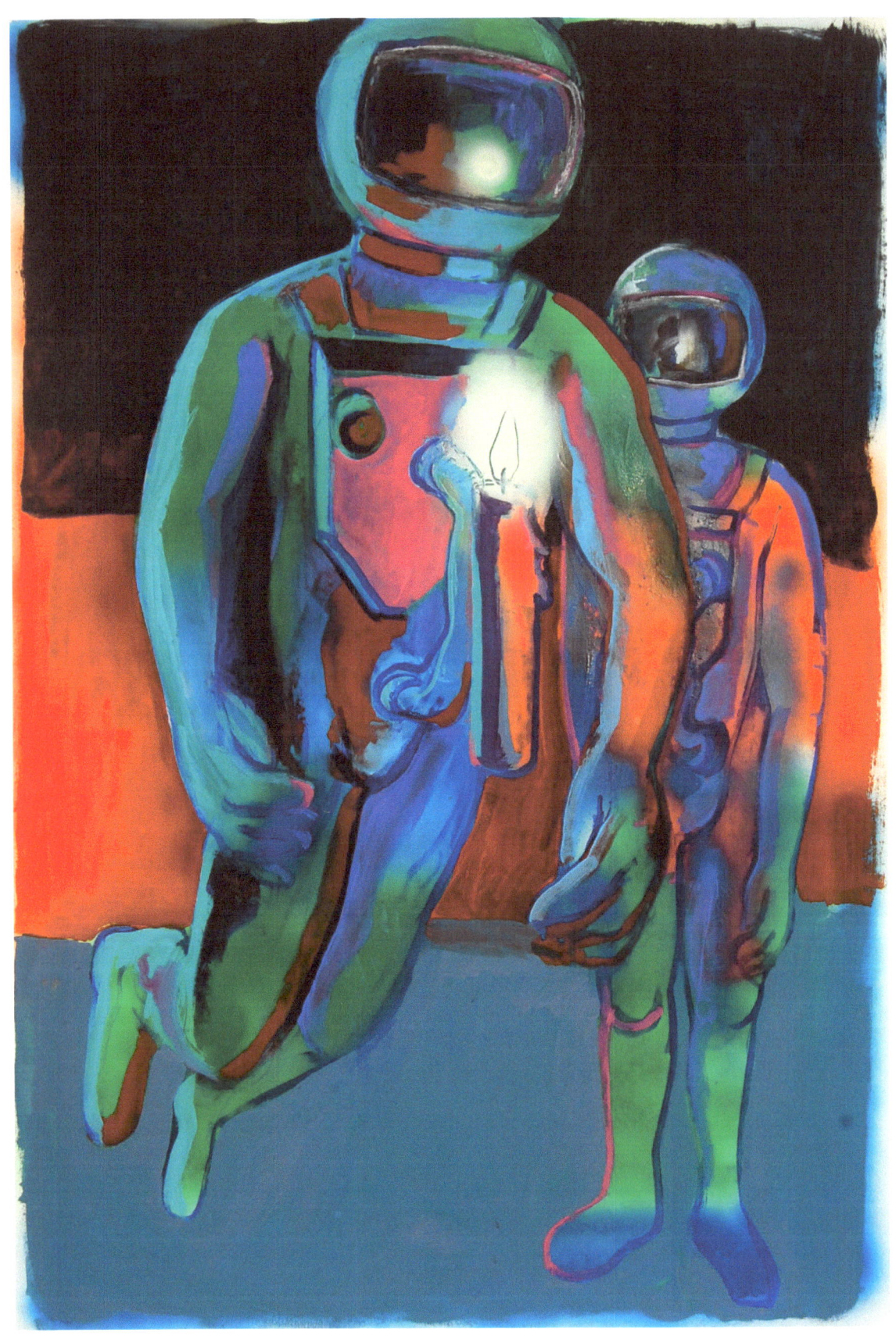

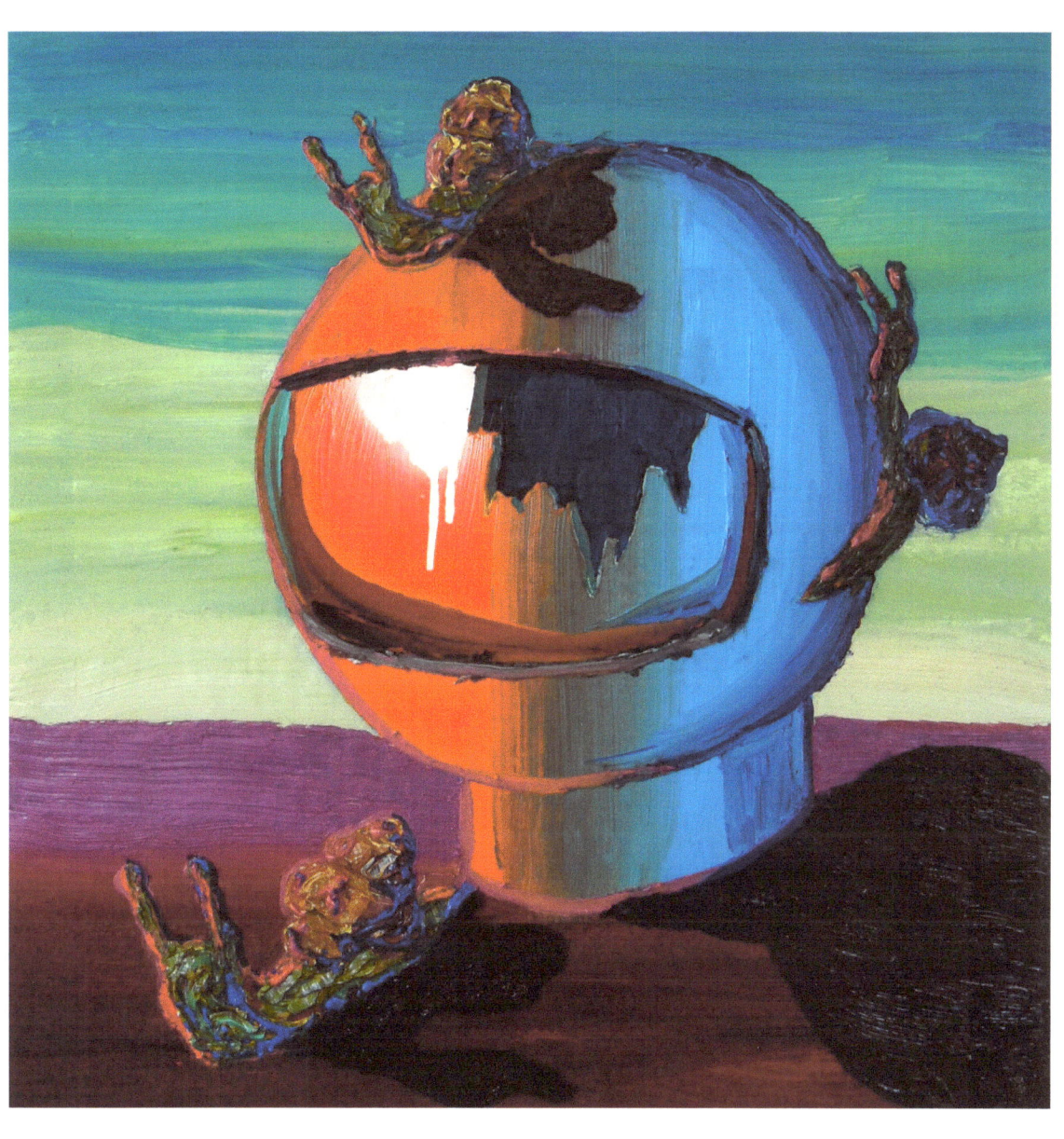

Candle, 2011
acrylic on paper, 100 x 70 cm (39" x 27 ½")

Memento Mori (Snails), 2012
oil on canvas, 55 x 55 cm (21 ½" x 21 ½")

MOON
MONKEY
CANDLE

The still-life always seemed pretty boring. We looked at Morandi in an undergrad critique, an artist's artist, making space with subtle shifts in colour. And there are Cezanne's apples, the cosmic signifigance of which I would still like to understand. But I recently realised that the still-life, a bunch of objects on a table, can contain a whole world, the mark can endow it with an emotional symbolism. The glass is the fragile spirit, the rose is the (dying) hope for the future, the candle-stick is the past, and the monkey brings his own unpredictable, stupid and anarchic character. The whole piece becomes a kind of unconscious allegory. These are winter works, made in November and December 2012, entering the dark tunnel of night before the solstice. At this time of year we feel more clearly that life is a mystery, our thoughts become more internalised. We are like monkeys staring at the flame in the darkness of our souls. There are no easy answers.

"We sit in the mud... and reach for the stars."
Ivan Turgenev

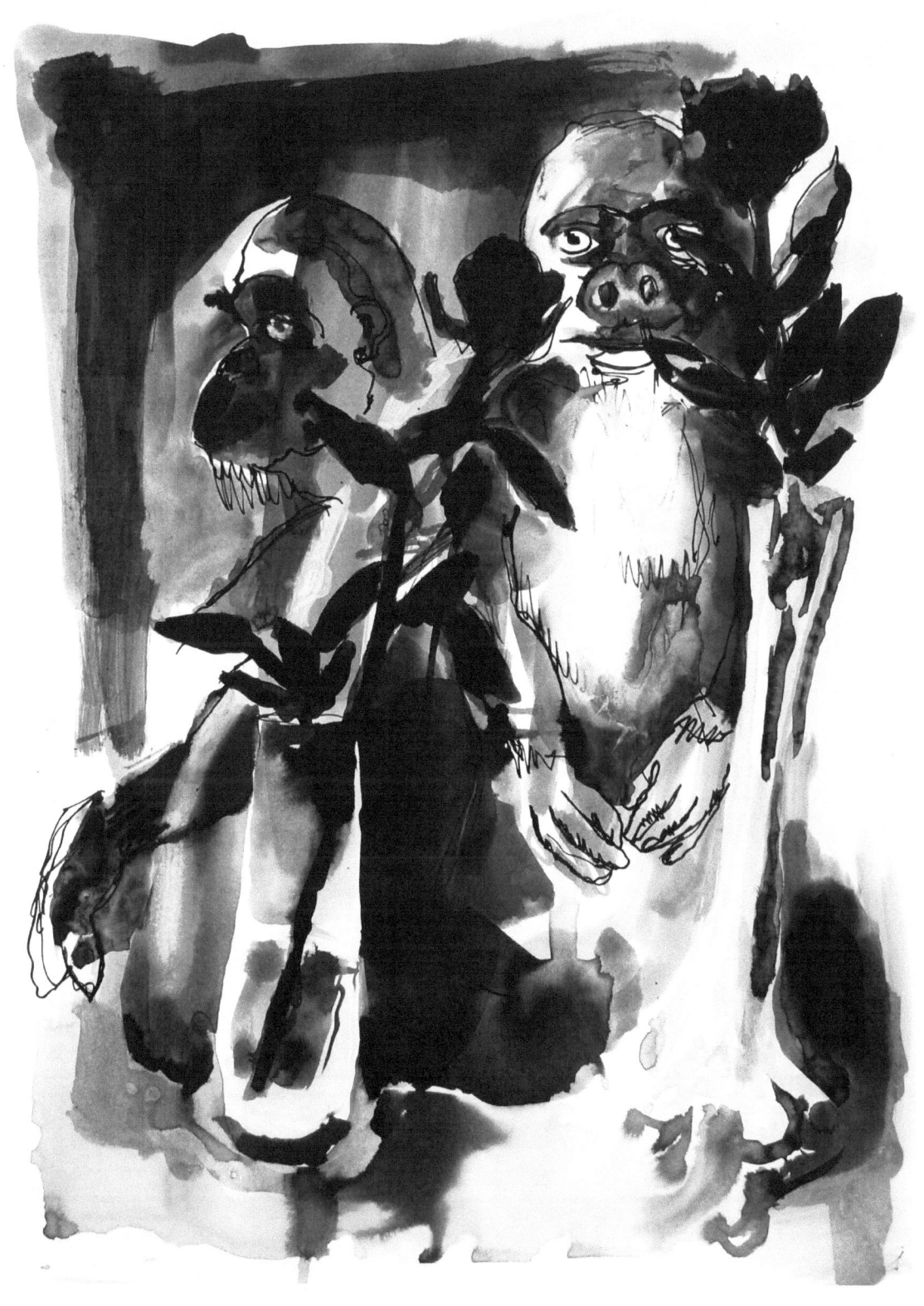

Roses and Monkeys, 2012
ink brush on paper, 70 x 50 cm (27 ½" x 19 ½")

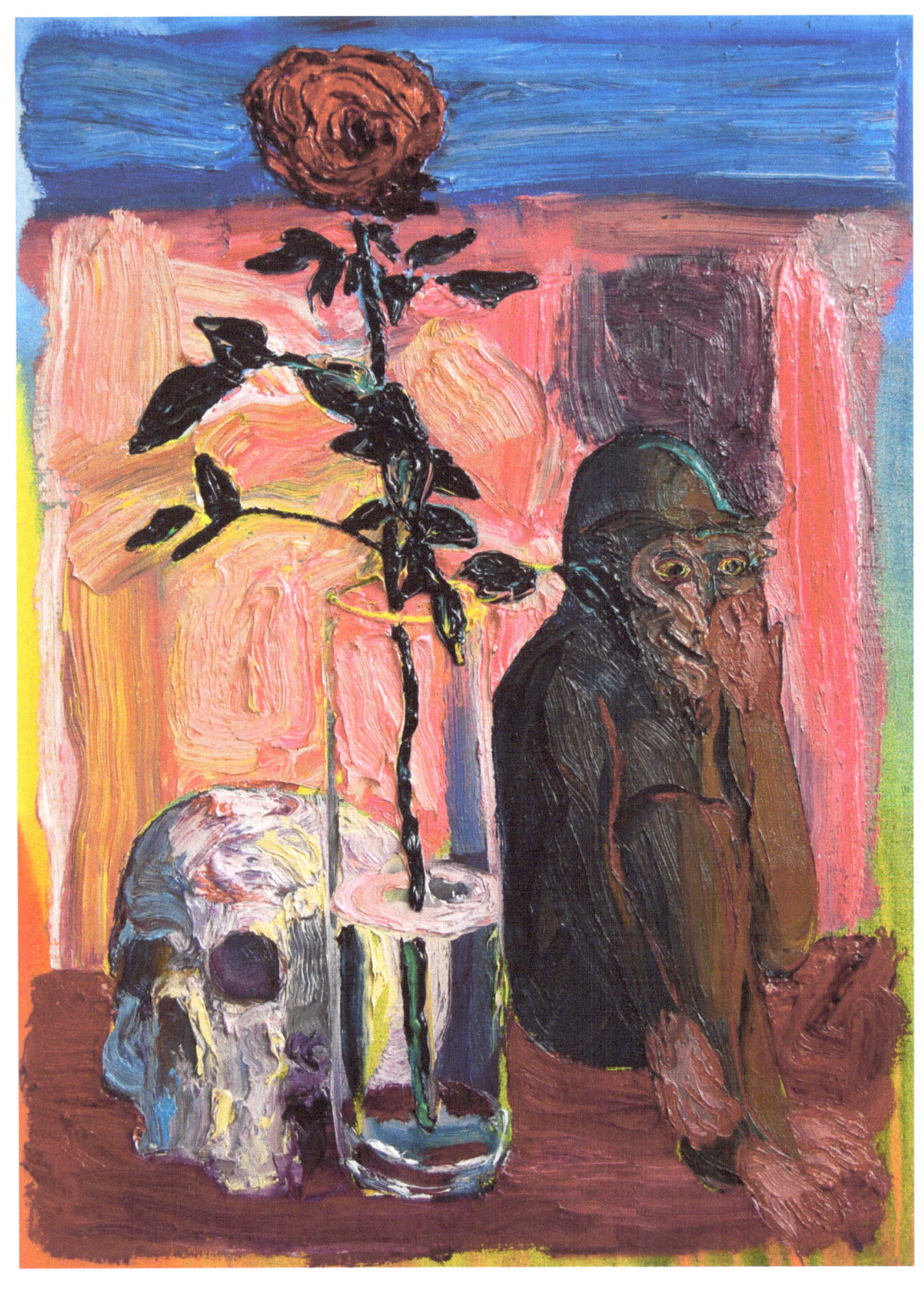

Still-life with Monkey, 2012
oil on canvas, 80 x 65 cm (31 ½" x 25 ½")

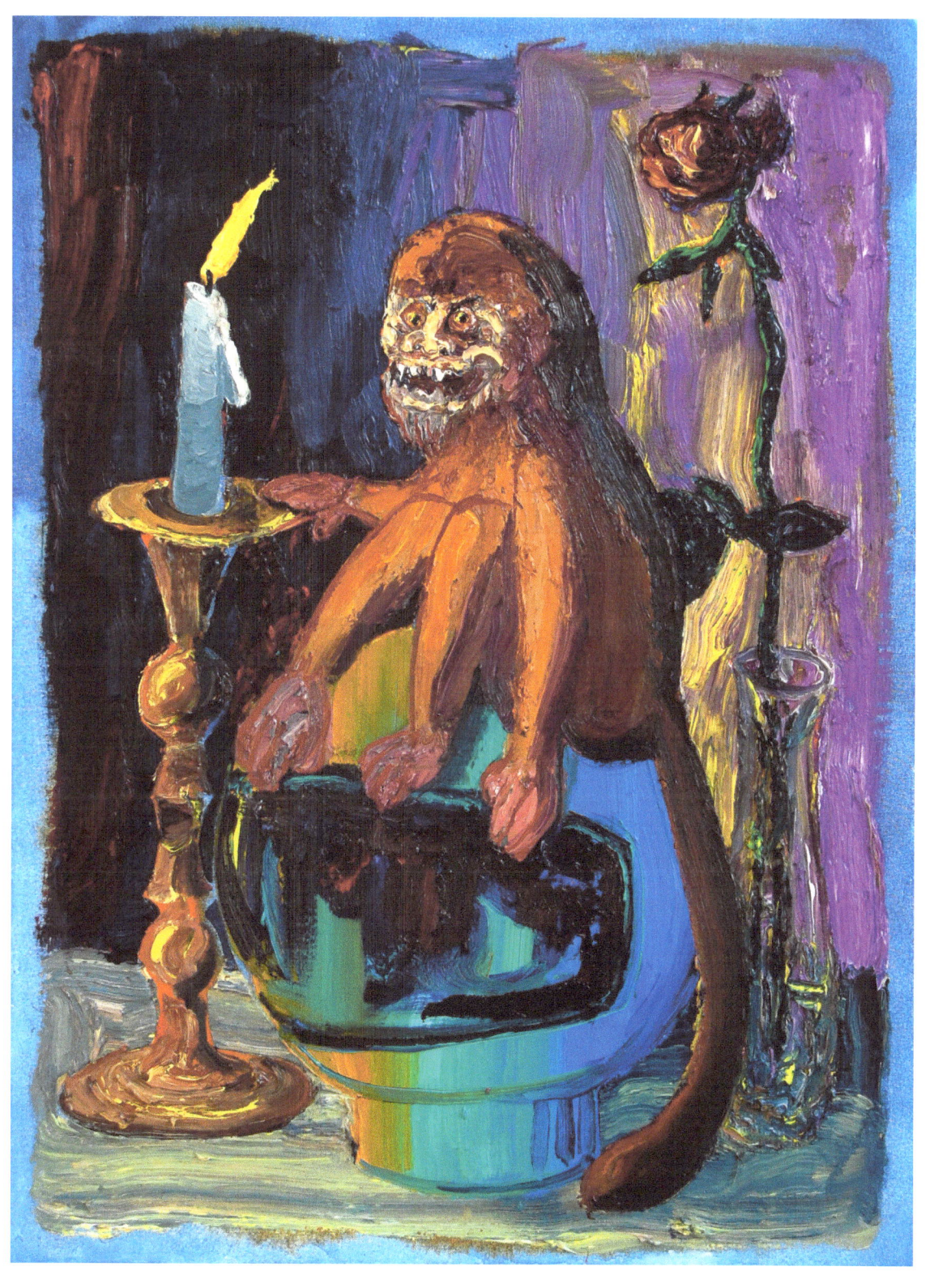

Still-life with Monkey, 2012
oil on canvas, 80 x 65 cm (31 ½" x 25 ½")

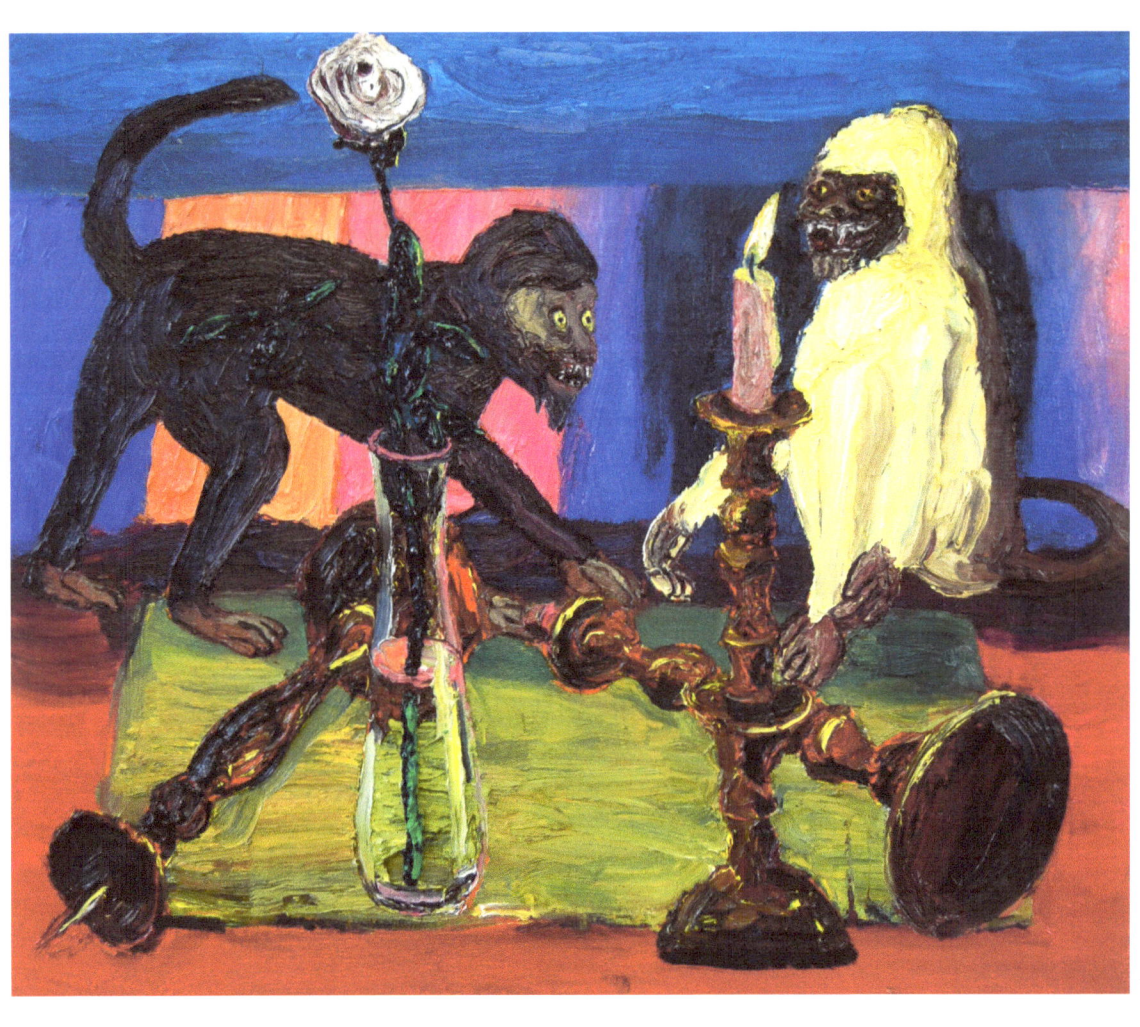

Monkeys, Rose and Candlesticks, 2012
oil on canvas, 65 x 90 cm (25 ½" x 35 ½")

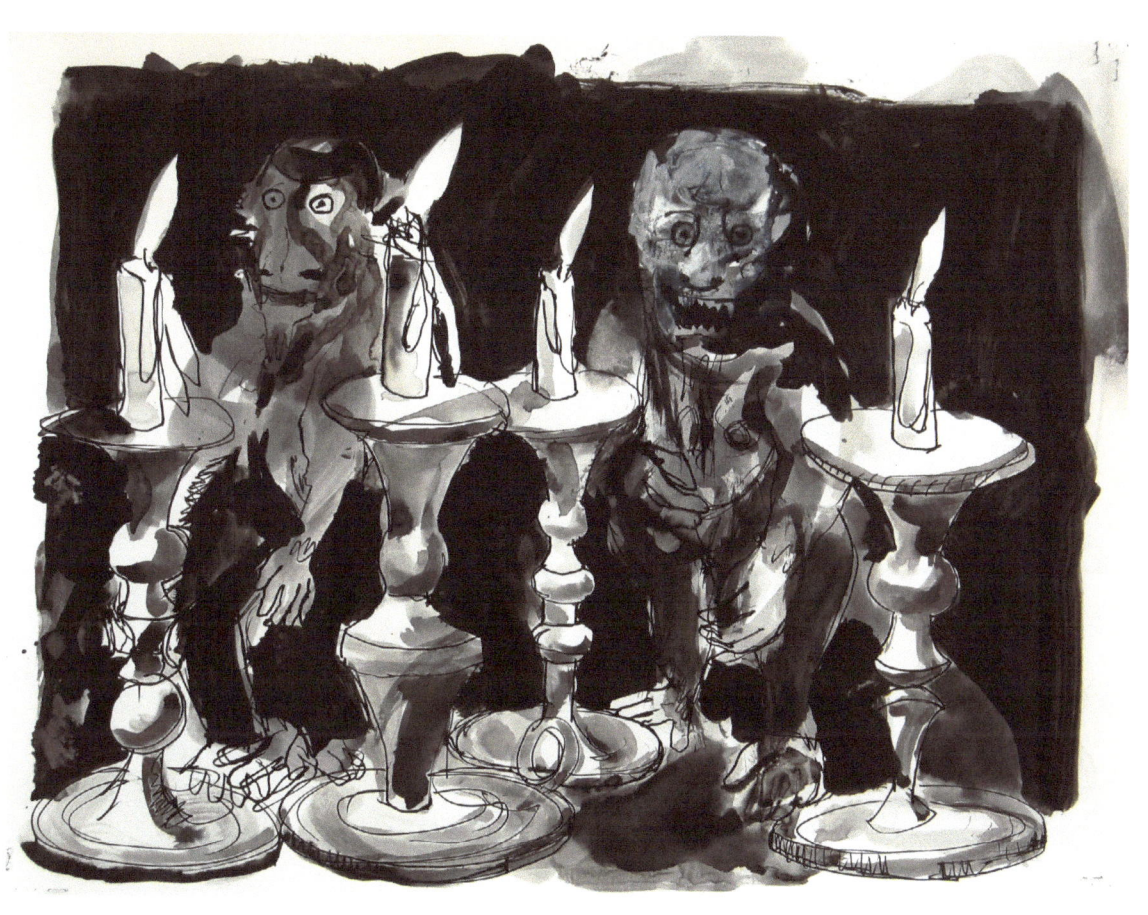

Four Candlesticks, 2012
ink on paper, 50 x 70 cm (19 ½" x 27 ½")

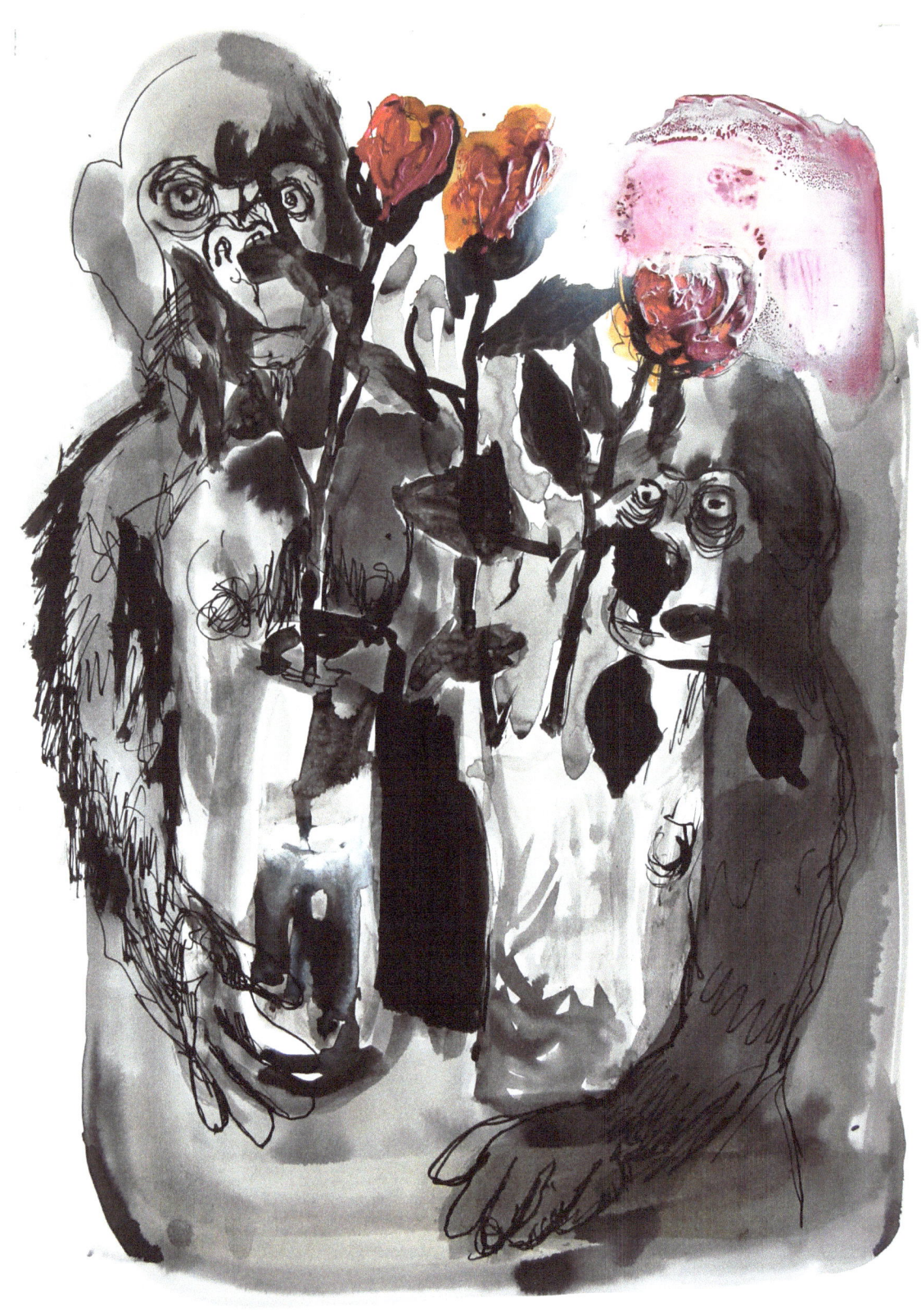

Chimpanzees and Roses, 2012
ink on paper, 70 x 50 cm (27 ½" x 19 ½")

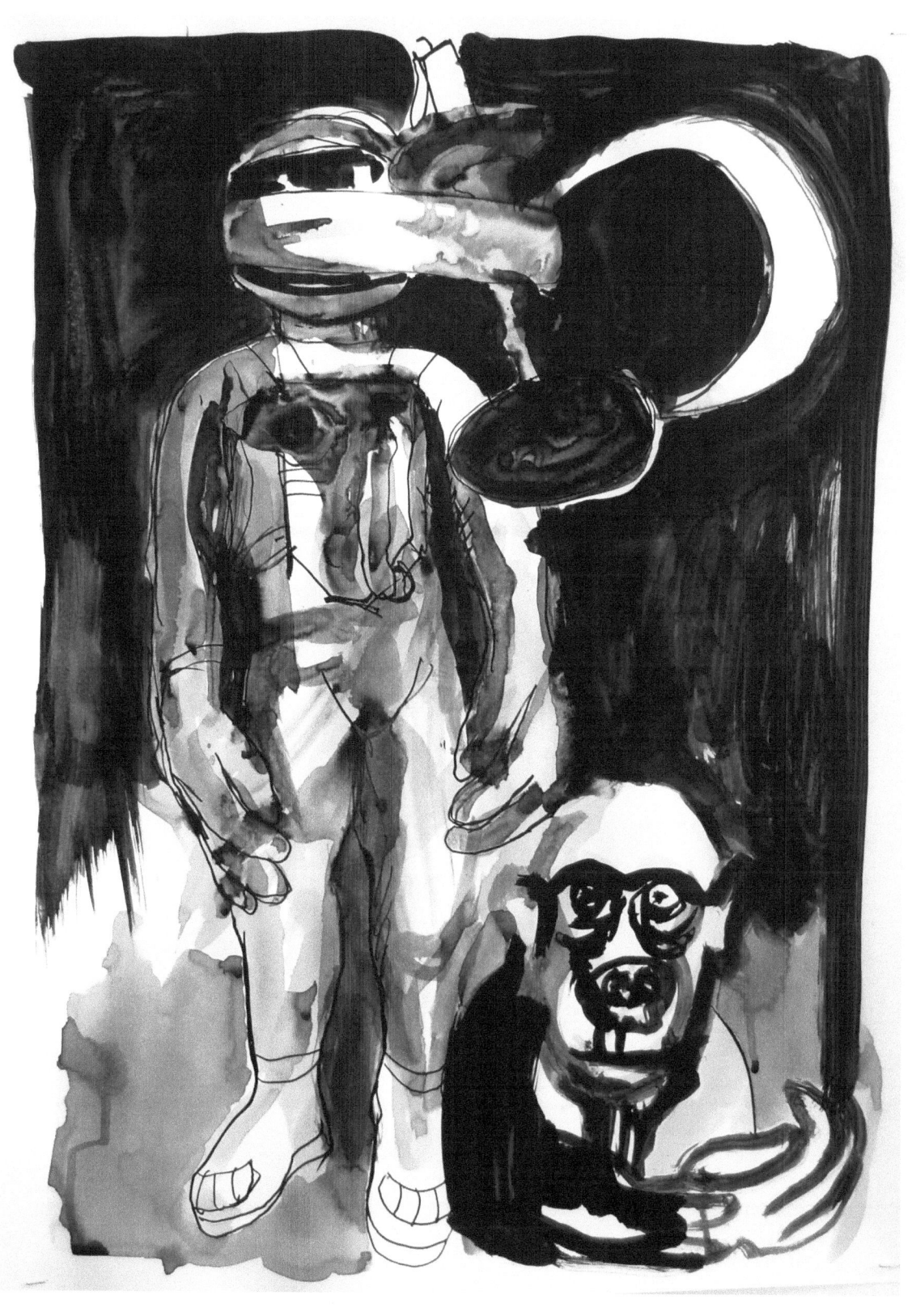

Astronaut, Candlestick and Monkey, 2012
ink on paper, 70 x 50 cm (27 ½" x 19 ½")

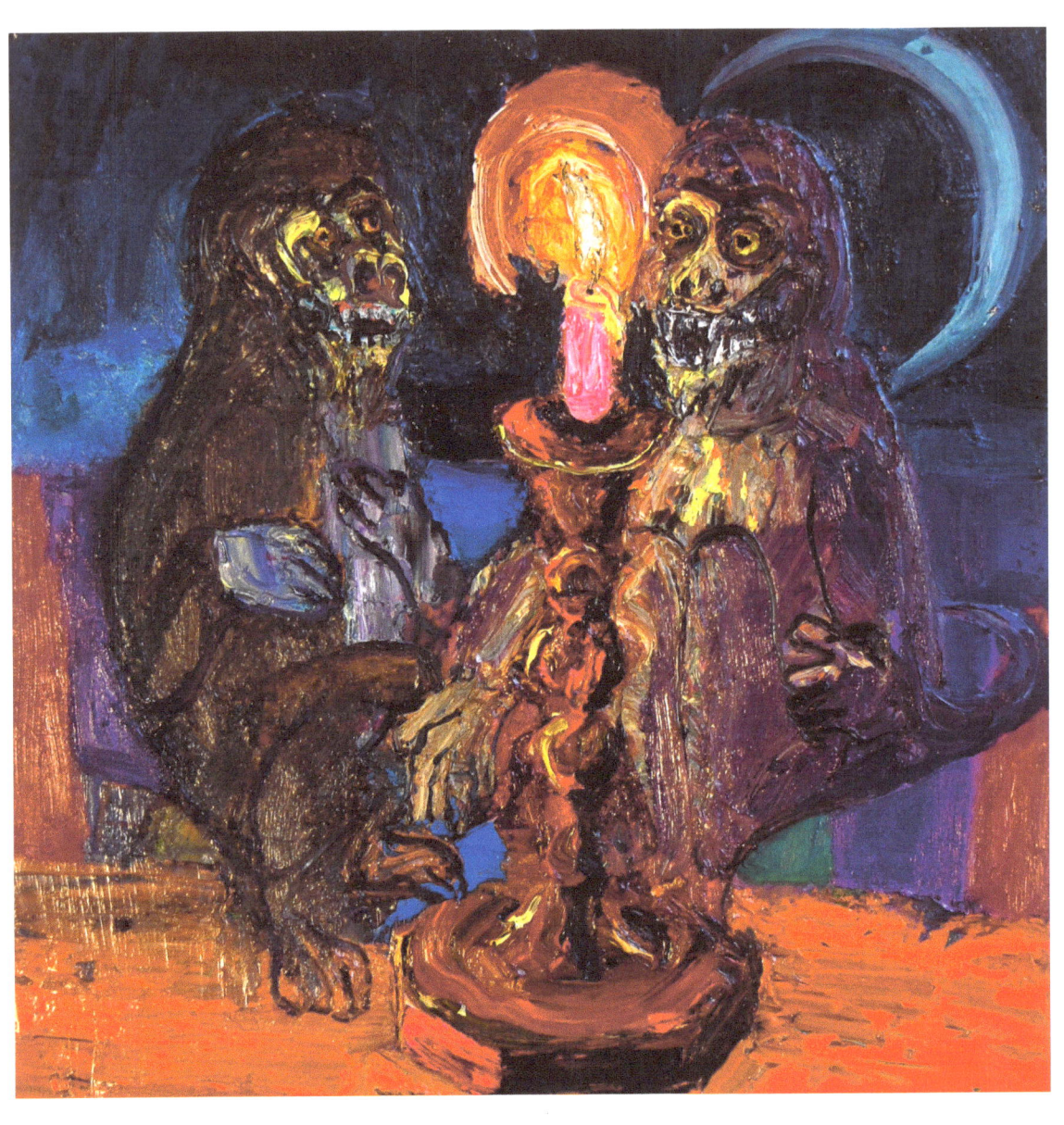

Two Monkeys (Night Creatures), 2012
oil on canvas, 60 x 60 cm (23 ½" x 23 ½")

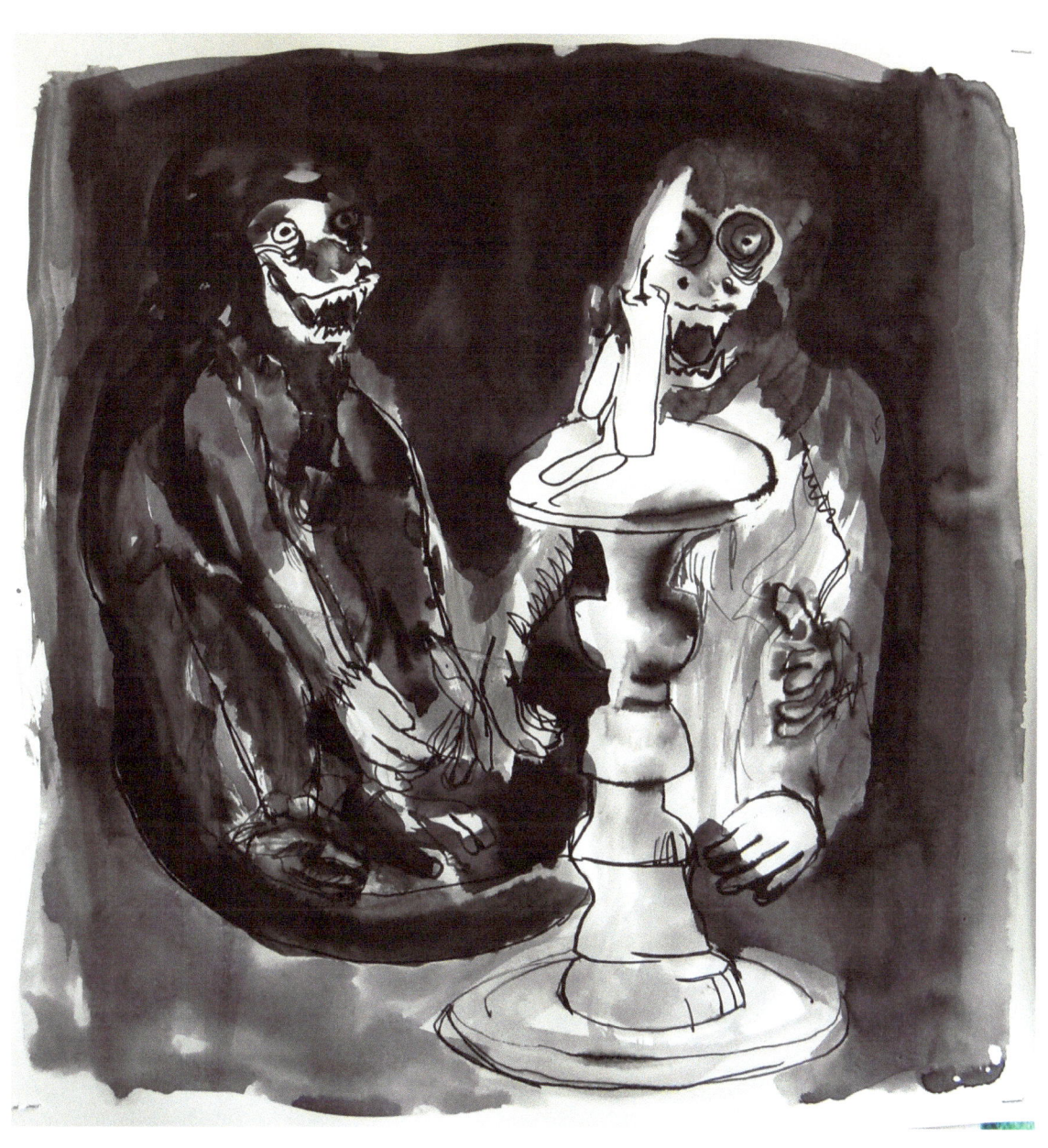

Two Monkeys (Night Creatures), 2012
oil on canvas, 60 x 60 cm (23 ½" x 23 ½")

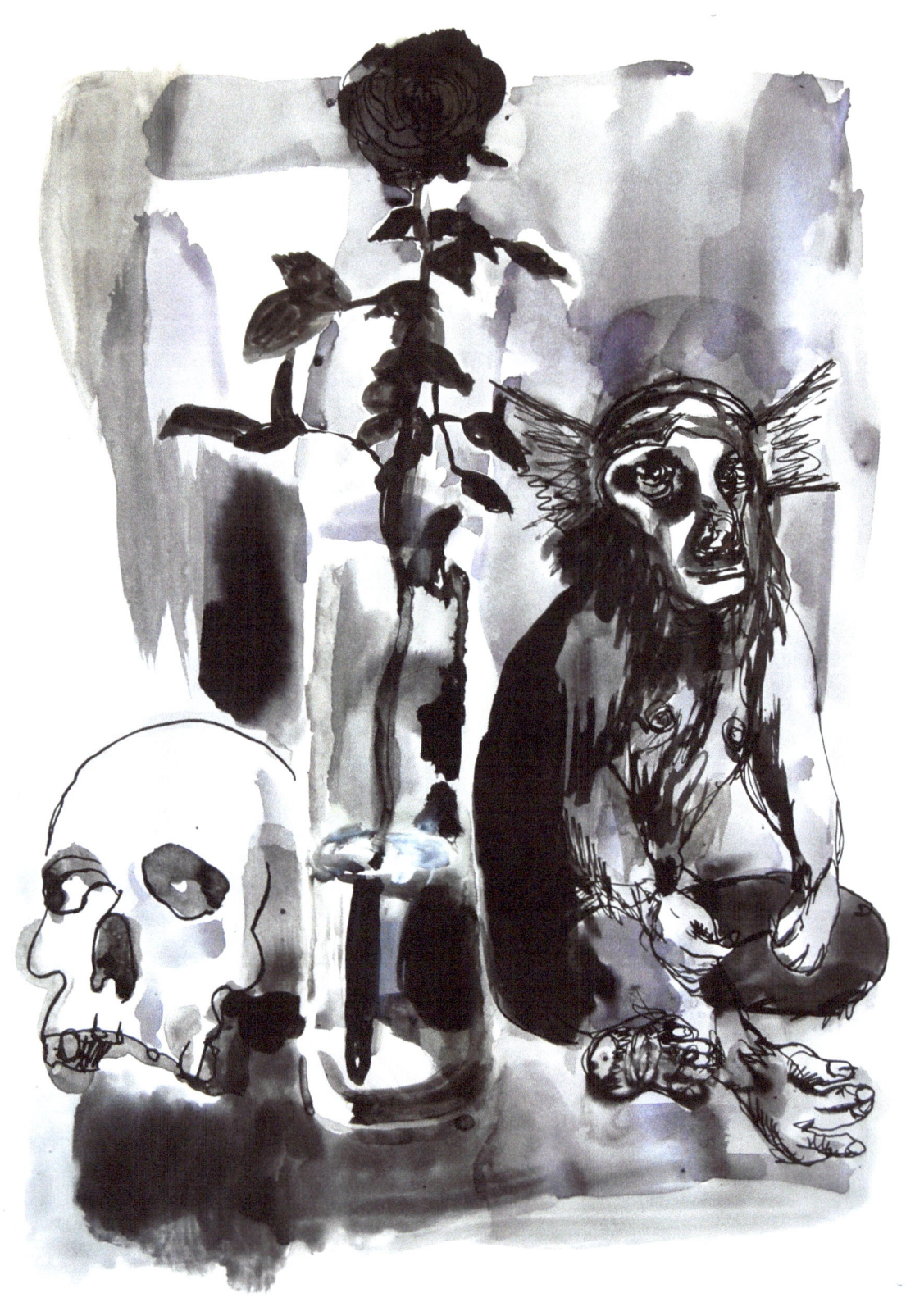

Still-life with Monkey, 2012
ink on paper, 70 x 50 cm (27 ½" x 19 ½")

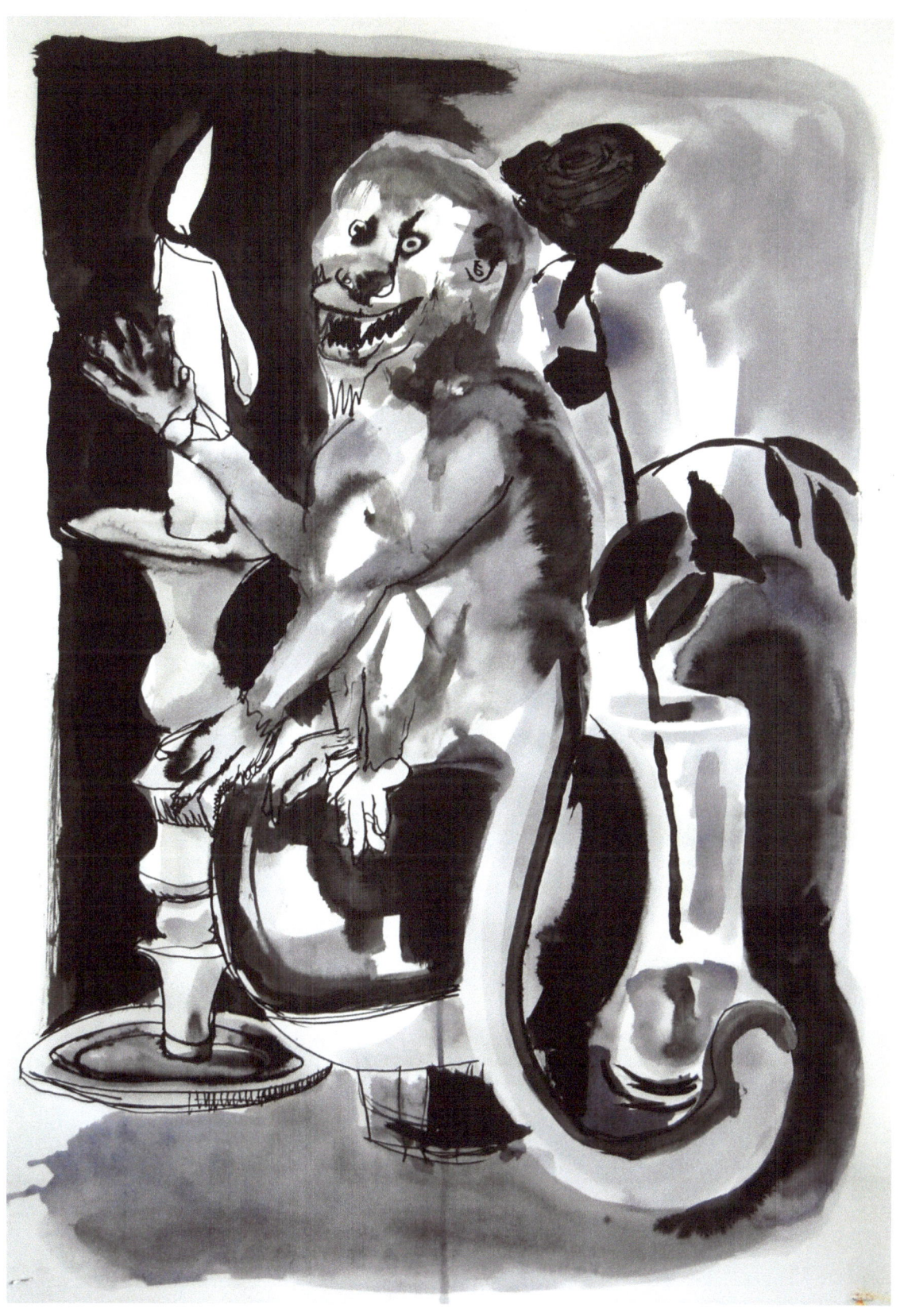

Still-life with Monkey, 2012
ink on paper, 70 x 50 cm (27 ½" x 19 ½")

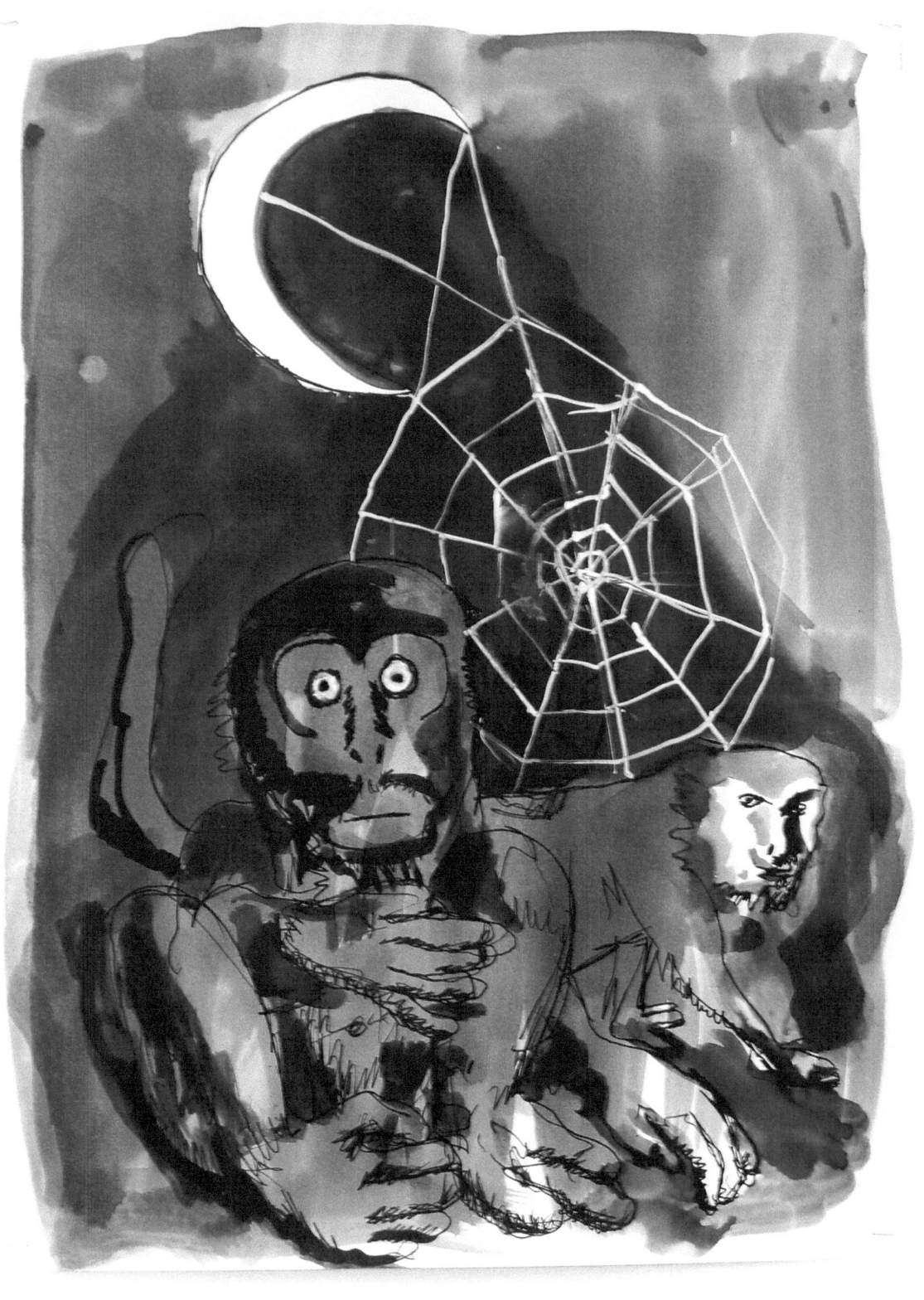

Moon Monkey III, 2012
ink on paper, 70 x 50 cm (27 ½" x 19 ½")

INTERVIEW
JANUARY 2013

HM: We noticed that you were from the Czech Republic but did most of your formal studies in the US, in MS and IN.... how do you feel that education reflected on your work and your progress as an artist? Did you have a reason to go to the US other than to study art? We're just curious about your journey and discovery.

LW: I'm not Czech actually. I am an American expat and I have lived in Prague for over ten years now. I studied painting in Indiana where I got my BFA and in Mississippi where I graduated with an MFA in 1992. I'm 46 and have been painting for around 25 years, but I feel that only in the last few years has the work started coming together more. One reason that I chose to become an artist is that it is a field that is always changing, one is constantly growing as an artist, and I like that. It's not over till it's over, if you know what I mean. I moved to Prague from New York just before 9/11. I'd been here before in the early 90's and I missed it, plus I found it hard to produce work in New York where its just too stressful. But now I miss New York too .. haha

HM: We are quite amazed by the volume of work that you produce and publish, how often do you paint and how often do you complete a painting? We notice that many paintings carry on the same themes almost as evolving narratives starring your favorite characters, is this true?

LW: Thanks for the compliment. I try to get over to the studio as much as I can. I used to work more slowly, but I realized that one can't be too precious about the work and also thinking too much just spoils it.

I try to maintain a thread through the work, one piece leads to another. I started working with the theme of astronauts and Indians last year (2011) when I got my new studio. I had started writing a novel for Nanowrimo the year before about Indians on the moon and images from that were still floating around in my head. I wanted to turn away from the type of work I had done in 2007–2008 which was more about my reactions to living in the Czech Republic and had focused on history and a kind of faded dream of the fin-de-siecle, which one can feel very strongly here. In the new work I wanted to be much more colorful and juicy, as a kind of opposite reaction to the gray skies of Central Europe.

HM: How do you come about choosing the characters to represent and their stories? We will point directly to your series including astronauts and candles which we have posted on hyperreal.me. There seems to be many others including Indians, skeletons, astronauts, cupids, and melting candles....With the interaction of these characters with color and symbols do you intend to create a metaphor or even a prolonged narrative?

LW: I don't mean for the narrative between these various characters to be clear or direct. I don't even know myself and I think that's important. Painting is a kind of unveiling, or a sort of dreaming, and I want to find the symbols, colours, and surfaces which resonate with the viewer in such a way that he/she can't quite define or know. In this way the painting becomes a cipher that hopefully nags at the viewers memory, that calls forth a sympathetic response.

Painting is an extremely slow medium in the sense that unlike film the image doesn't move, so art is fundamentally about a feeling of mystery, or an unresolved tension, that evokes feelings within the viewer. In that way one lives with a painting and meditates on it. That is the power of the single image or of the painting as an object.

I was thinking of the astronaut as a kind of tragic figure, in a sort of retrofuturist way. Retrofuturism is a kind of hauntological attitude to the lost dreams of the past, and I do feel that the space program is basically dying and that the journey to the moon will come to be like an ancient myth. In this time of resource depletion and late capitalist turmoil, I sincerely wonder if we will ever send another man into space, or at least out into space as an explorer. It's a symbol of the end of manifest destiny. And so in this way the astronaut becomes an endangered figure, like a brother perhaps with the native, with the so-called indigenous peoples. With our technology we have become divorced from nature and the Western/European response to the Other has always been a loaded one, loaded with colonial or romantic Rousseauian projection. I can't help but be caught up in that historical process, but I feel like the planet is in crisis and if we don't learn to live together with all our differences, then we are lost and our Enlightenment project will come to nothing. Perhaps we should ask if we are so enlightened, then why does our society still rely on leveraging cheap labour in "third world" countries?

So the relationship of the indian with the astronaut is fraught with difficulties and I think we all know that, at least at a subconscious level. Of course it's complicated for me as a white suburban guy from Kentucky transplanted to Prague to approach the image of native peoples. Some people will always be offended by appropriation, they would feel that my use of these figures, for example, is only a part of the continuing colonial discourse. In response I can only suggest that we share each others' stories and we are enriched by the wide variety of cultures and dialogues that springs from this relationship. If we only focus on ideas of "authenticity" or "identity politics", then we continue to be trapped in opposing camps. I've always felt that the artist's role is to go into the danger zone and to take risks. The risk I take is that I will only reinforce stereotypes through the work, like with loin cloths/feathered headdresses, and so on. I suppose living in the Czech Republic I felt that I could more comfortably approach this type of imagery, without worrying about being politically correct.

As an American here I'm an outsider so I can deal with this topic with perhaps a bit more authority than a Czech painter, nor do I think Czech painters are interested in this theme anyway. My work is about America, because I realised as a foreigner that I would always be defined by my nationality. Living here I have the space to see the country and its history from a distance. And I also think I'm drawn to the lives of indigenous peoples because they belong to a tribe, whereas I have become a man with no country in some regards. Art is about the visual, and representational art is bound to have some political or psychological relationship with the surrounding culture.

HM: If there is a narrative, such as in the Astronaut and Candle paintings, what is that story?

LW: In some ways these works are all memento mori, reminders of death. As I said the astronaut is endangered too, our way of life is in trouble. The candles represent a kind of phallic energy, but they also represent time, so our time is running out. They stand, like the figures, as a kind of witness. But lately I've moved away from combining all these symbols together and am focussing on working with the tropes individually, so in an exhibition setting the paintings can play off of each other.

HM: We were introduced through a brief discussion about Fritz Scholder, who we are appreciate, there appears to be a strong influence here from his work. Did his work have a lasting influence on you, is that one reason you use Native American imagery? But more than the figures, it is the boldness of blocked color, softening edges, and ghostly appearance of light that makes us notice a connection, what do you think?

LW: I was already painting Native Americans when I discovered his work, but what I really like about it is his use of color and the way the figures stand and look at the viewer. This is something I'm doing in my work as well. Scholder studied under Wayne Thiebaud and his work is like an amalgam of Thiebaud's use of color and

Francis Bacon's approach to the figure. There were many artists across the States working in a similar way to Scholder in the 60's and 70's and this shows that art was still functioning on a social level. It was the end of movements and although I think there are some great artists working today, I think our culture is more and more fragmented. That's not necessarily a bad thing, but I heard Erik Davis on his podcast Expanding Mind the other day refer to our time as "the twilight of the analog" which I think is such a good turn of phrase .. in a sense the analog is dying off and painting is the ultimate form of that kind of hand-crafted object. It will never disappear altogether. In fact the future may very well see a return to the tribal, with all the localised art-making and self-modification that entails. The analog could come back in a big way.

HM: Being a huge fan, we really enjoyed your insight on Scholder and the article you sent me titled "Who's Afraid of Fritz Scholder," by Paul Chaat Smith. It discusses Scholder's many contributions as a prominent American artist but shows how he was instead cast off only as an Indian Artist by most critics. We think that this is a great topic for discussion as we enter a more connected world where real-world locations may be losing power to the Internet.

HM: Do you have any upcoming shows or projects you are working on?

LW: I have a show lined up in September at a small gallery in Litoměřice, a town north of Prague. It's an old Gothic interior apparently with vaulted ceilings and I'm looking forward to seeing my new work on display. I've shown in cafes in Prague but the scene is pretty small here. While I have the studio I just want to produce as much as I can and hopefully expand my career.

HM: What is the art scene like in Prague and the Czech Republic? What is your favorite art hangout or art venue in your city?

LW: Considering the size of the scene (Prague has about 1.5 million inhabitants), there are a number of exceptional artists here. The Czech Republic has always been overshadowed culturally by their big neighbour, Germany, and Prague doesn't hold a candle to Berlin, for example. But the power of these small countries in Europe with their long history can't be denied. A lot of painters here are dealing with different ways of applying paint, using drips and stencils, etc, and some of that way of working has rubbed off on my approach.

The coolest art scene here, at least in terms of an underground vibe, is around the A.M. 180 collective and their gallery space in Klub Utopia. The brother/sister team who set up the space are inspired by indie culture and the LA/Brooklyn/Williams-burg/London/Berlin art axis. They also put together a summer music festival called Creepy Teepee which is held in Kutná Hora. Highly recommended.

HM: Do you use any digital devices or technology to create or influence your work?

LW: I sometimes cut stencils for my work, but it's all done by hand. I've played around with trying to make some 3D animation based on my motifs, but its hard to find the time. So much work nowadays is complimented by video, sculpture and performance and I have some ideas along those lines. But generally my approach is pretty traditional, just brushes and canvas.

(Source: Hyperreal.Me, via hypereal)

KULTURNI UDALOST / CULTURAL EVENT

Culture, like democracy, is a fragile thing. Like a plant you have to provide it with a place to grow, nourishment and care. But like a plant, culture is often ignored or taken for granted. We forget about it, it's just there. Like a painting on the wall.

On my trip to Croatia this summer I saw a photo of a cultural event in Rijeka from 1978, people lined up in the street, smiling for the camera. I love old photos of artist groups from various places, all these little regional groups working in parallel, all around the globe. There's something romantic about it, the urge to create in some little corner of the world. And then I thought about the revolutionary impulse, people taking to the street, how it shares a certain bravery and recklessness with the impulse to make art, to communicate. What has happened to the revolutionary impulse? Did somebody forget to water it?

Last year I was painting about astronauts and Native Americans on the Moon. Those paintings were about technology as a dead end, about the empty future, about the end of the world. I needed to get away from that place. Rather than projecting into the future, I turned to the past, which I find is vanishing just as quickly. If you look at old photographs they show worlds gone by. It's like magic, but also filled with sadness. We can't get the lost time back. I draw diagrams over the actors from the past, looking for clues in the surface of time. Is there a pattern, some underlying structure that lies hidden in the most mundane corners of existence? Back behind the plants on the shelf or on the window sill where the revolution lies forgotten?

The Vit Soukup retrospective had a big impact on me. His use of photographs as source material, his approach to the banal, his interest in Czech popular culture and the period of normalization. Normalization seems to live on – just as many people have internalised totalitarianism, only understanding power and betrayal in their interpersonal relationships, the cultural stasis in the 80s seems to still be inside us too, we're stuck in it like a kind of quicksand. Time vanishes, but in other ways it seems to keep returning. We're trapped in the Eternal Return, like hamsters on a wheel.

The immigrant is the person who stands at a crossroads where different cultures meet; the immigrant becomes a cultural hybrid whose experience falls somewhat to the side of the national cultural dialogue. Immigrants never fully belong to their new home, nor to the one they left. We are like uprooted plants, trying to send a tap root down to find new water. The wind blows us around like dust.

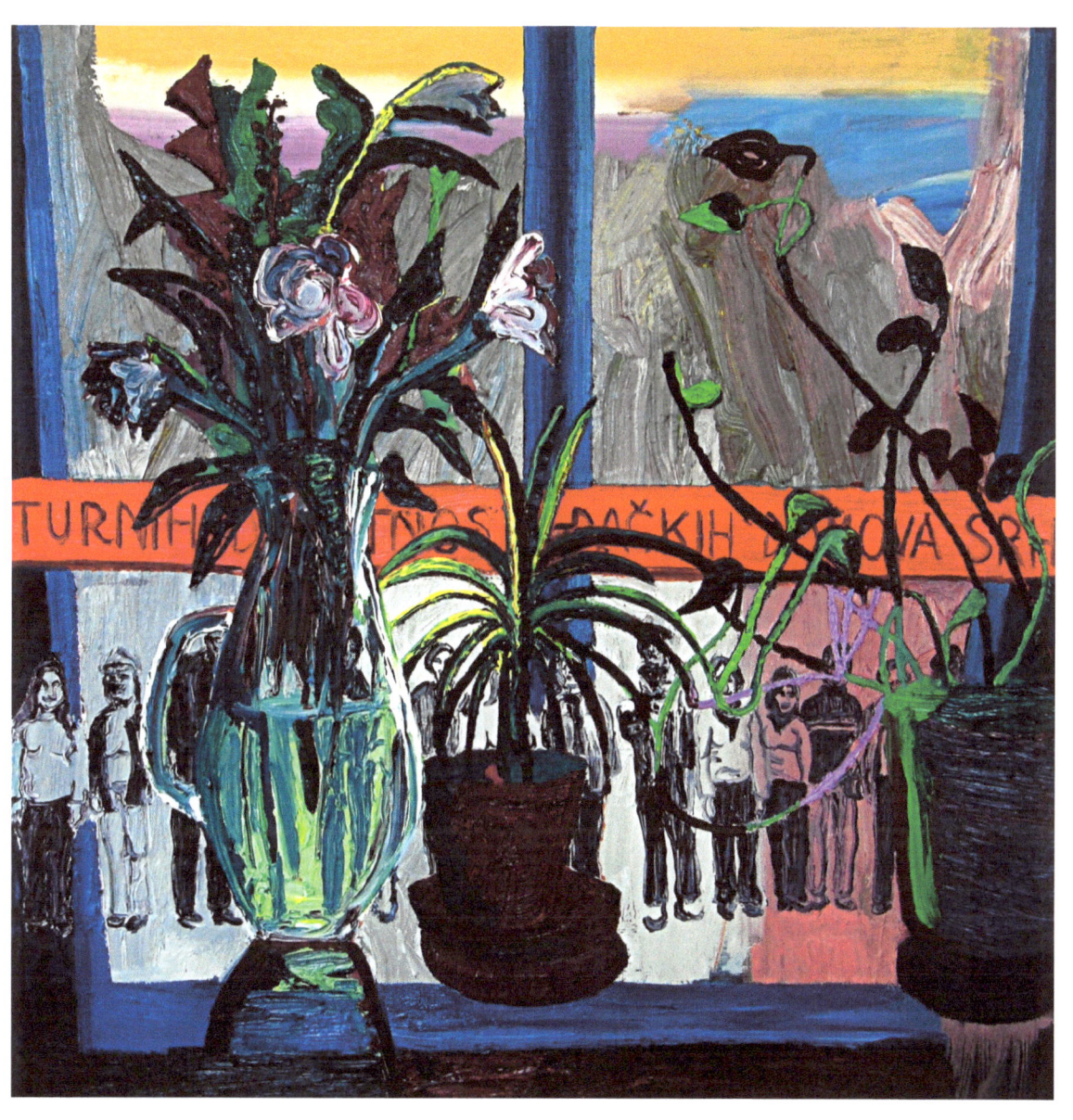

Window (Cultural Festival), 2013
oil on canvas, 100 x 100 cm (39" x 39")

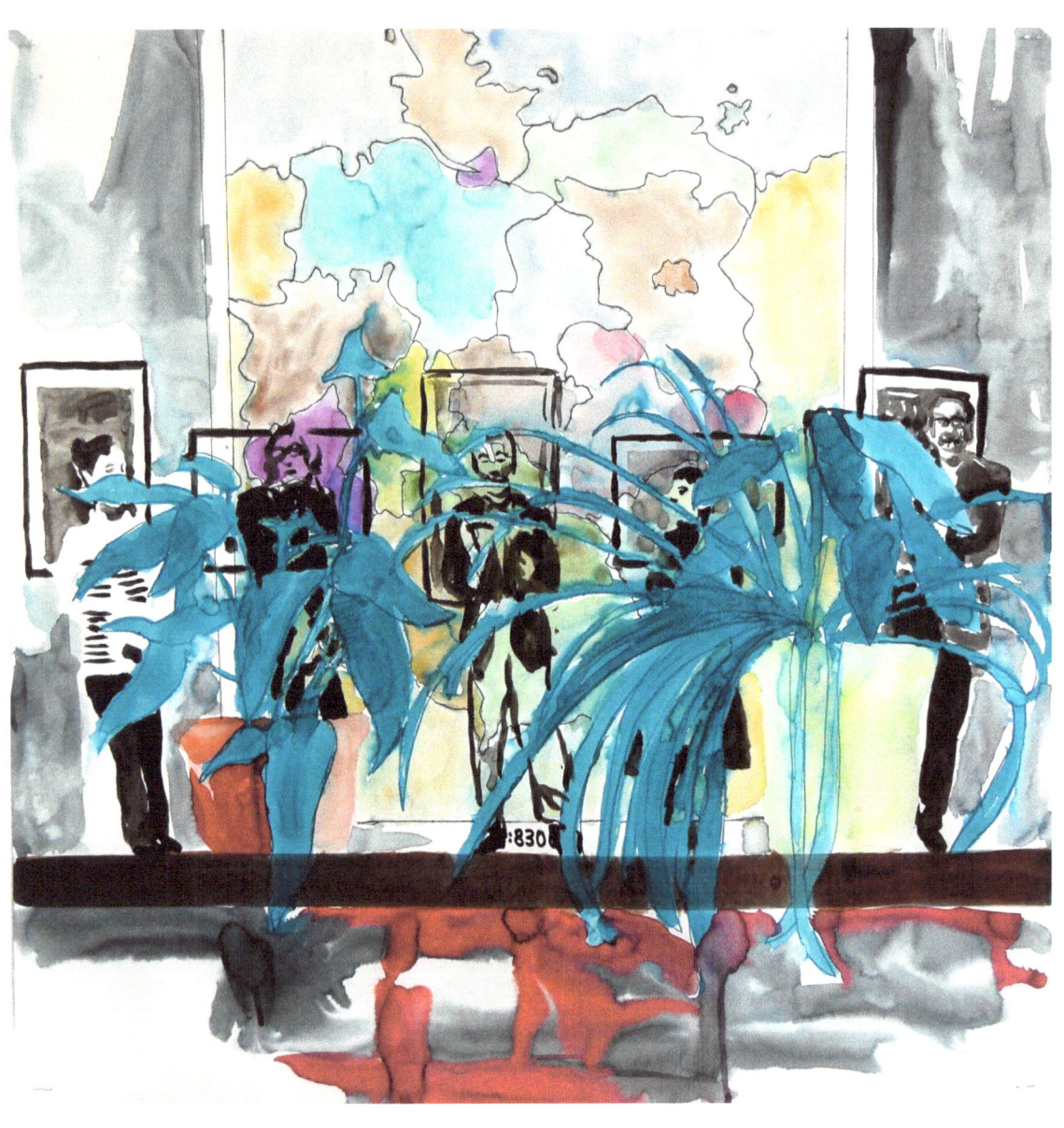

Deutschland (Exhibition on a Shelf), 2013
ink and watercolor, 70 x 70 cm (27 ½" x 27 ½")

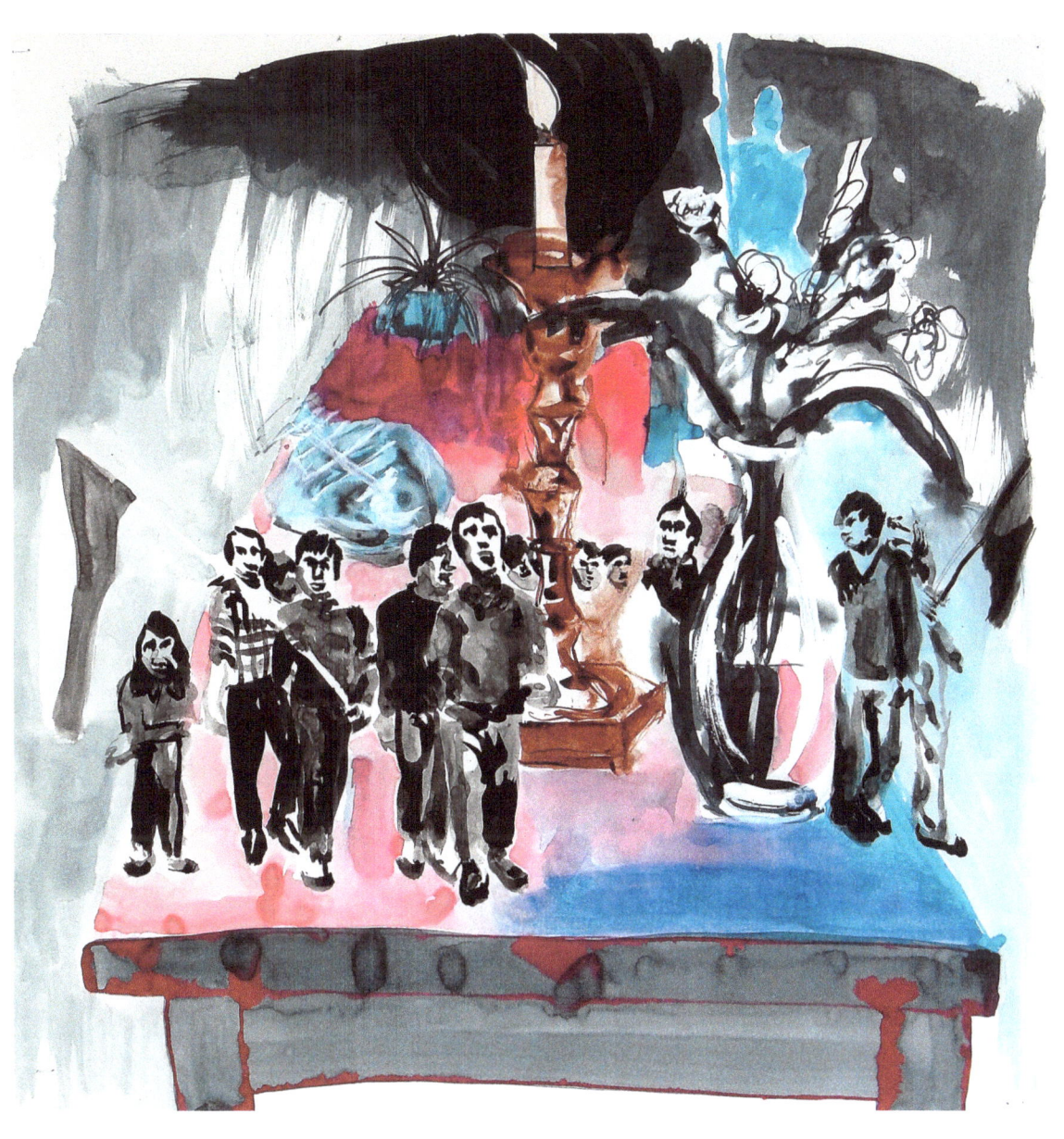

Table (Revolution), 2013
ink and watercolor, 70 x 70 cm (27 ½" x 27 ½")

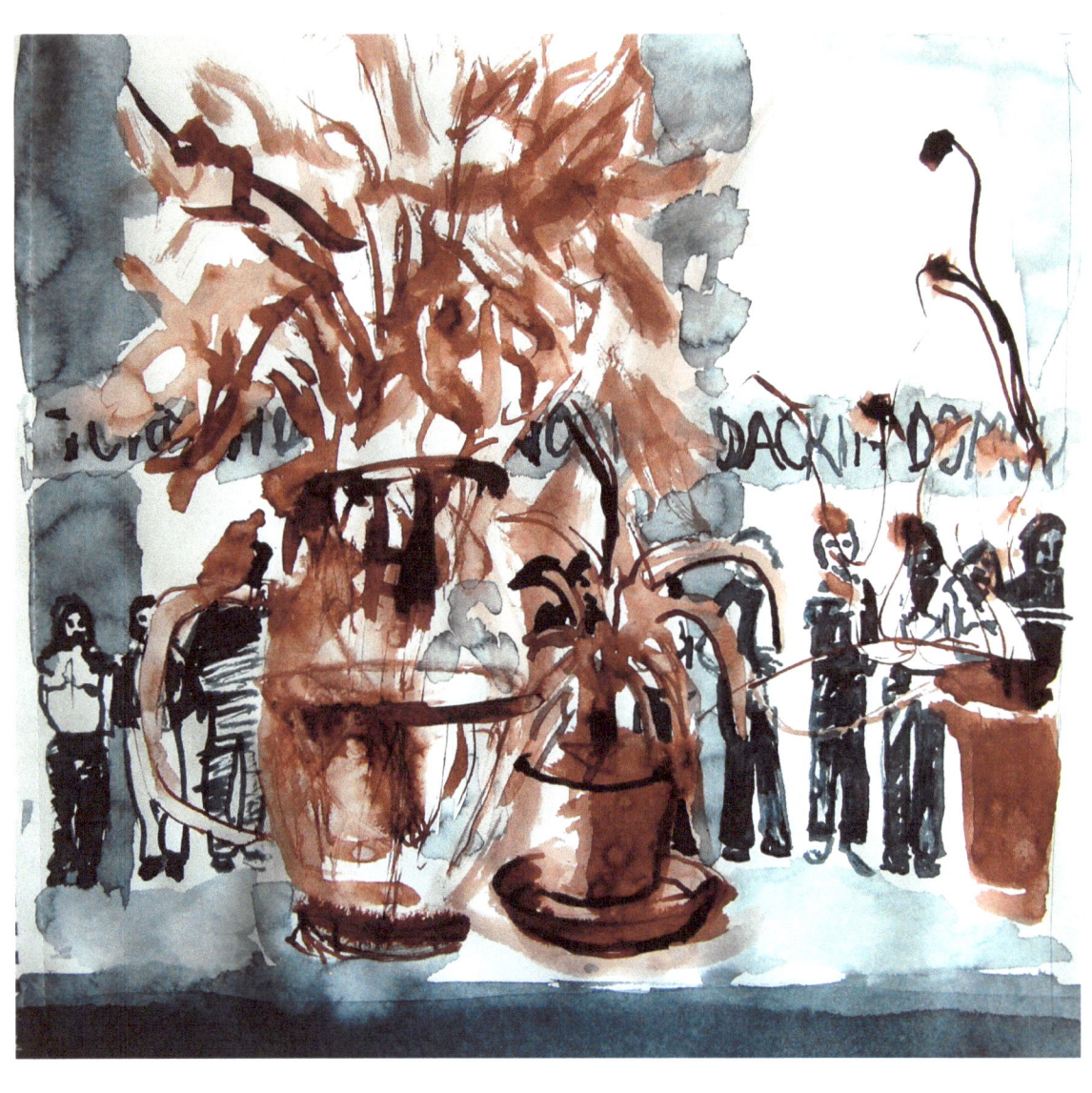

Window, study, 2013
ink on paper, 30 x 30 cm (12" x 12")

IMAGINARY FRIENDS

This group of work grew out of the idea to paint portraits of people from memory, or to invent them altogether. The challenge was to instill a personality into the face, to create a presence, like a character in a novel, which suggested some back story, or some unseen events. I was also dealing with particular types: shy teenage girls, cowboys, heavy metal fans, crying women, old rockers, etc. In a sense these characters came to represent a sort of self–portrait through others; in a Jungian sense, a kind of collective unconscious expressing itself through the psyche, the anima and animus of the world's soul. They are my imaginary friends who come to help me, like familiars, in the world of the imagination.

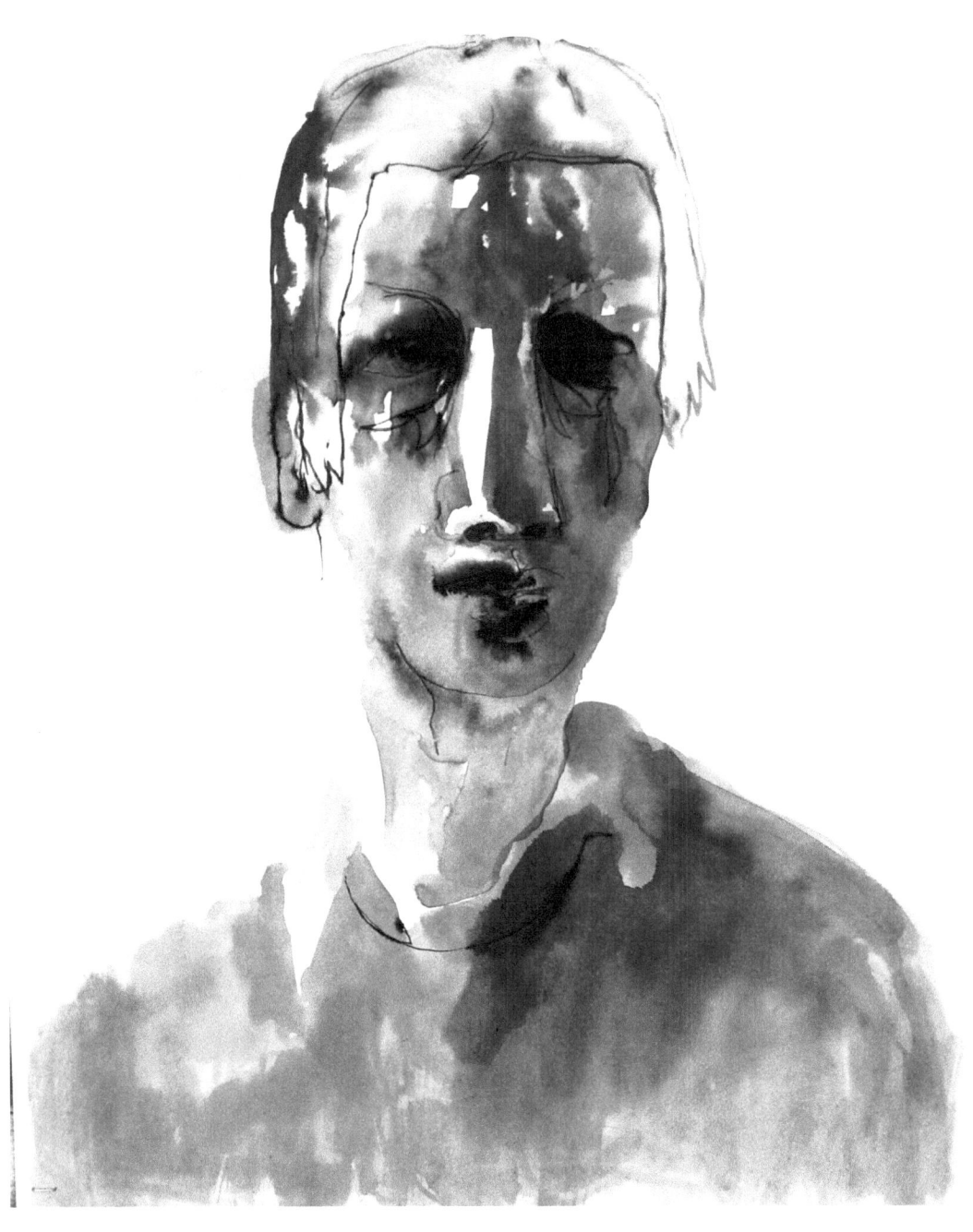

Portrait XIII, 2013
ink brush on paper, 65 x 50 cm (25 ½" x 19 ½")

48

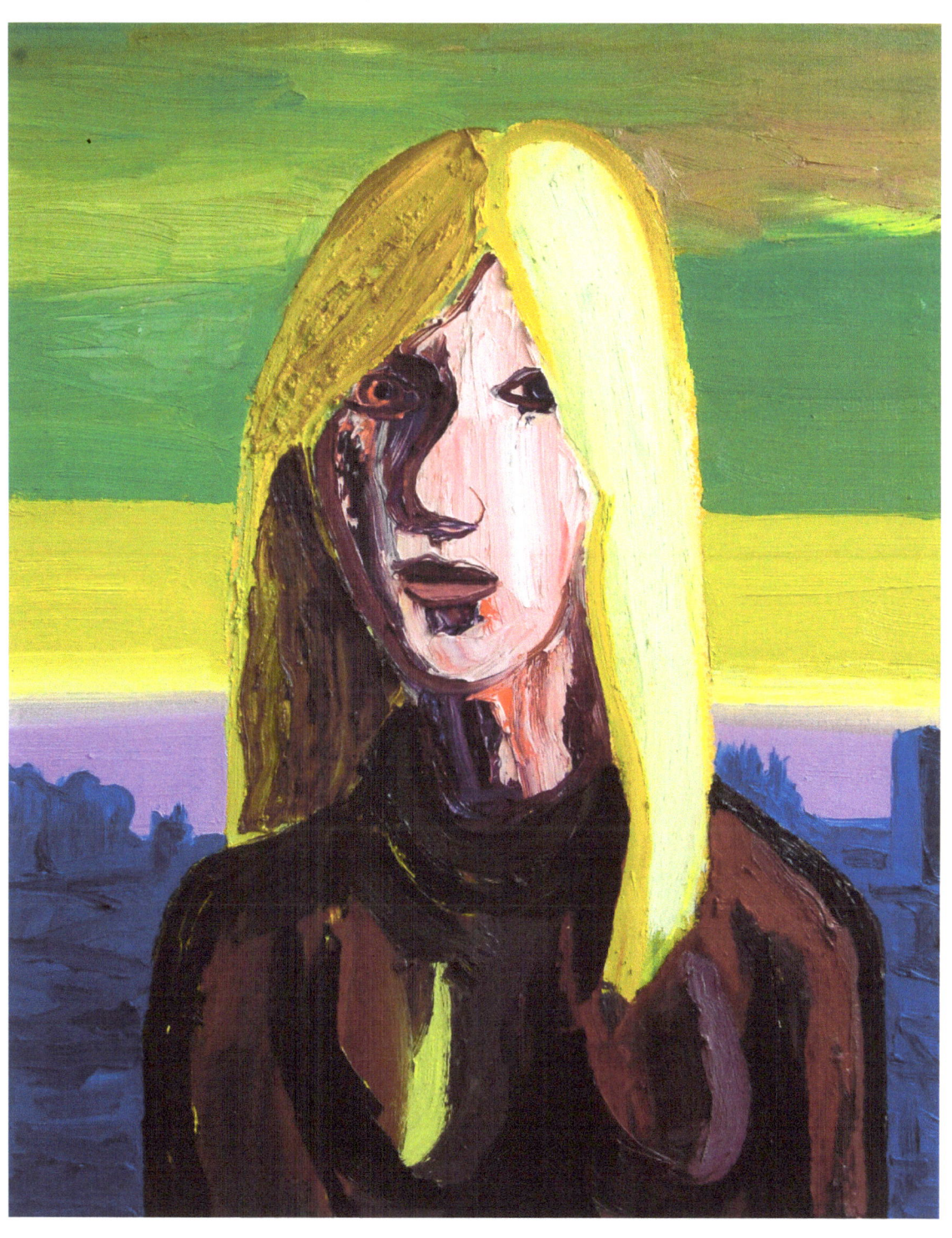

Girl, 2013
oil on canvas, 80 x 65 cm (31 ½" x 25 ½")

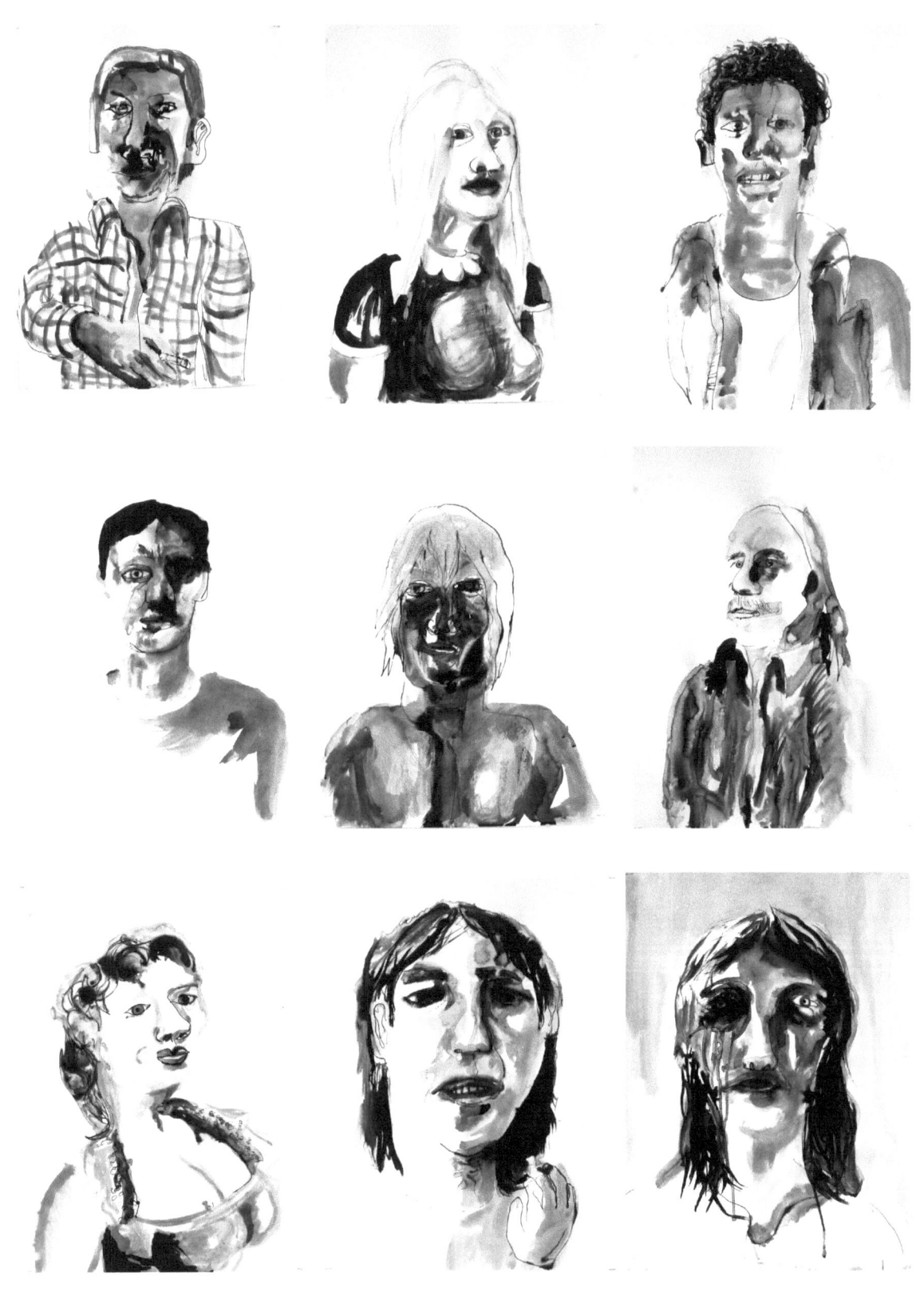

Portraits (various), 2013
ink brush on paper, 65 x 50 cm (25 ½" x 19 ½")

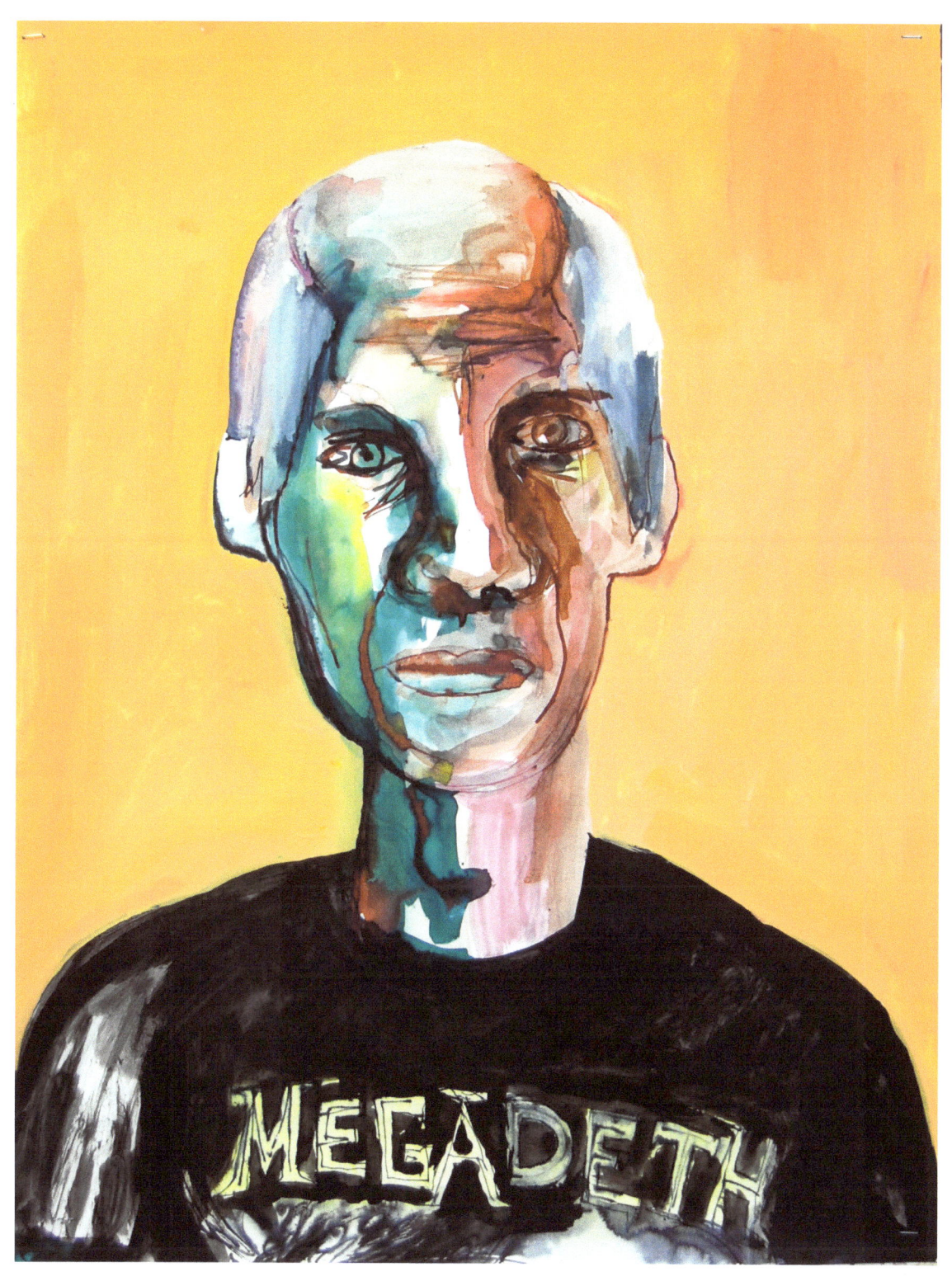

Man in a Megadeth Tshirt II, 2013
ink and watercolor on paper, 65 x 50 cm (25 ½" x 19 ½")

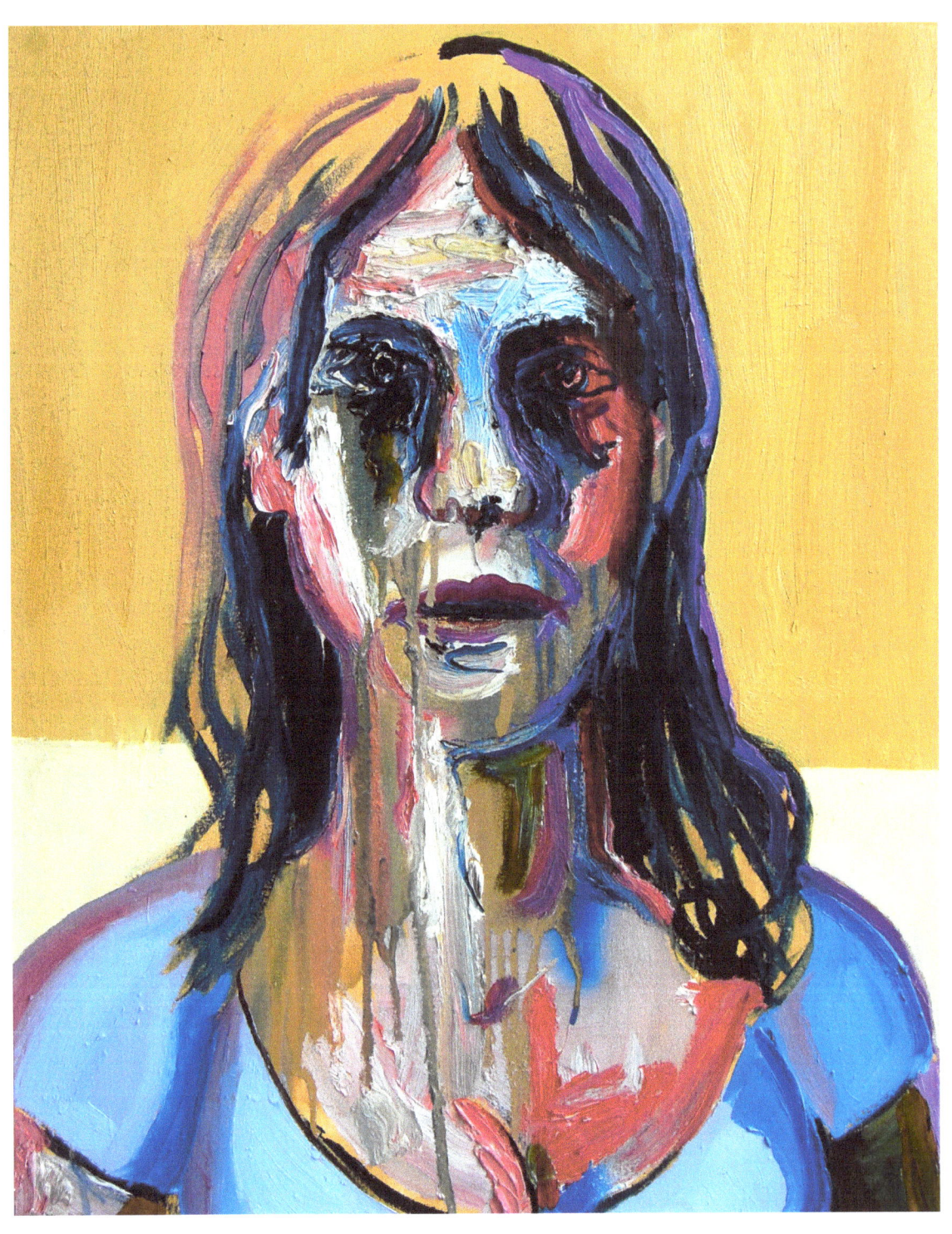

Weeping Woman, 2013
oil on canvas, 80 x 65 cm (31 ½" x 25 ½")

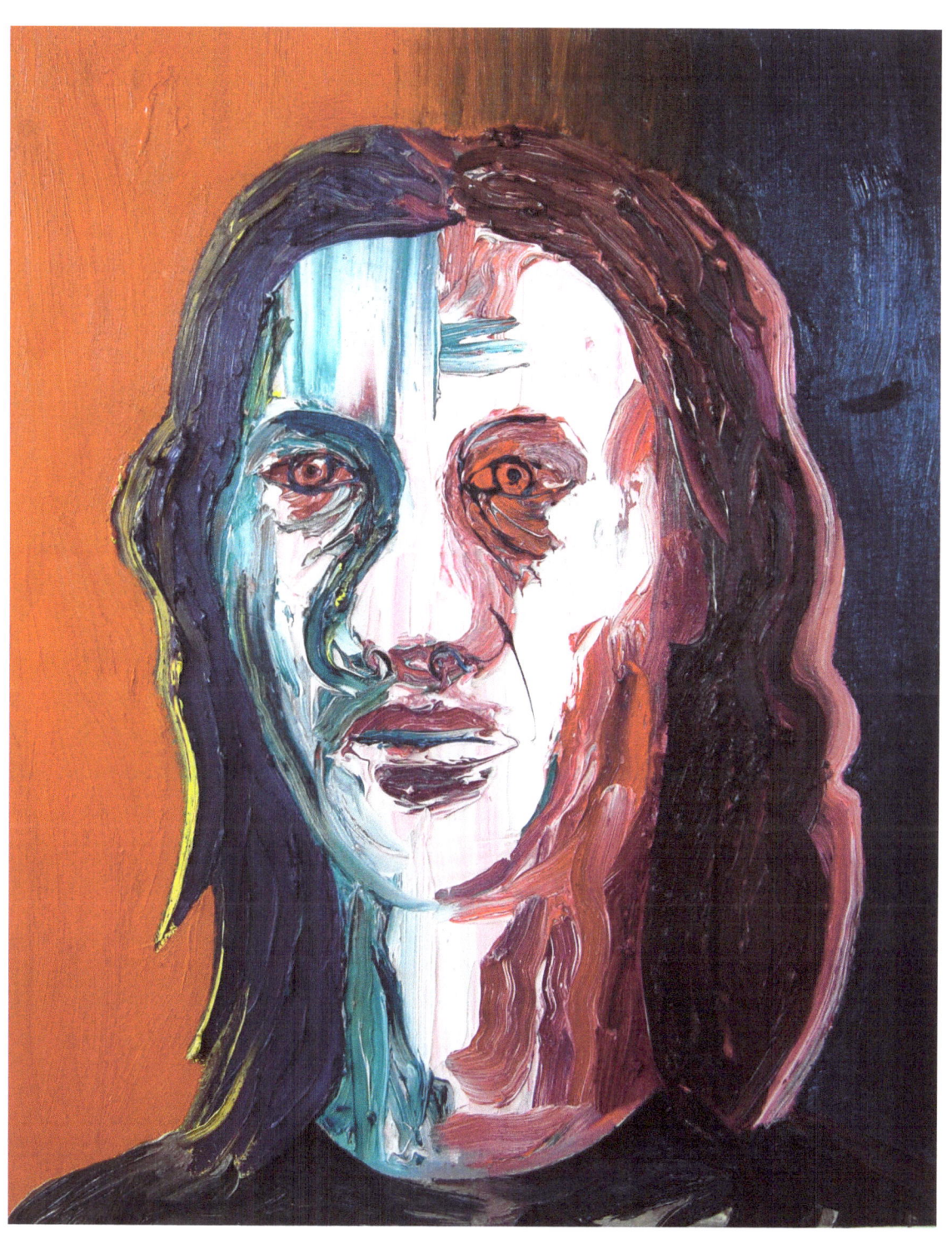

Rocker, 2013
oil on canvas, 80 x 65 cm (31 ½" x 25 ½")

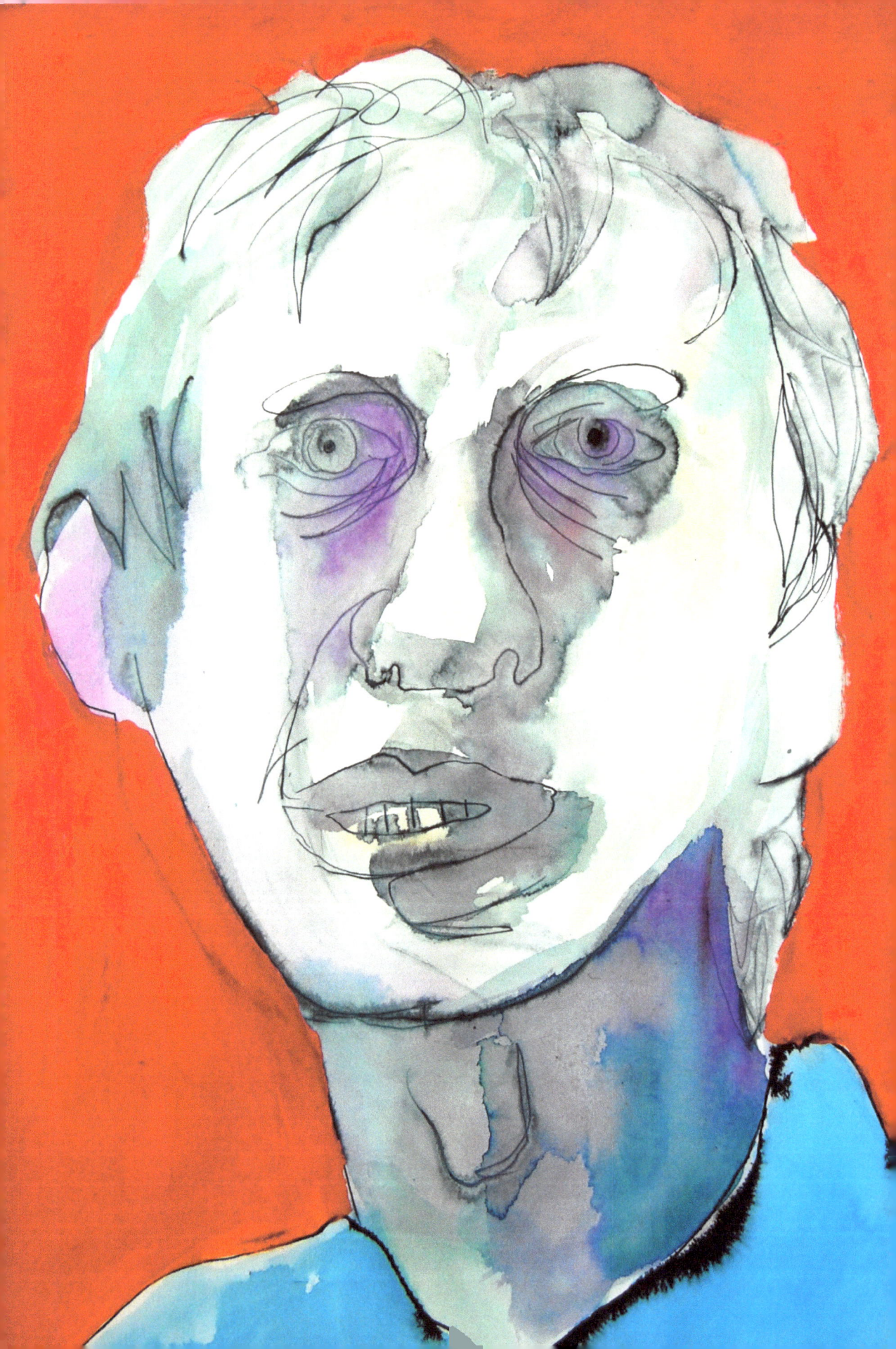

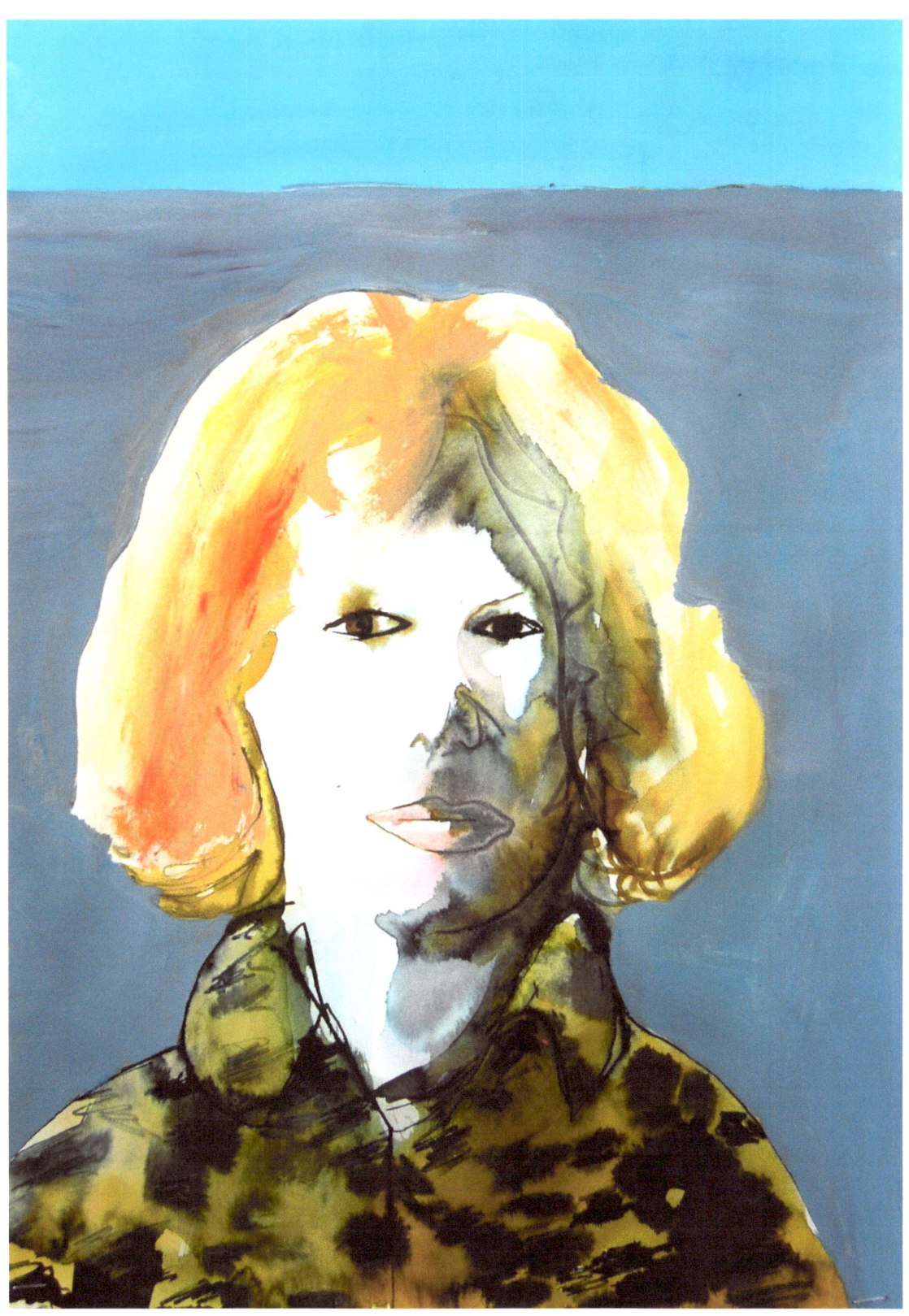

British Dad, 2013
pen and ink and watercolor,
40 x 32 cm (15 ¾" x 12 ½")

Redhead, 2013
pen and ink and watercolor,
40 x 32 cm (15 ¾" x 12 ½")

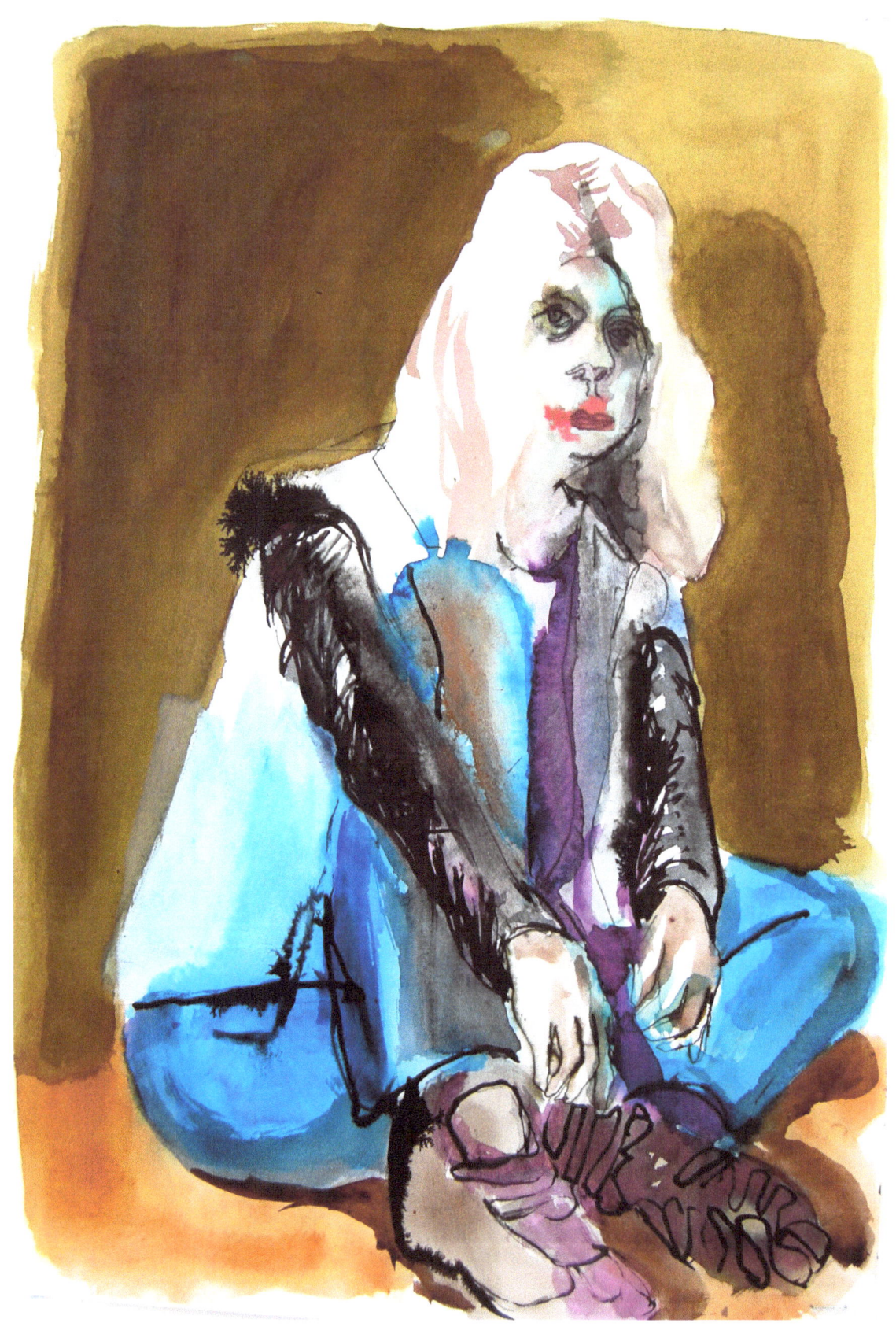

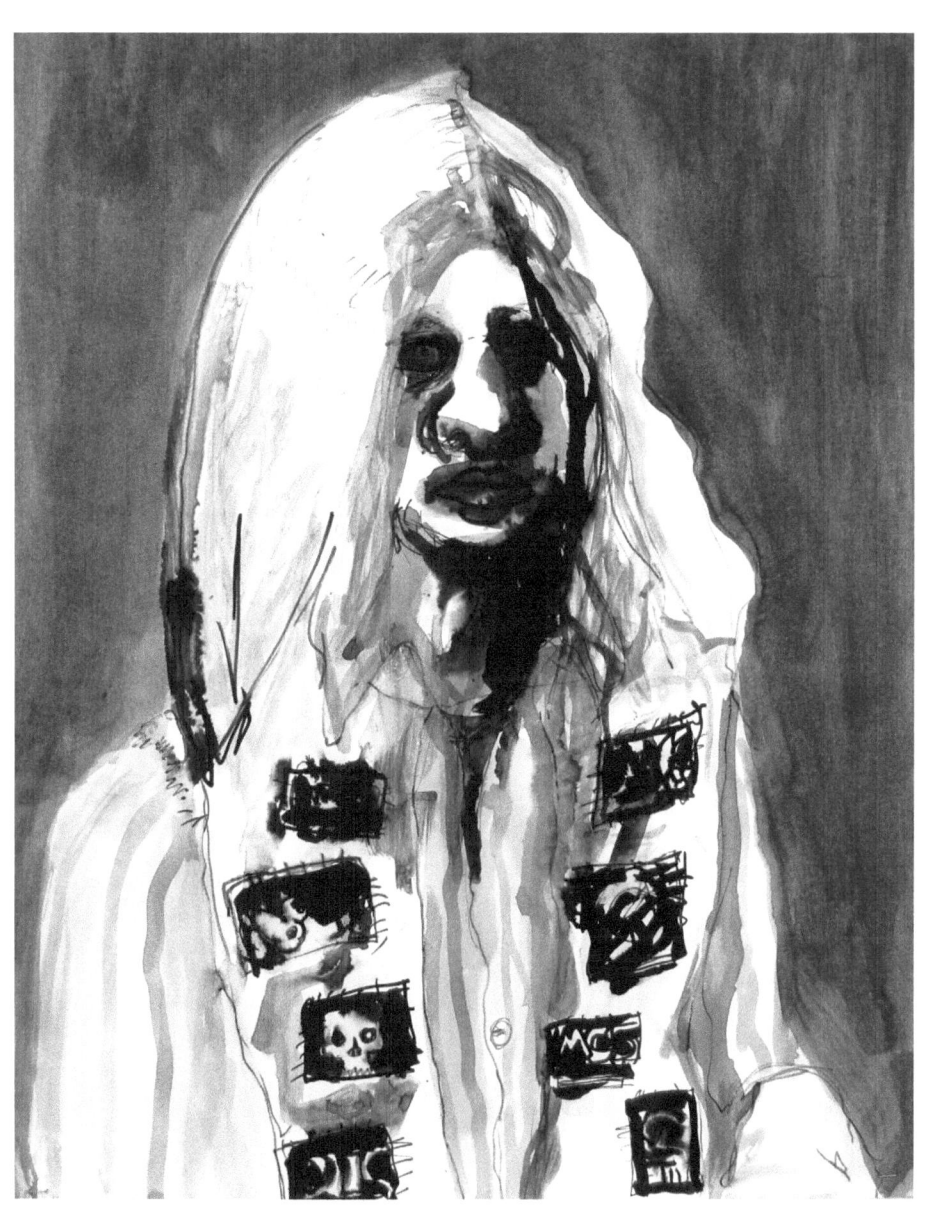

Metalhead, 2013
pen and ink and watercolor on paper,
40 x 32 cm (15 ¾" x 12 ½")

Metalhead, 2013
ink on paper,
65 x 50 cm (25 ½" x 19 ½")

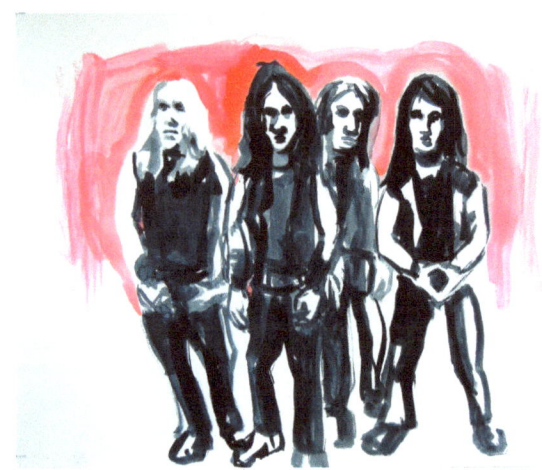

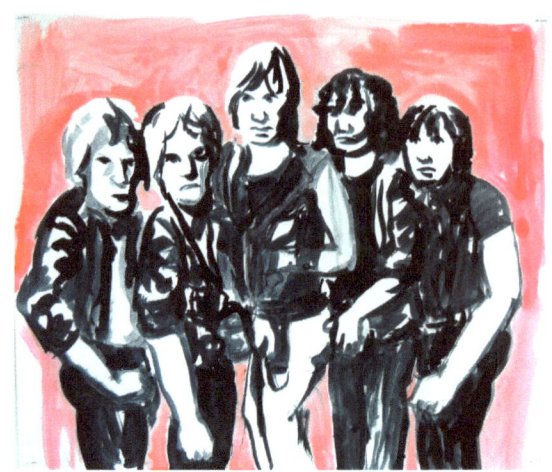

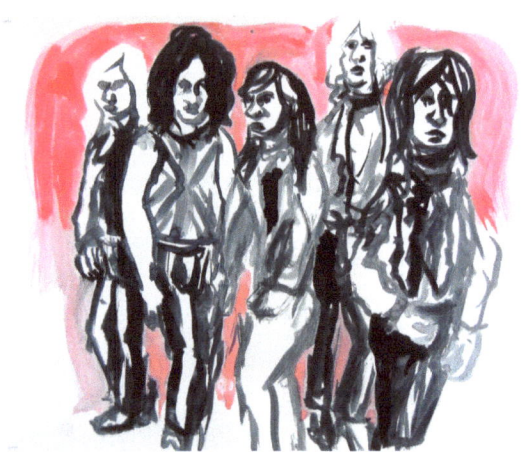

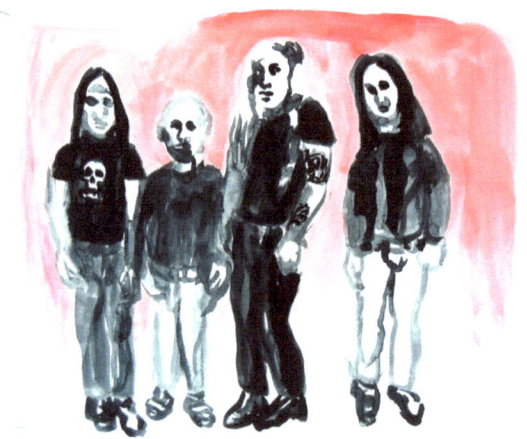

Rock Band II, 2013
ink on paper, 50 x 65 cm (19 ½" x 25 ½")

Rock Band I, 2013
ink on paper, 50 x 65 cm (19 ½" x 25 ½")

Rock Band IV, 2013
ink on paper, 50 x 65 cm (19 ½" x 25 ½")

Rock Band III, 2013
ink on paper, 50 x 65 cm (19 ½" x 25 ½")

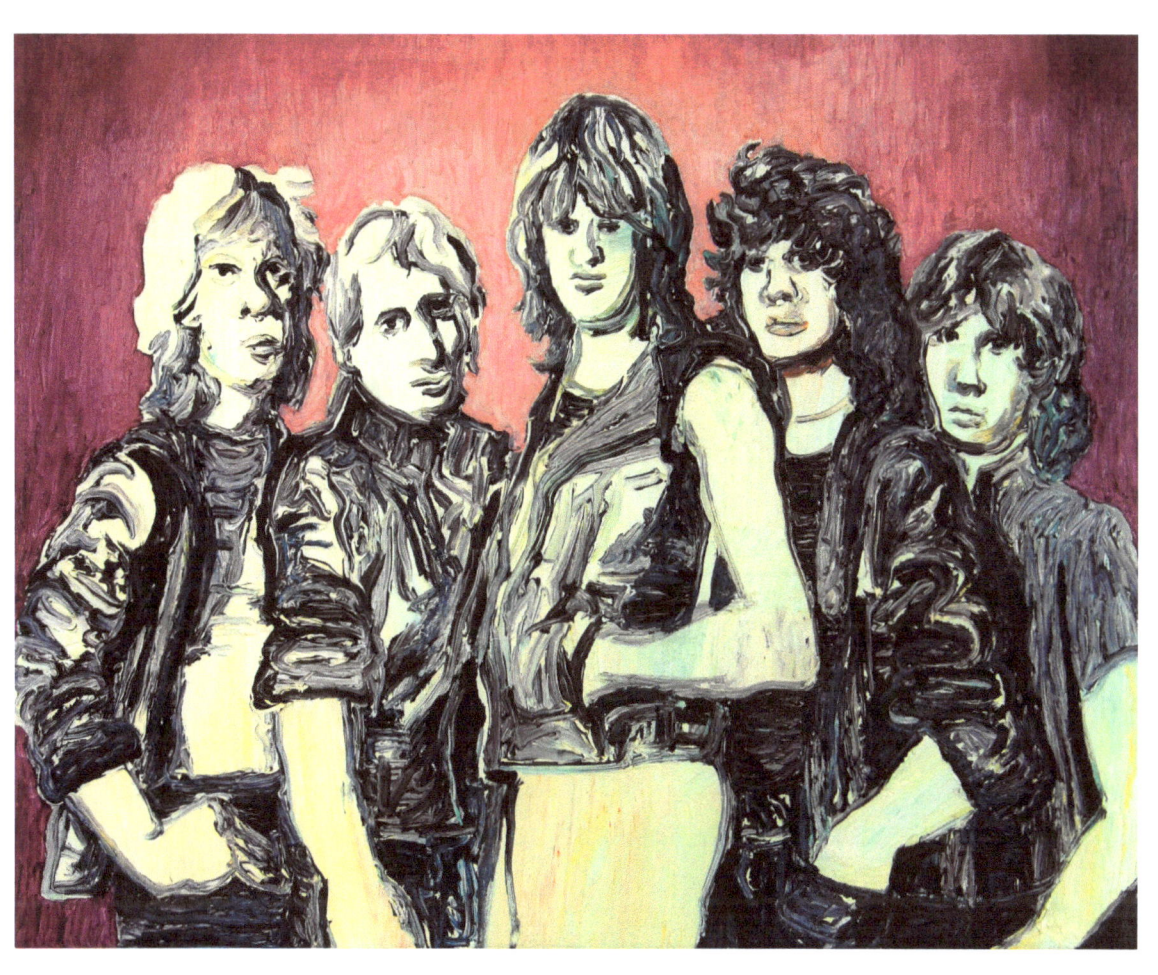

Rock Band, 2013
oil on canvas, 55 x 70 cm (21 ½" x 27 ½")

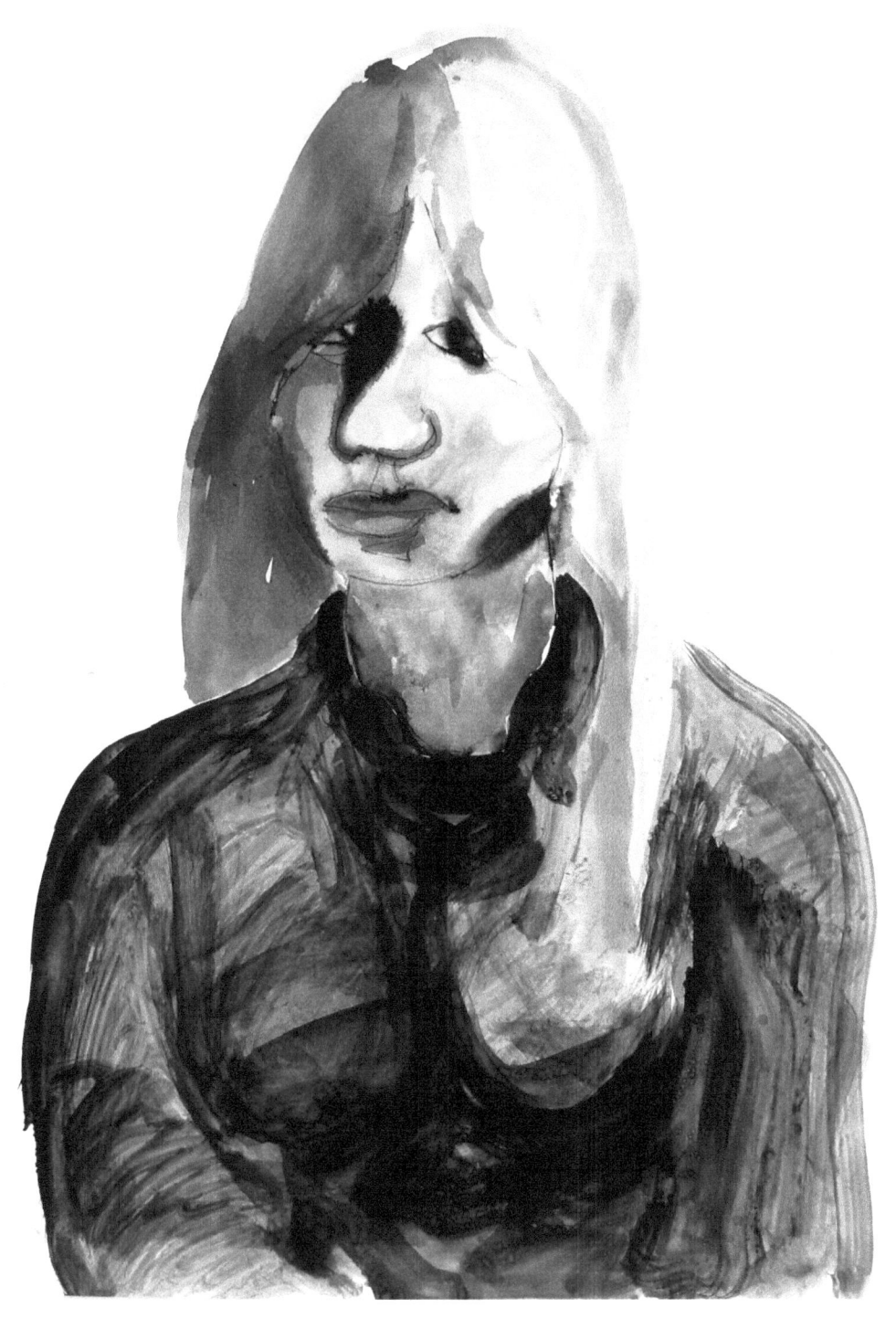

Portrait IV, 2013
ink brush on paper, 65 x 50 cm (25 ½" x 19 ½")

SACRED GEOMETRY

These drawings on old film publicity stills arose from my interest in early Greek philosophy, geometry with a protractor and compass, combined with my search for a connection with Czech culture. They were made in 2008 when I had my studio in the Meetfactory residence center. The mystery of the golden mean overlaid on the banal objects and faces in the photographs suggests some deeper meaning, some important conjunction of time and space, everything in its right place. Do the compositions reveal some invisible locus of power, some occult mystery hidden in photographs? It is meant to be ironic and absurd, nothing really holds together, everything is slipping, and the degraded sense of history and media in the photographs do not hold any clues. But they try.

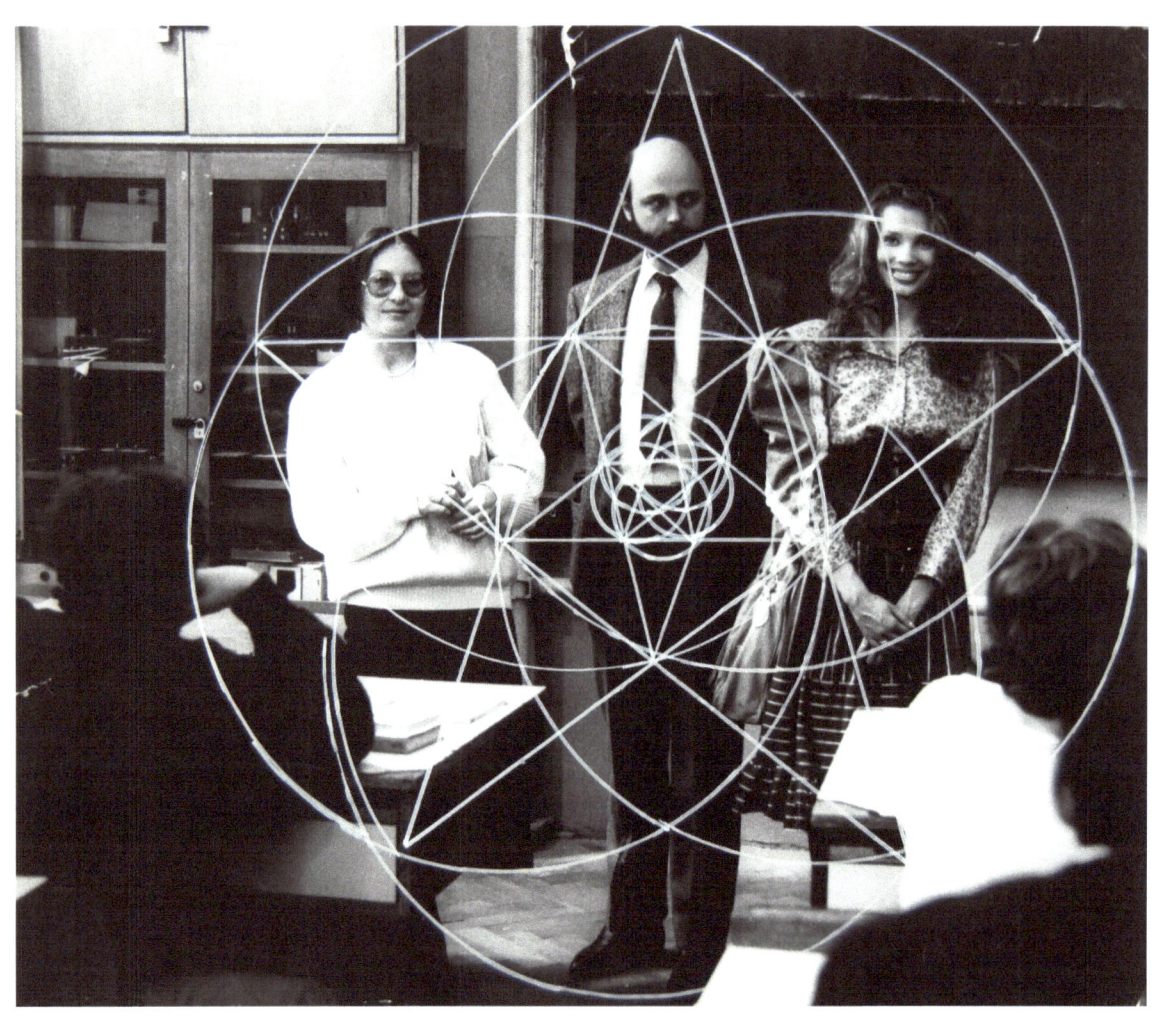

Sacred Geometry series, detail, 2008
ink on film stills, 21 x 30 cm (8" x 12")

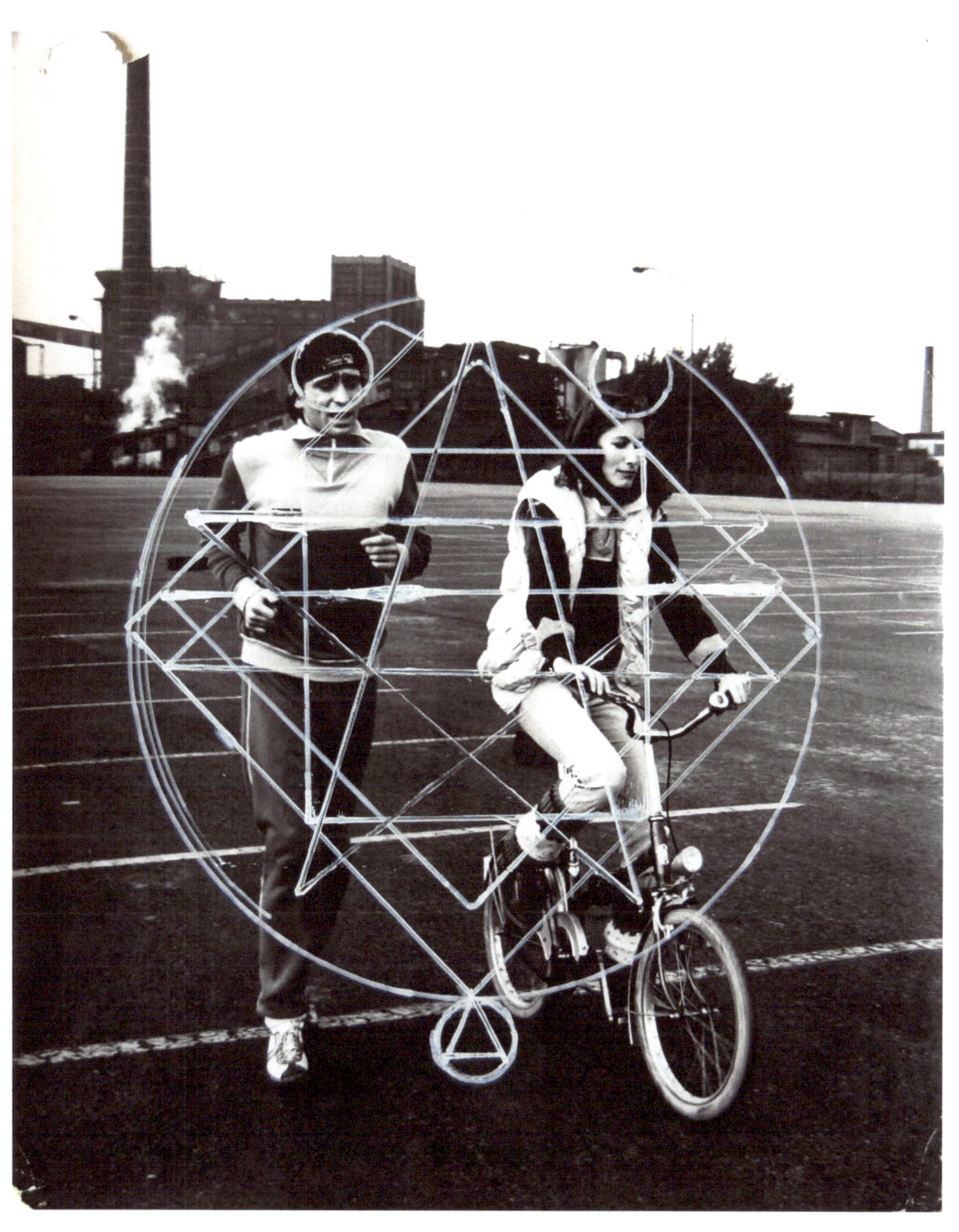

Sacred Geometry series, 2008
ink on film stills, 30 x 21 cm (12" x 8")

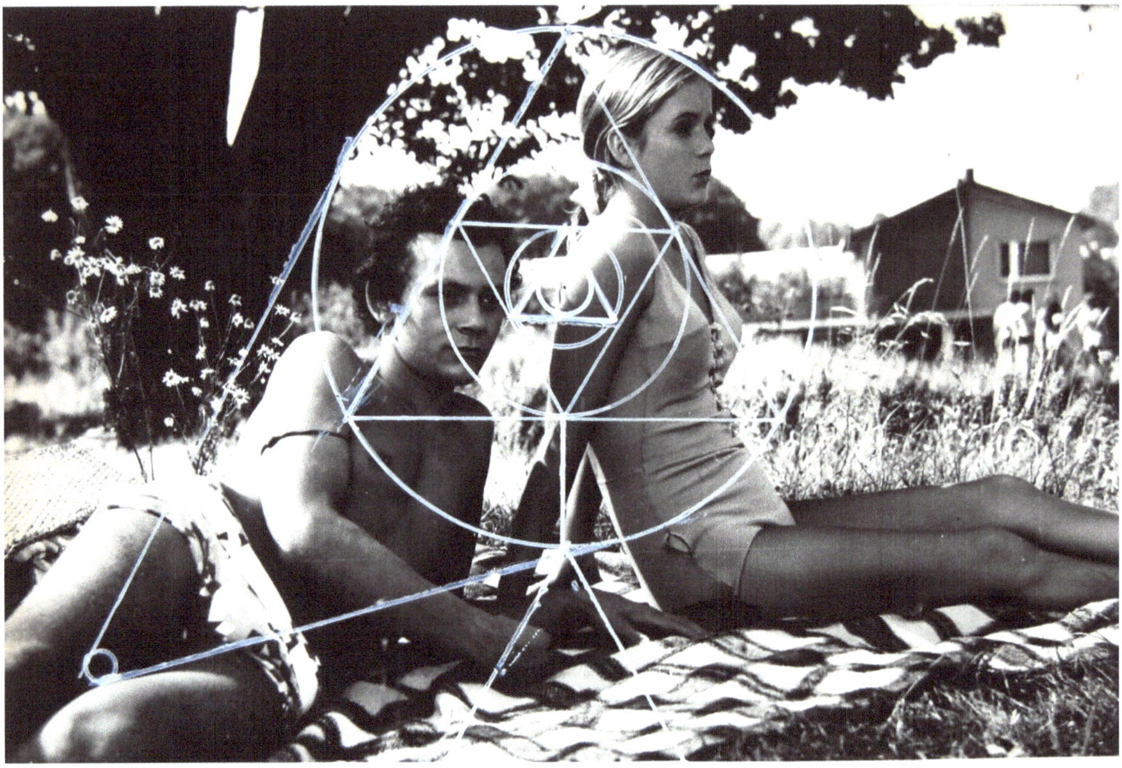

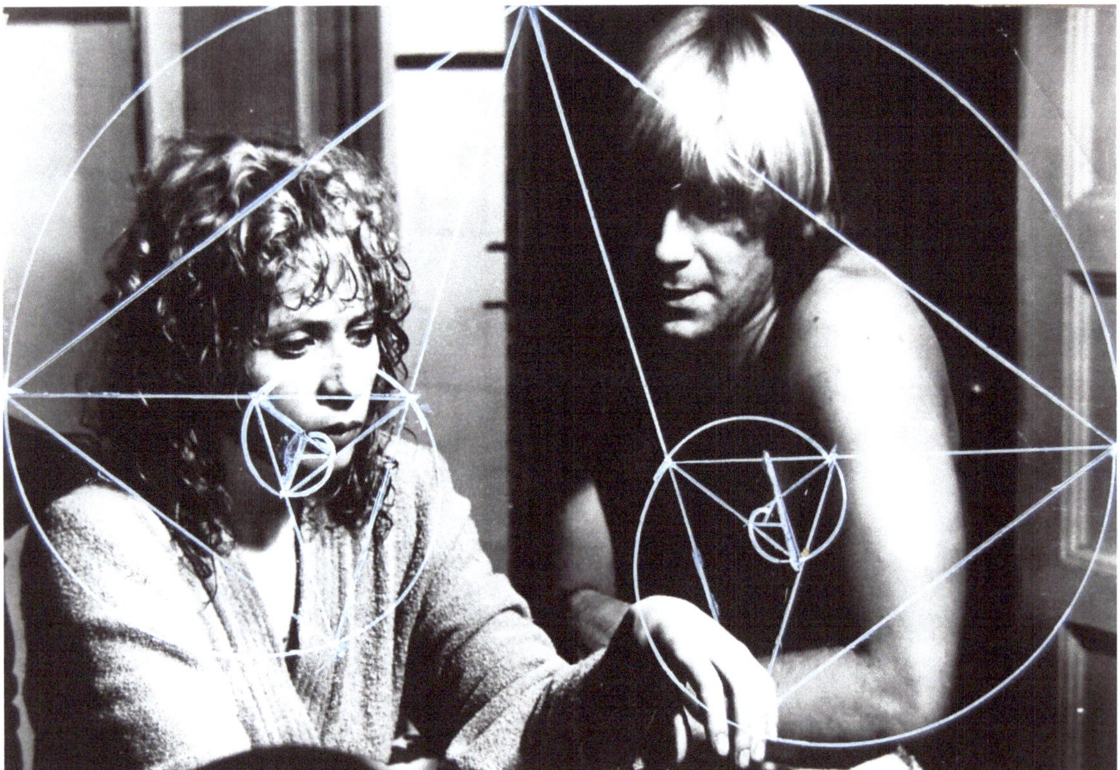

Sacred Geometry series, 2008
ink on film stills, 21 x 30 cm (8" x 12")

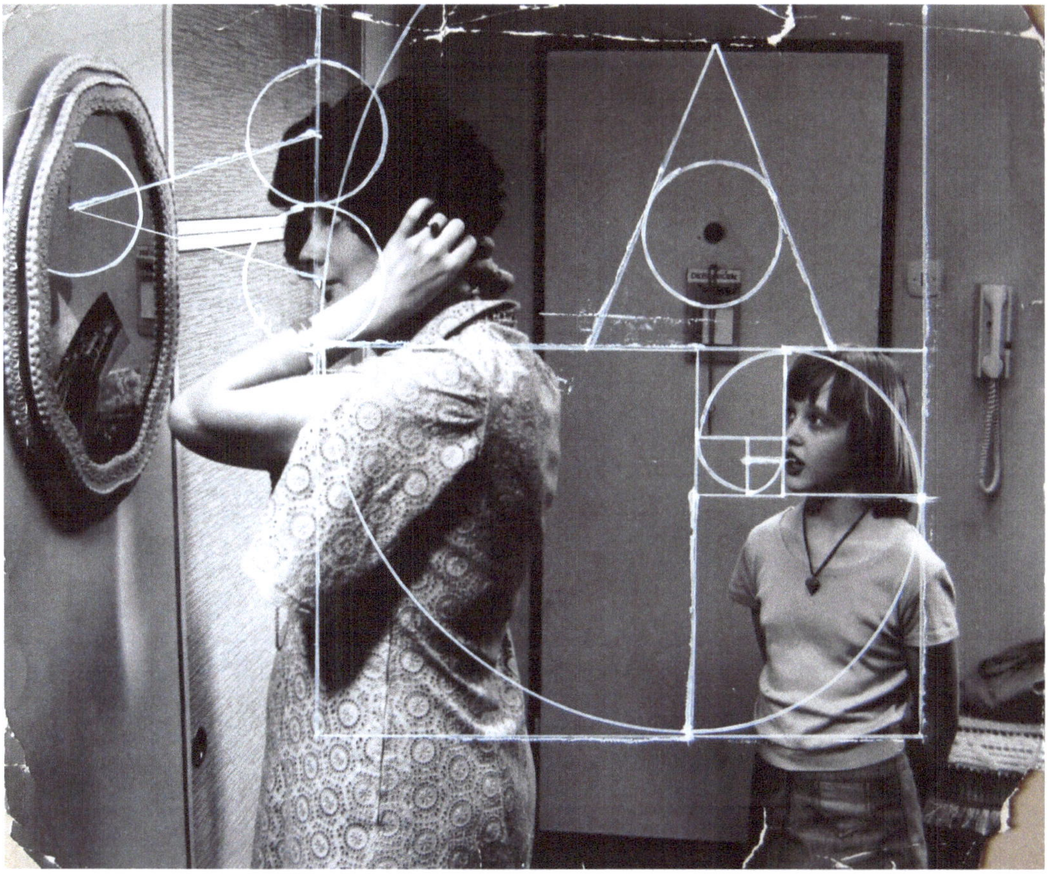

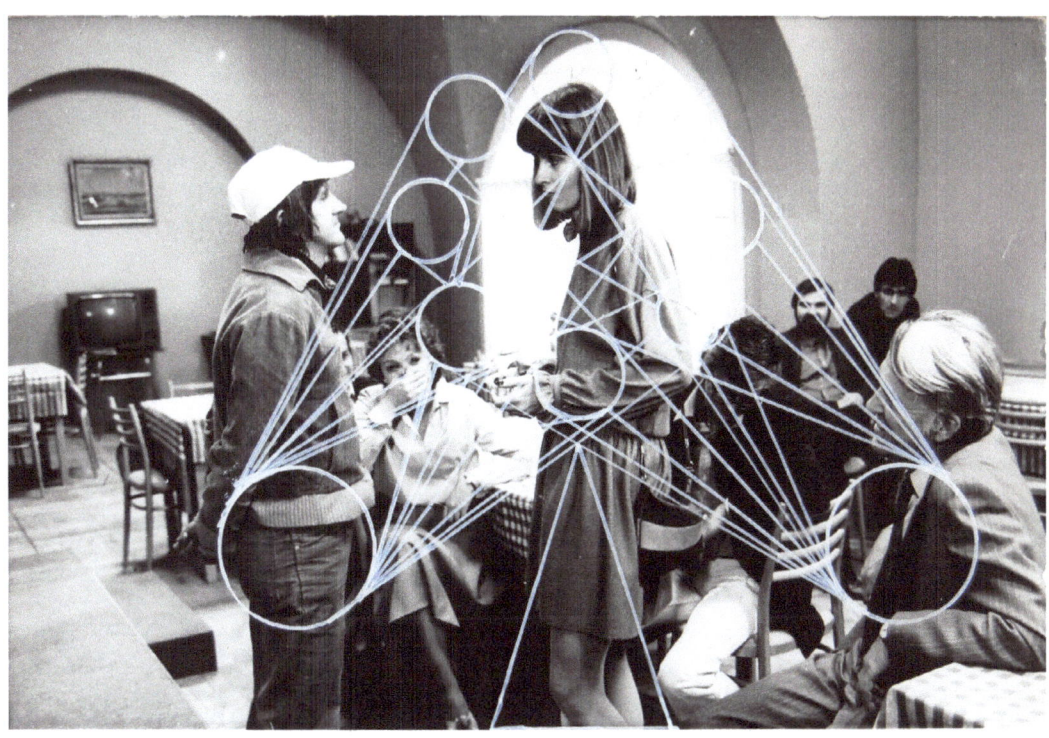

Sacred Geometry series, 2008
ink on film stills, 21 x 30 cm (8" x 12")

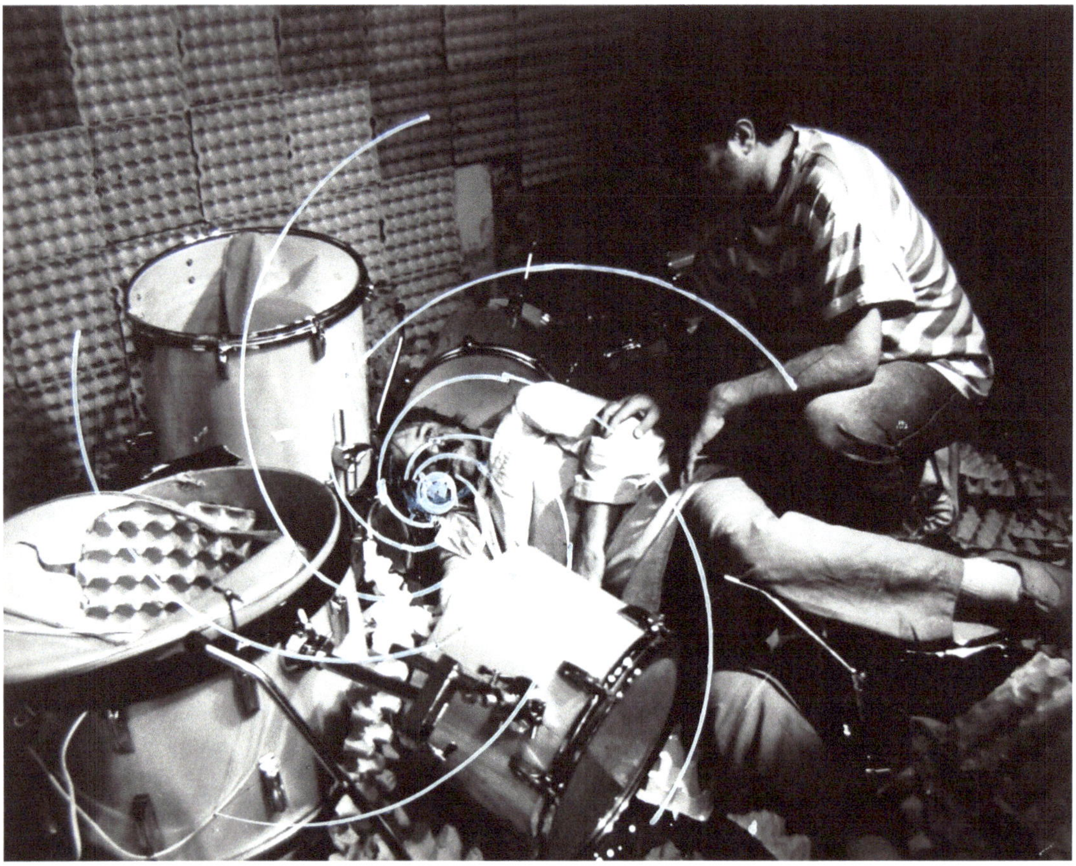

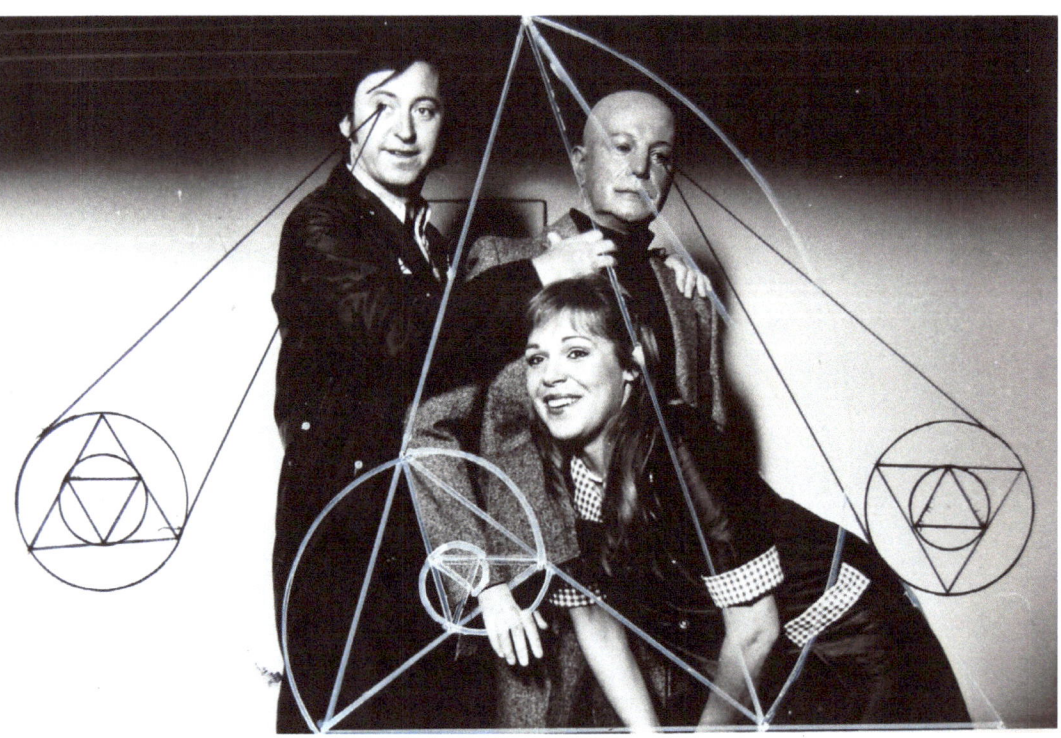

Sacred Geometry series, 2008
ink on film stills, 21 x 30 cm (8" x 12")

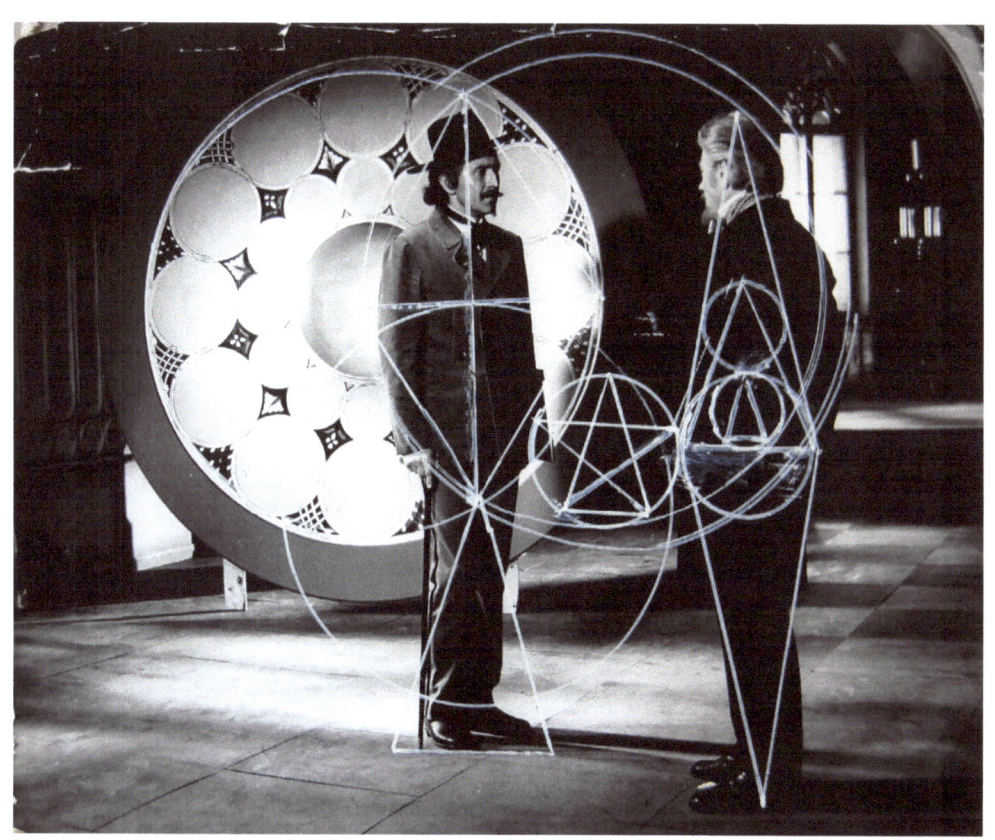

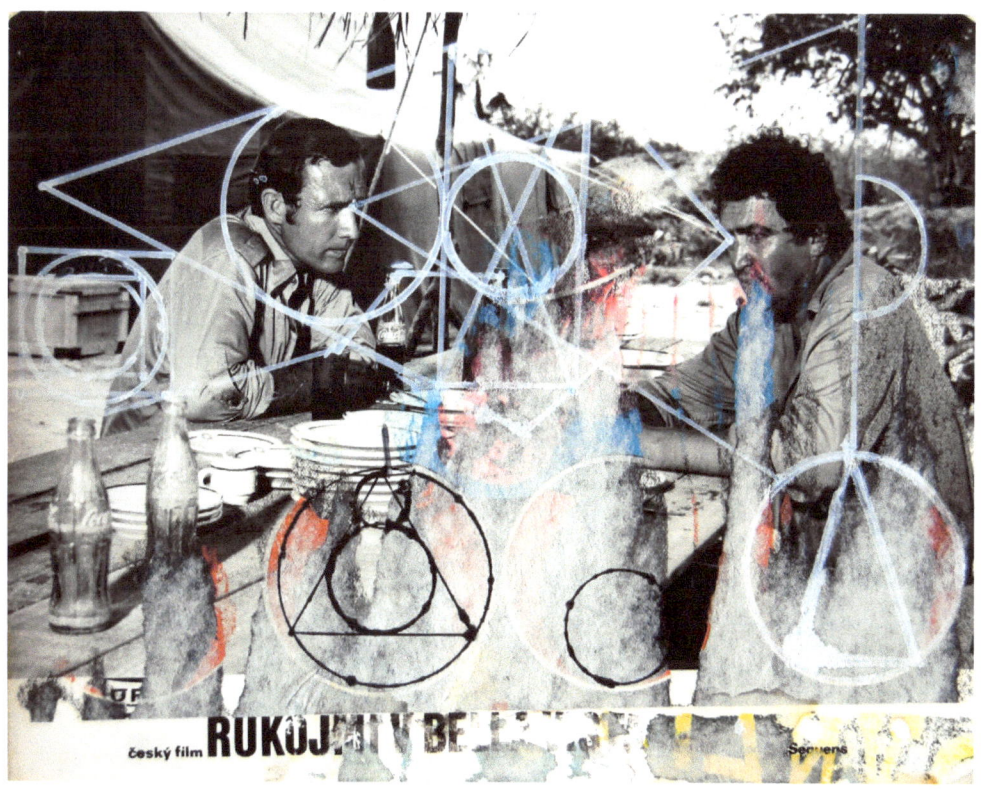

Sacred Geometry series, 2008
ink on film stills, 21 x 30 cm (8" x 12")

KONEC / THE END

This is the end, beautiful friend
This is the end, my only friend
The end of our elaborate plans
The end of everything that stands
The end
Jim Morrison – The End

Its probably not a good idea to have a skull in the studio. It sits on the shelf, empty eye sockets blindly gazing back at you. You start to have too many negative, even apocalyptic thoughts, and besides its in the air these days, environmental and economic collapse, mass extinction. Fun fun fun. What do we paint about at the end of the world? Is there a point to art anymore, if our grandchildren might be the last to walk the earth? Is this just some bizarre christian American obsession that got stuck in my mind from growing up over there? Or do our nightmares only come true when we keep thinking about them, giving them power?

A big ship on the horizon is evocative of travel, of times past, of the urge to escape. Like skulls, the Titanic has also become a kind of kitsch, almost all representational imagery suffers from this cynicism, the power of the image is being sucked dry. Can we say the word Titanic without thinking of Leonardo di Caprio? Hollywood is slowly but inexorably colonizing the imagination and the internet is destroying culture as we know it. In my paintings, the party's over, there's nothing left but a few sad monkeys, and the ship is moving away like a mirage. Are we going down like the Titanic, a one-way voyage to the bottom of the sea? When I emigrated I made my artistic journey explicit, and now I am like a ship at sea.

I might be tempting fate to call my exhibition The End. Will it be my last exhibition? To be a great artist, one needs a little black magic. It may all be smoke and mirrors, but you cant see the sleight of hand. The paintings group together and, like a good magic trick, become something greater than the sum of their parts. If I could clap my hands, spin around and vanish in a puff of smoke, I would. I've already disappeared twice, and every time I reappeared in the Czech Republic. I guess I'm a bad magician, it may take some time before I disappear again. That will be my last trick.

Postscript

This show like my show from a year before, "Moon Monkey Candle" at AM180, is made up of winter paintings and you can see from the text that there was a depressive, melancholic mood in the work. But after every end is a new beginning. The day after the opening my family and I flew to Italy on a trip to the heart of the Renaissance in Milano, Bologna and Florence. To see these beautiful altarpieces by Filippo Lippi, for example, reinvigorated my sense of the beauty and purpose of art. If I wrote here that the world may end in 100 years, well I'd like to contradict that, to make it clear that I don't long to embrace such a hopeless nihilistic position. Soon after my return to Prague I received news that my dear friend and former roommate Blaine Pitzer was in intensive care with colon cancer, and then the next morning came the news that he had died at the age of 47. I'm still meditating on what he meant to me and the meaning of our lives, but it underscored the fact that life is short and bittersweet. There is very little time and we must seek the light, hold on to joy and believe in love.

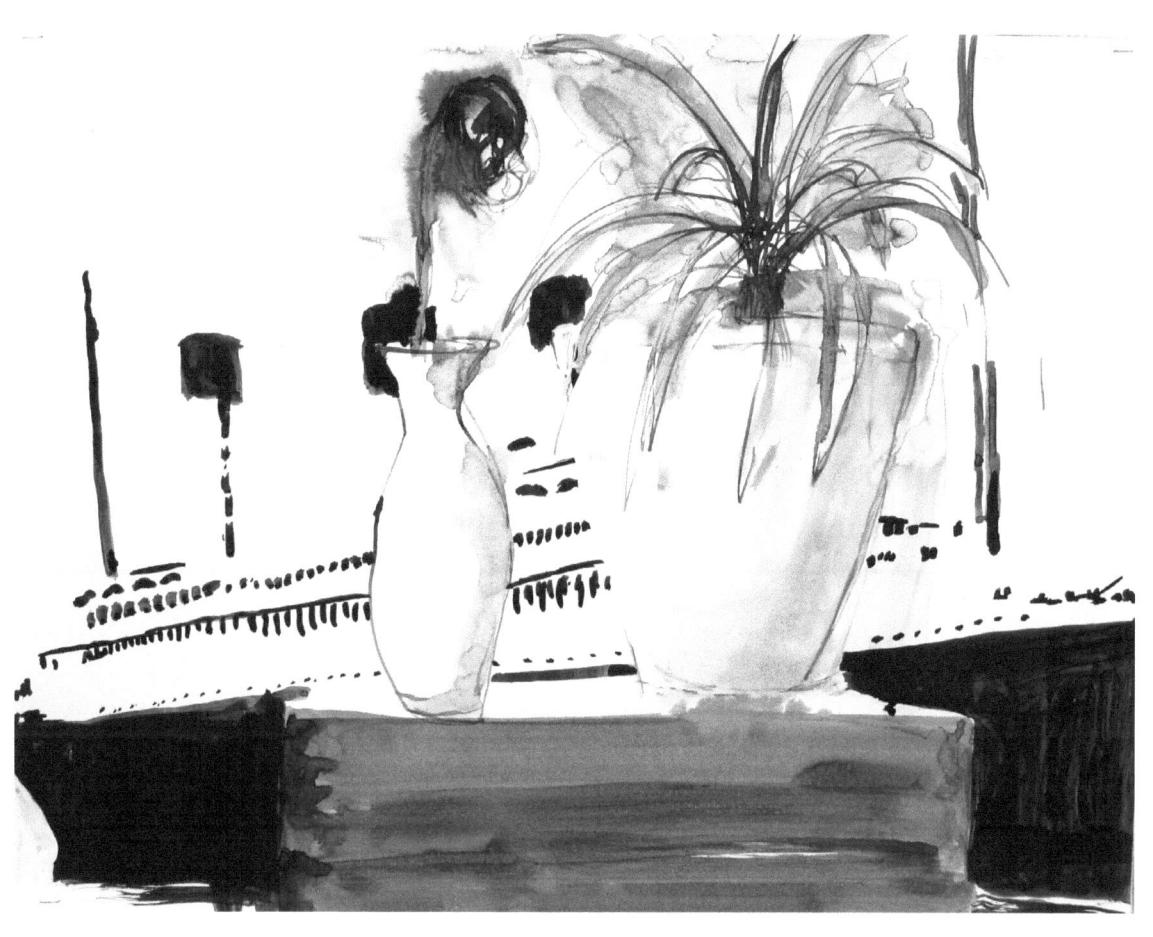

Titanic (Still Life), 2013
ink brush on paper, 50 x 65 cm (19 ½" x 25 ½")

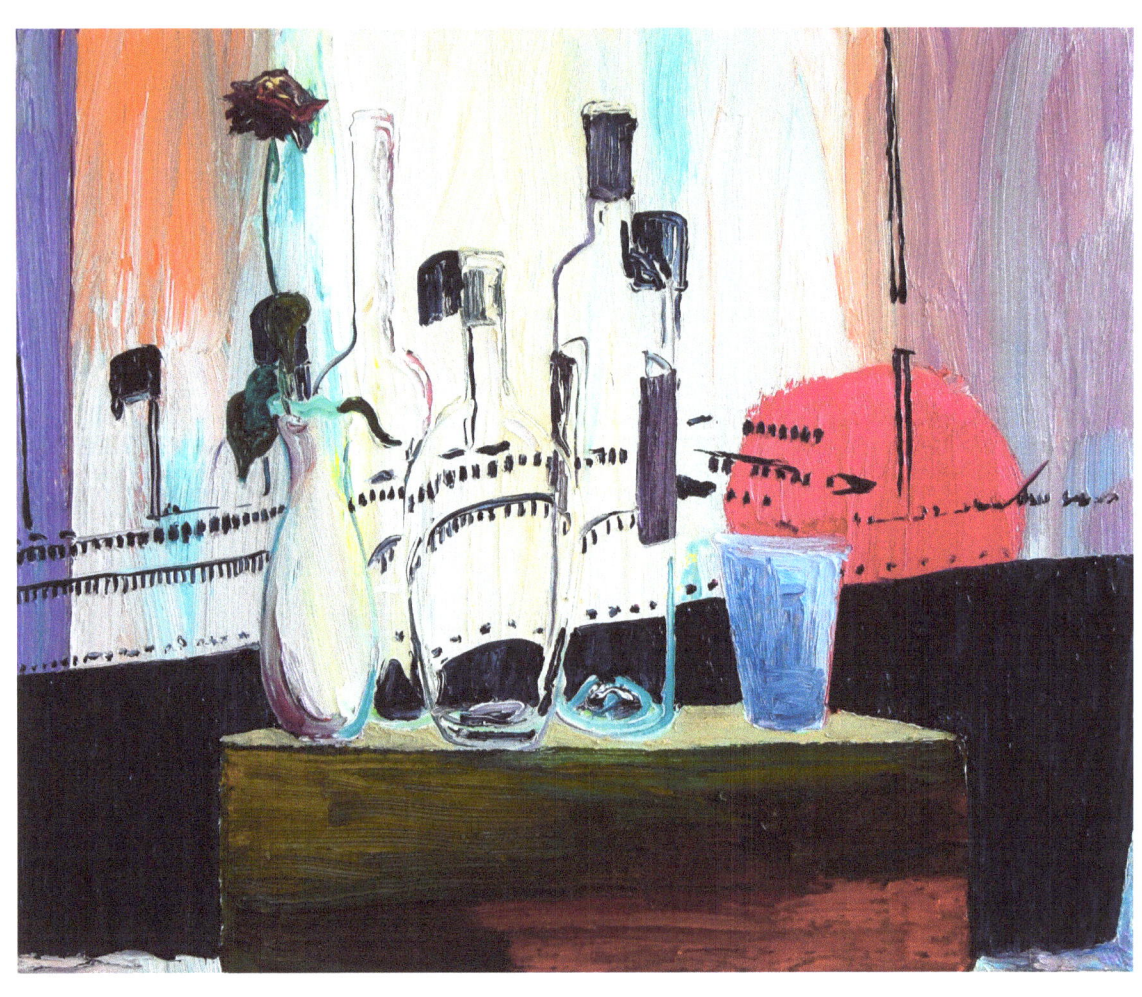

Still life (Empty Bottles and the Titanic), 2013
oil on canvas, 65 x 80 cm (25 ½" x 31 ½")

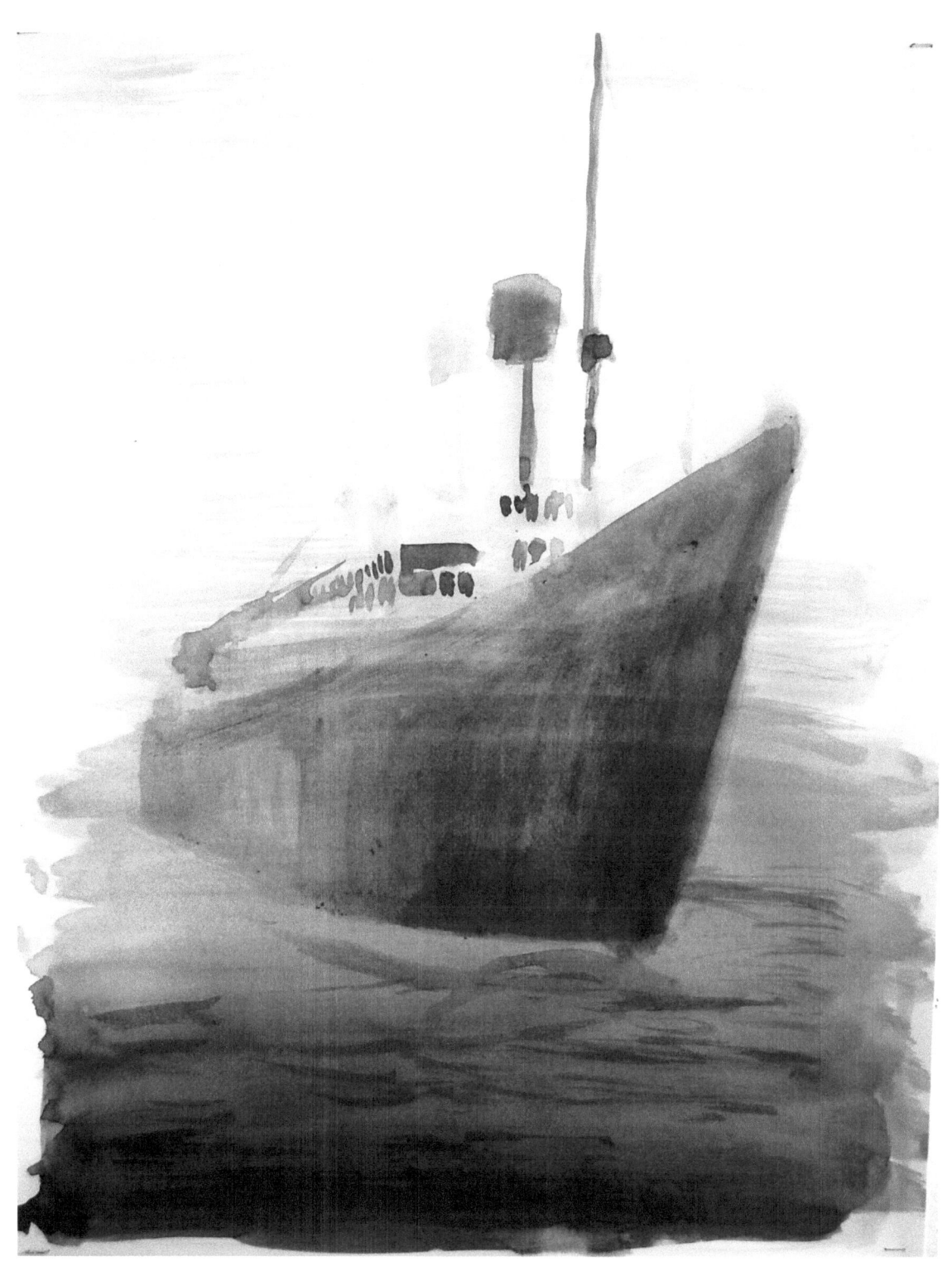

Ship in Fog, 2013
ink wash, 65 x 50 cm (25 ½" x 19 ½")

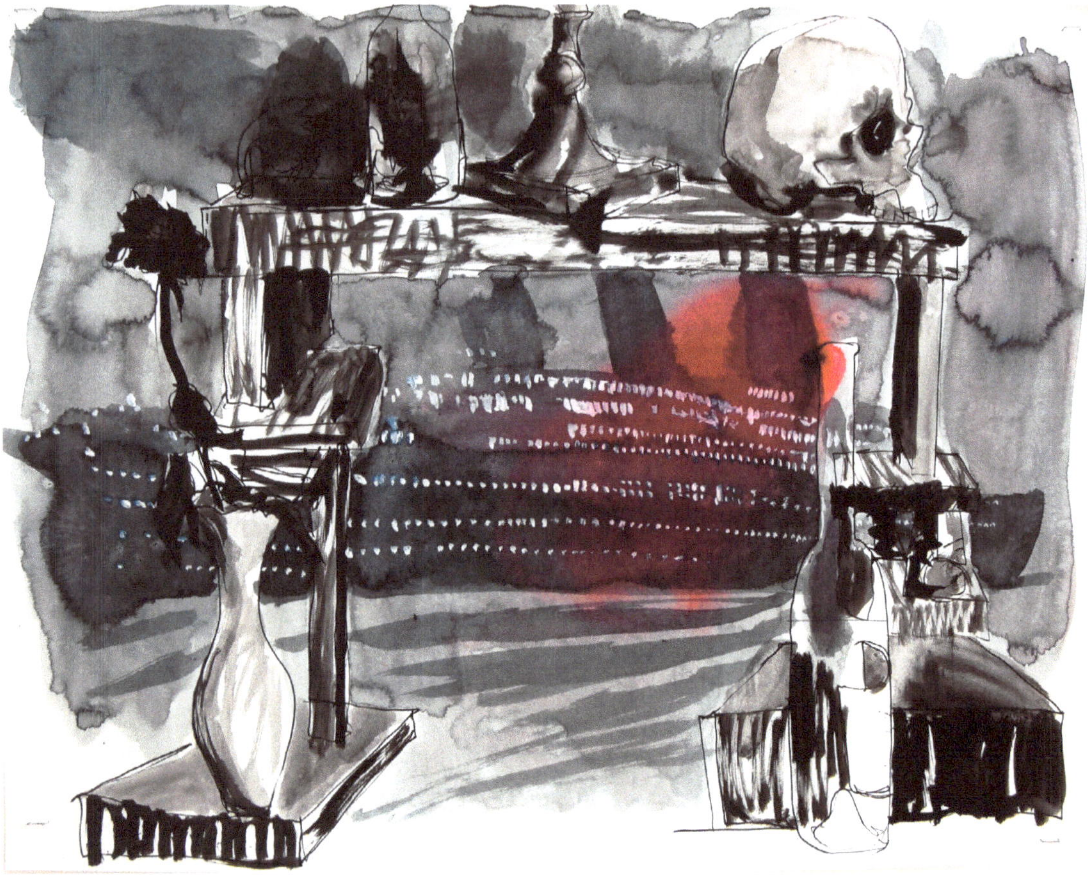

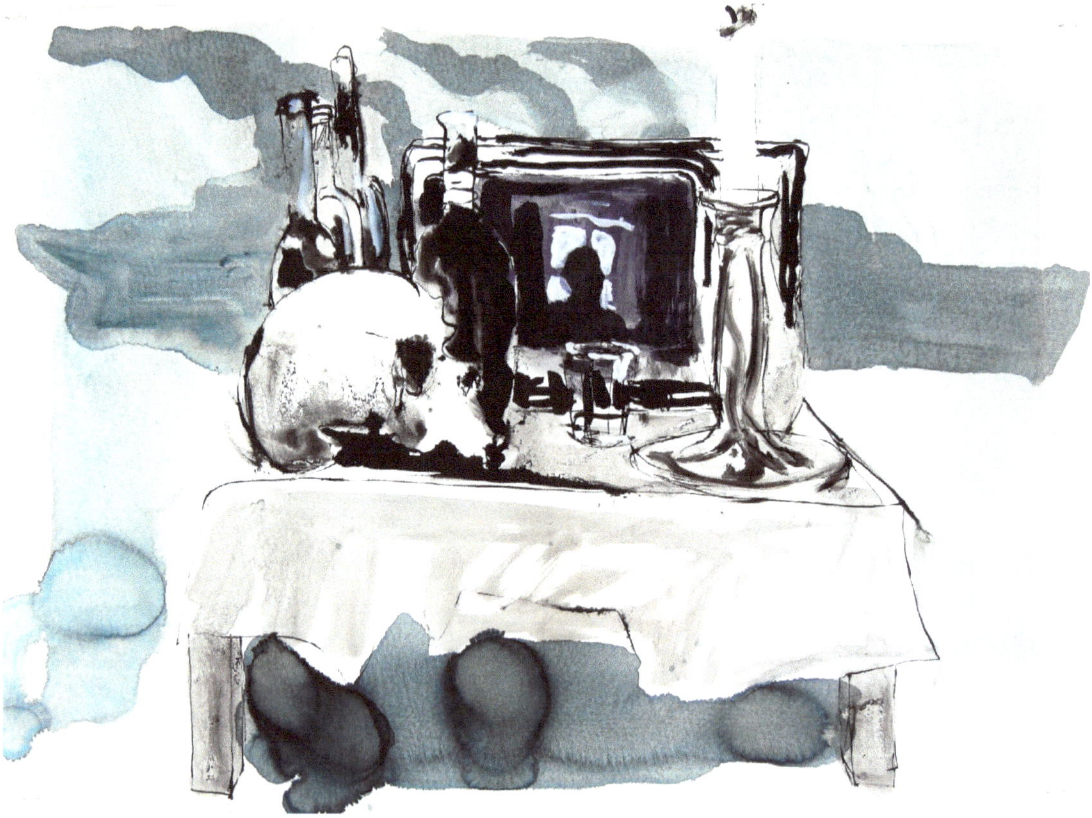

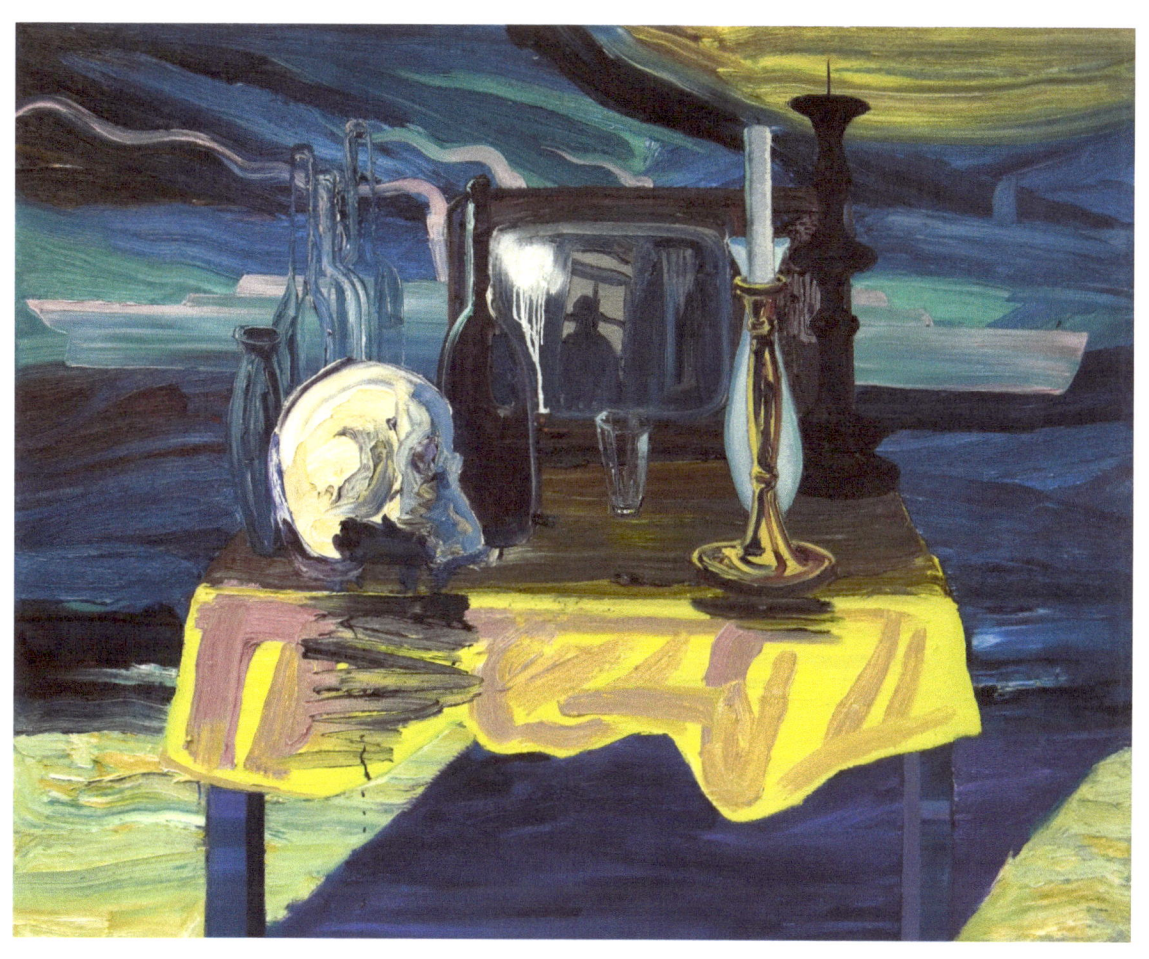

Titanic Still Life 3, 2013
ink on paper, 50 x 65 cm (19 ½" x 25 ½")

Still Life with TV, study, 2013
ink on paper, 50 x 65 cm (19 ½" x 25 ½")

Still Life with TV, 2013
oil on canvas, 120 x 150 cm (47" x 59")

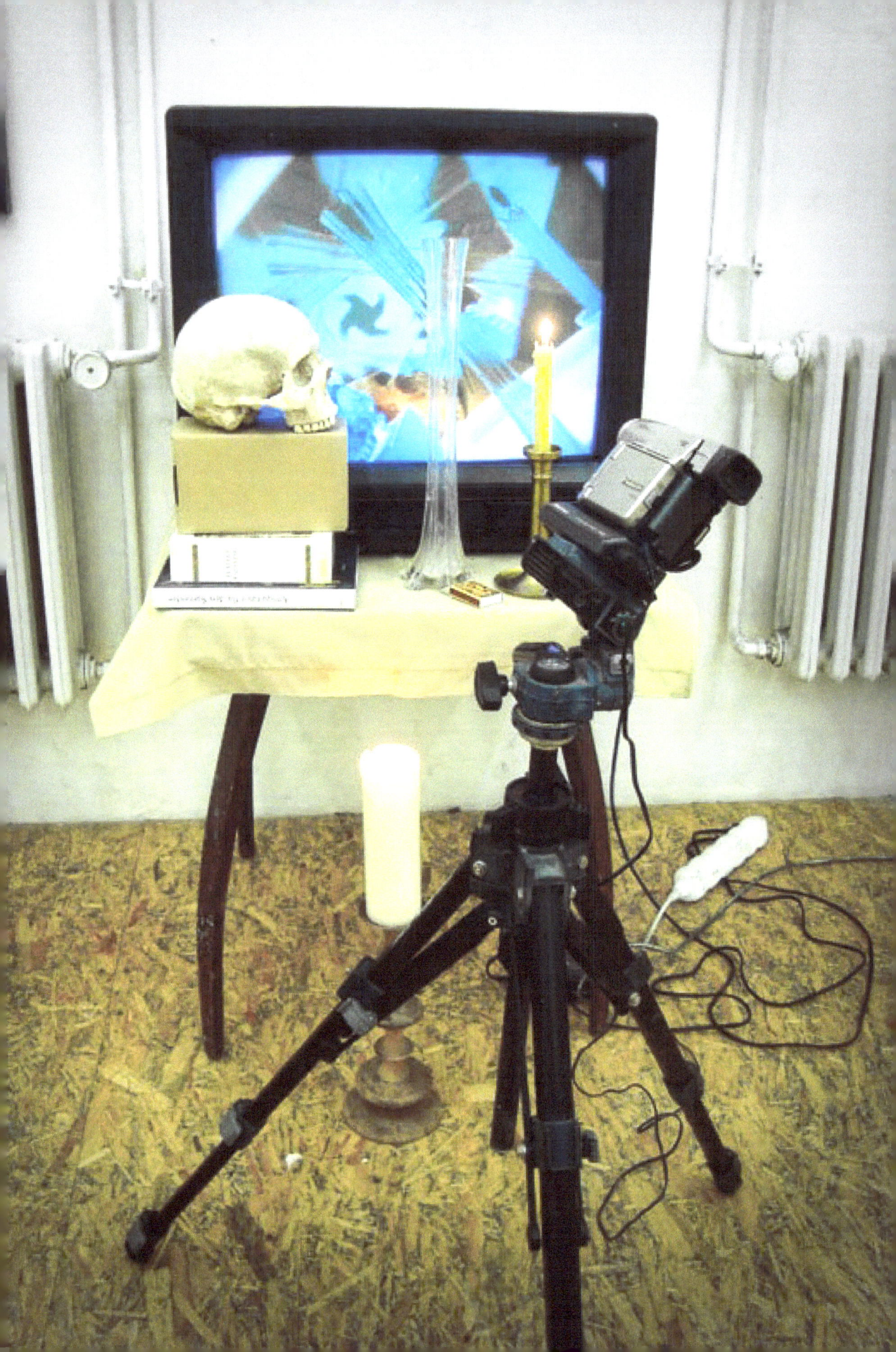

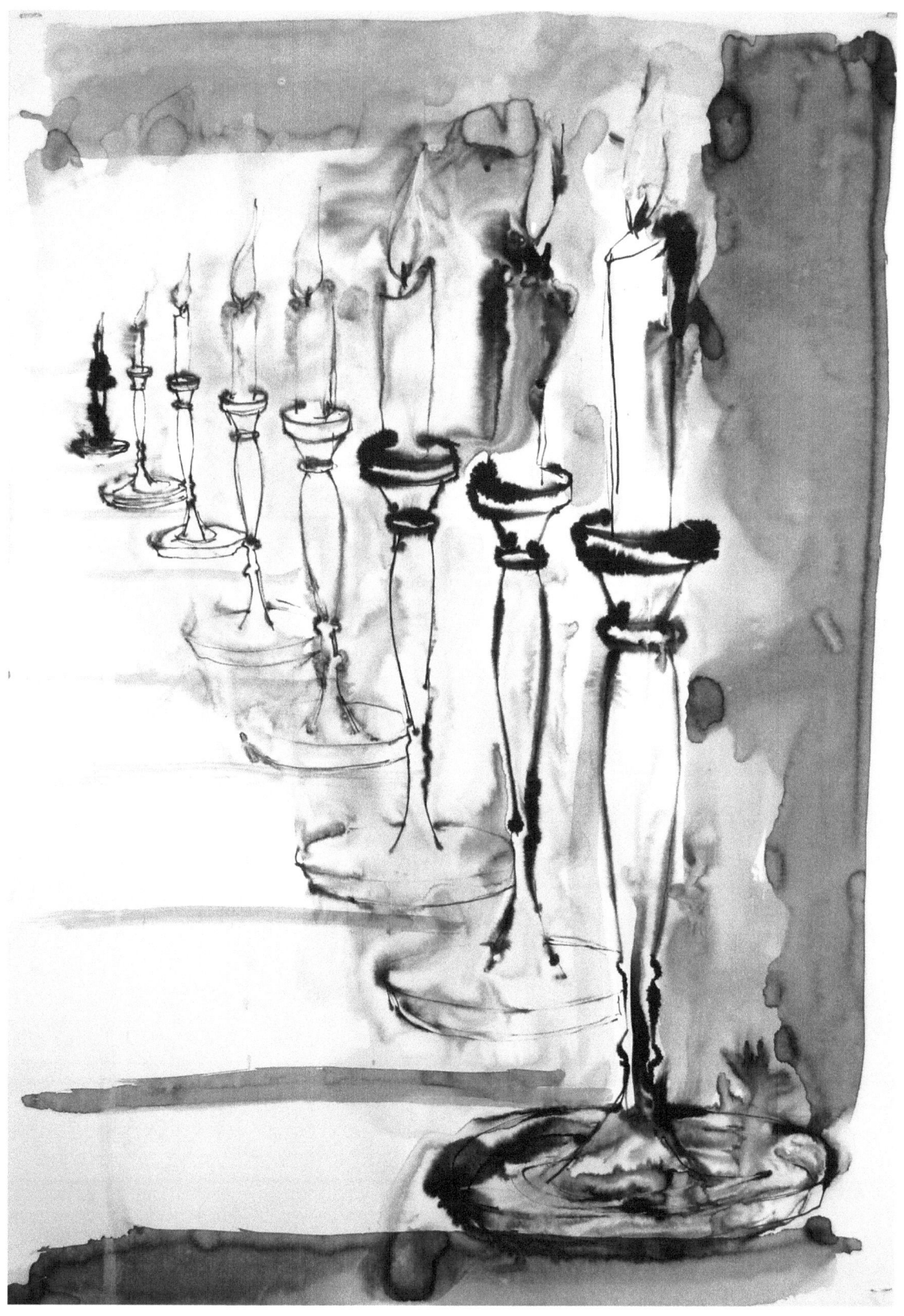

Skull Candle TV, 2013
video feedback installation

Candlestick Feedback, 2013
ink on paper, 70 x 50 cm (27 ½" x 19 ½")

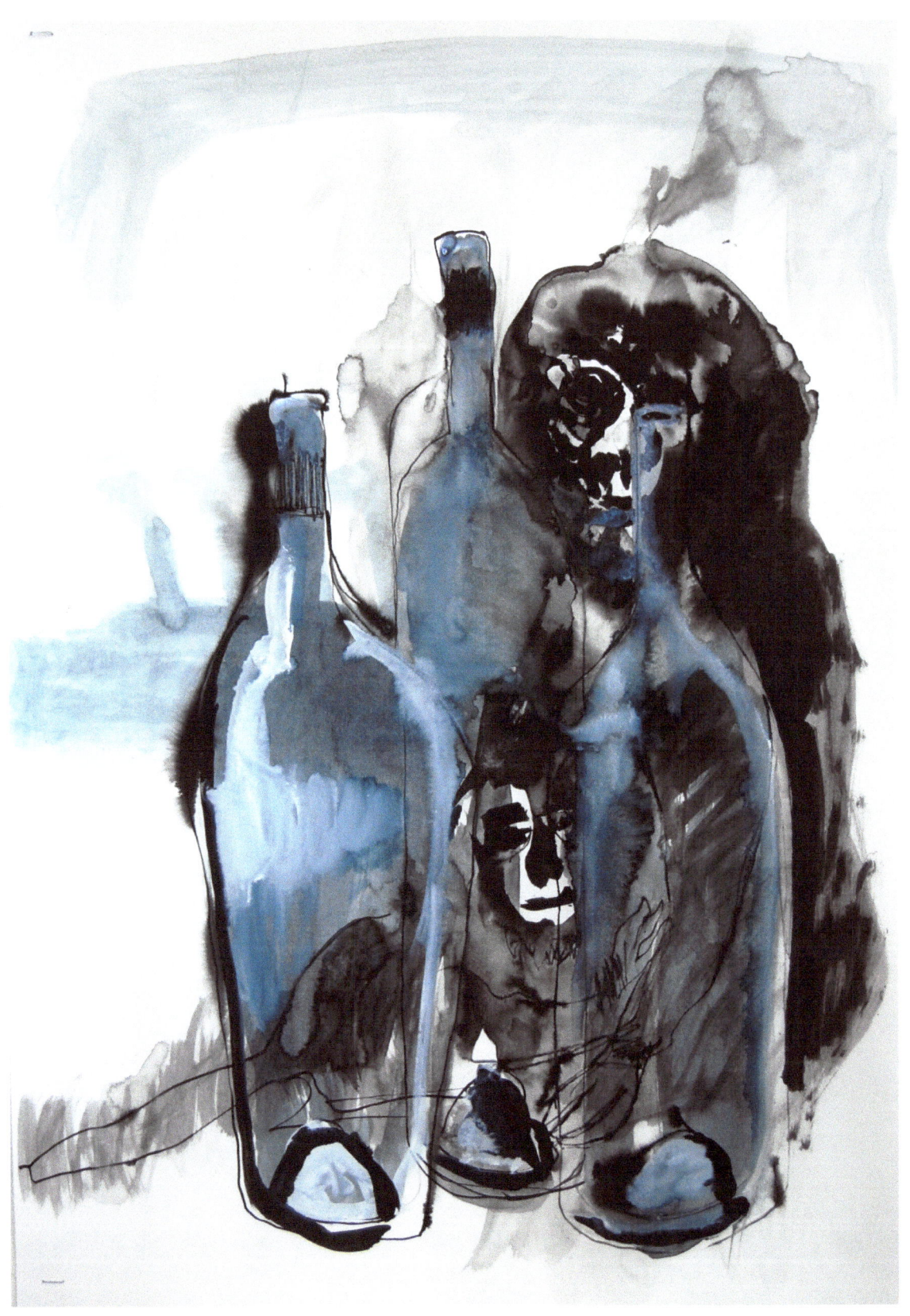

Bottles and Monkeys, 2013
ink on paper, 65 x 50 cm (25 ½" x 19 ½")

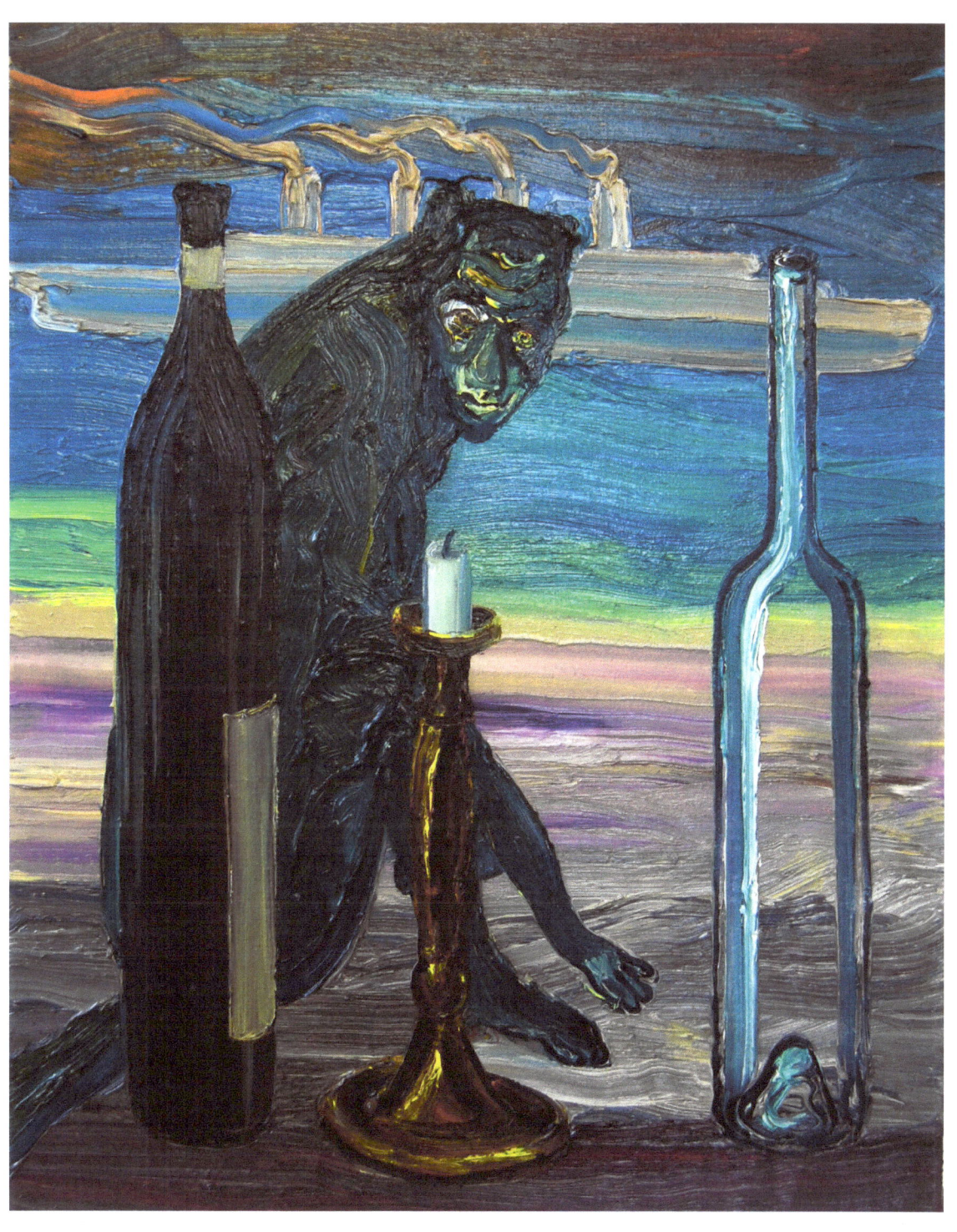

Bottles, Monkey and Ship, 2013
oil on canvas, 80 x 60 cm (31 ½" x 23 ½")

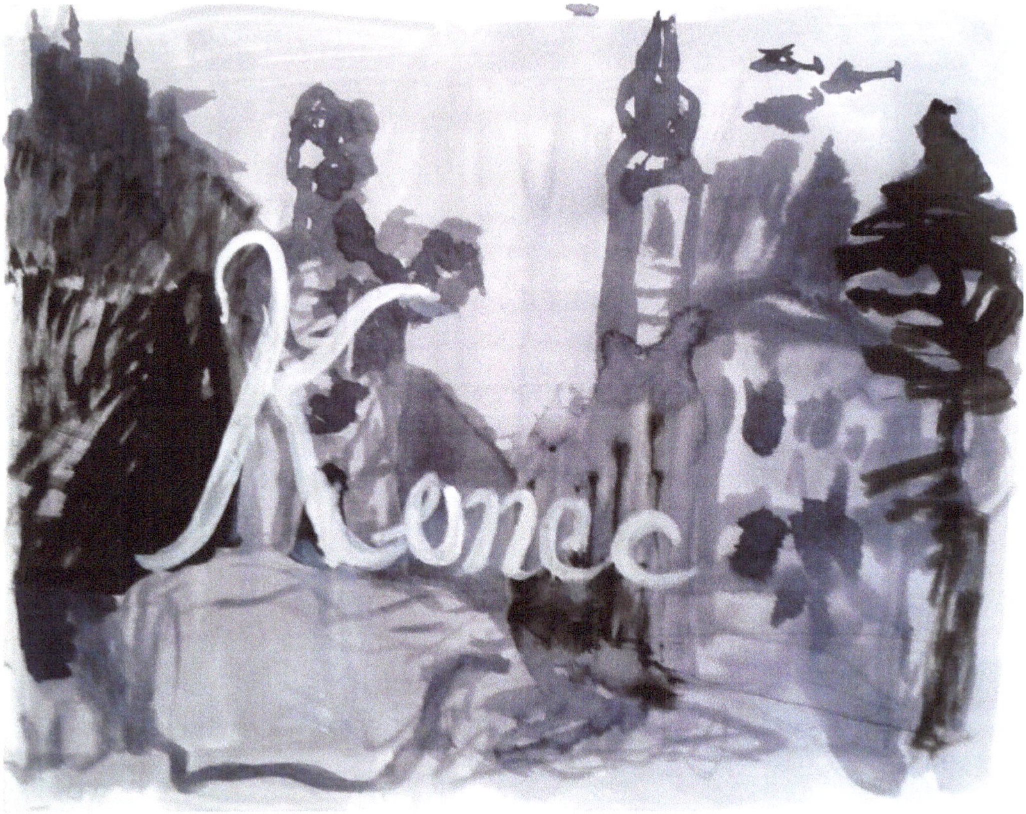
Конец

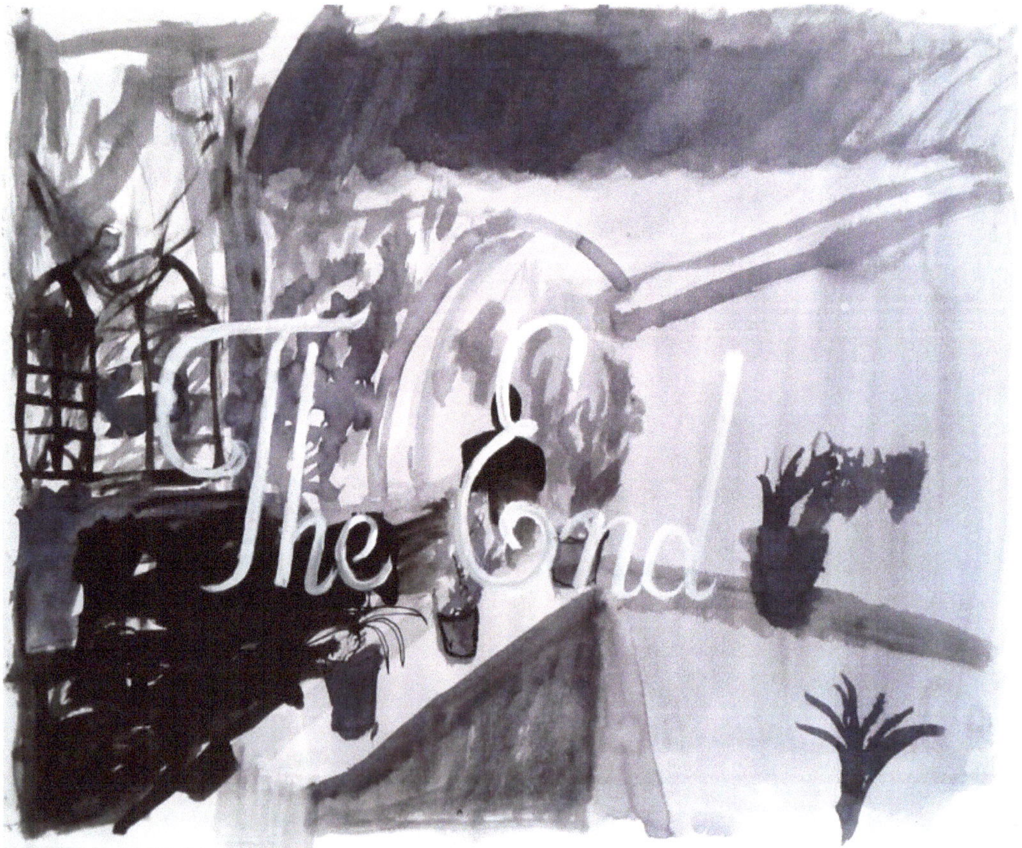
The End

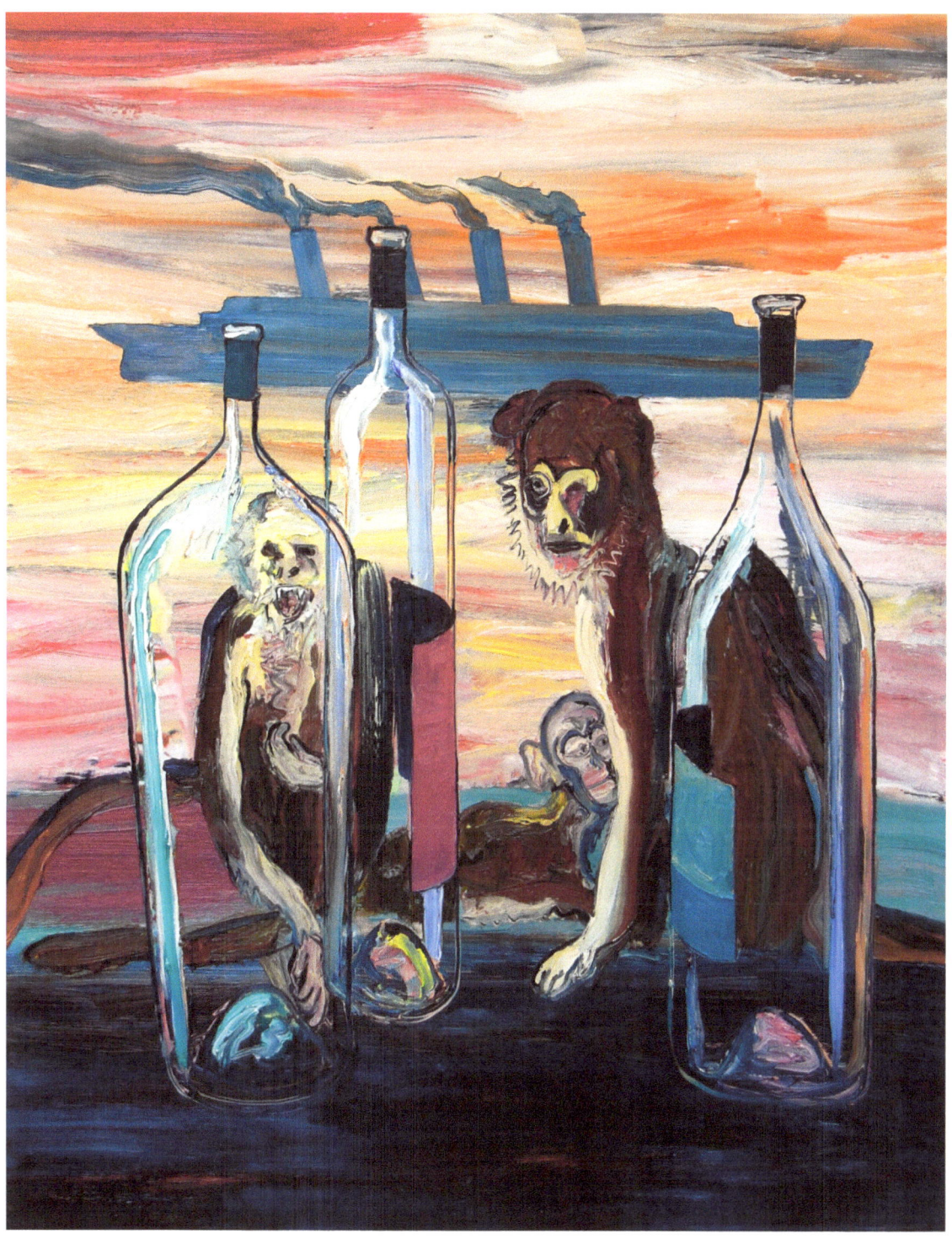

Konec, 2013
ink on paper, 50 x 65 cm (19 ½" x 25 ½")

The End, 2013
ink on paper, 50 x 65 cm (19 ½" x 25 ½")

Monkeys Bottles Ship, 2013
oil on canvas, 150 x 120 cm (59" x 47")

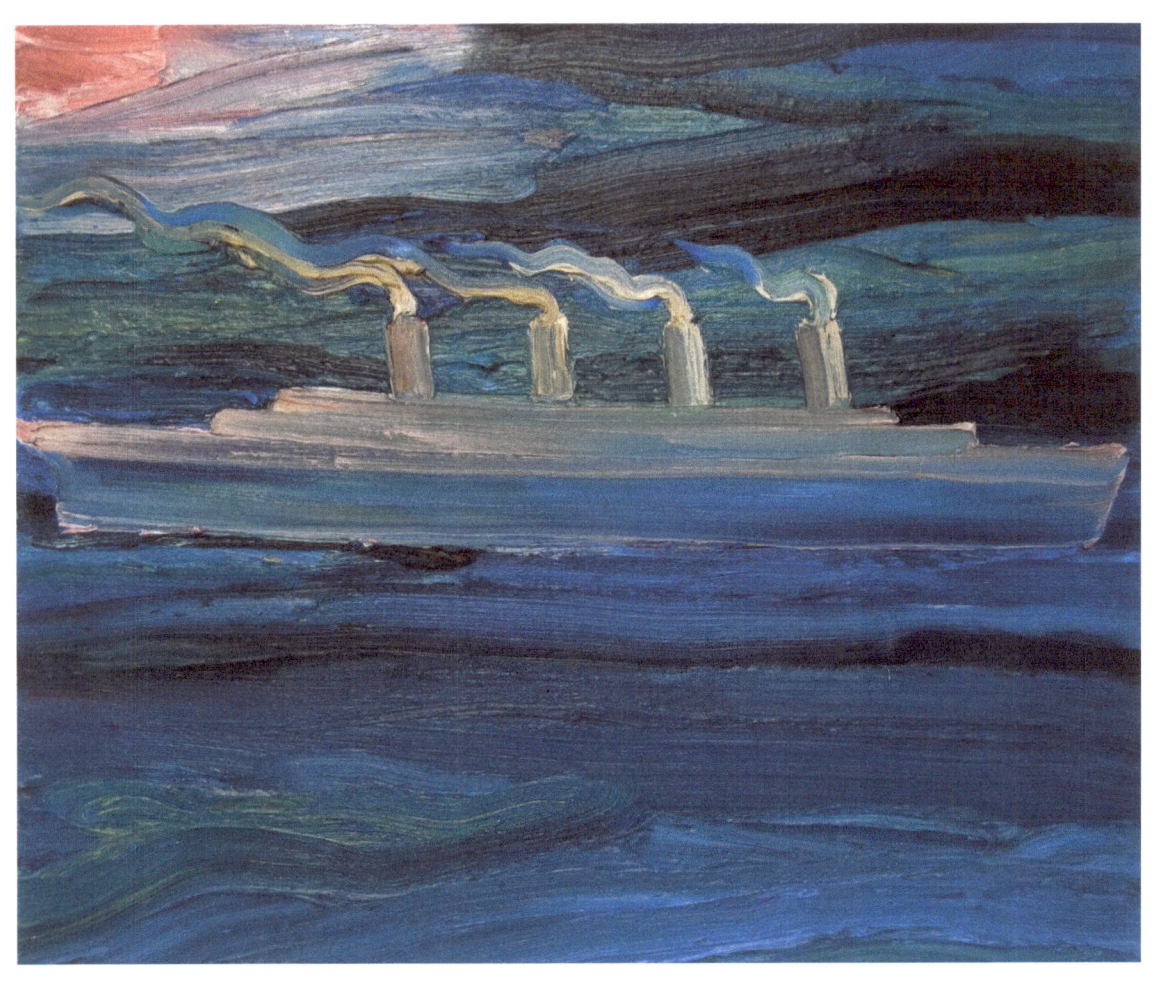

Ship at Sea (Blue, Pink, Green and Black), 2013
oil on canvas, 65 x 80 cm (25 ½" x 31 ½")

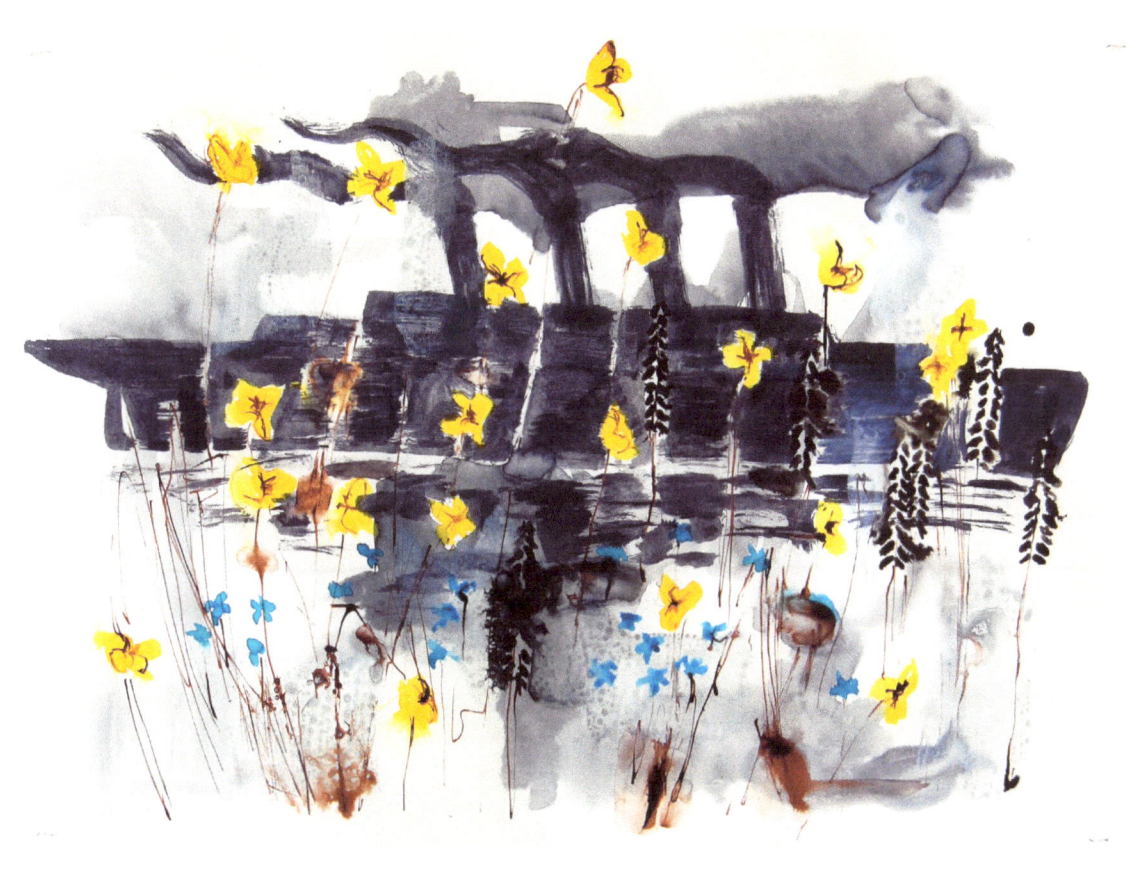

Ship with Flowers, 2013
ink on paper, 50 x 65 cm (19 ½" x 25 ½")

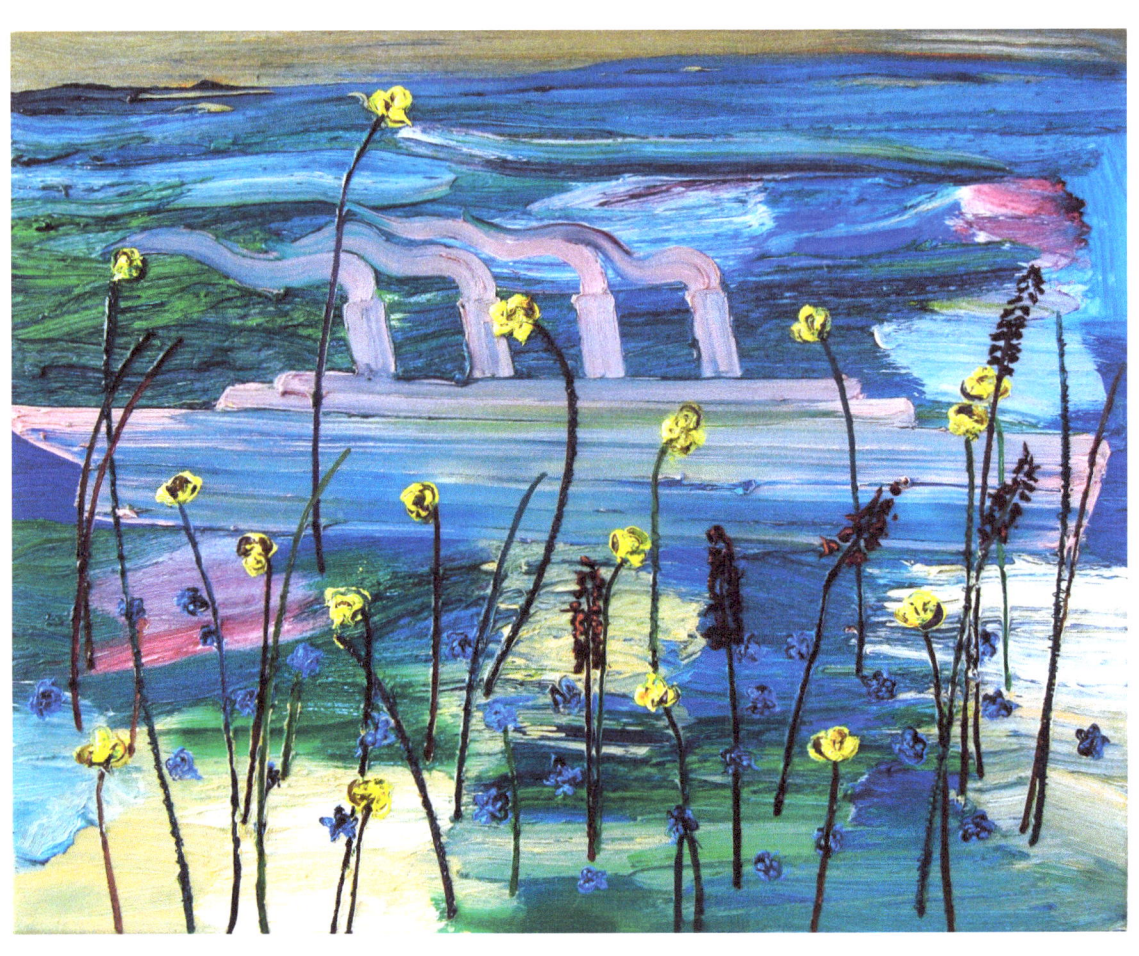

Ship with Flowers, 2013
oil on canvas, 70 x 90 cm (27 ½" x 35 ½")

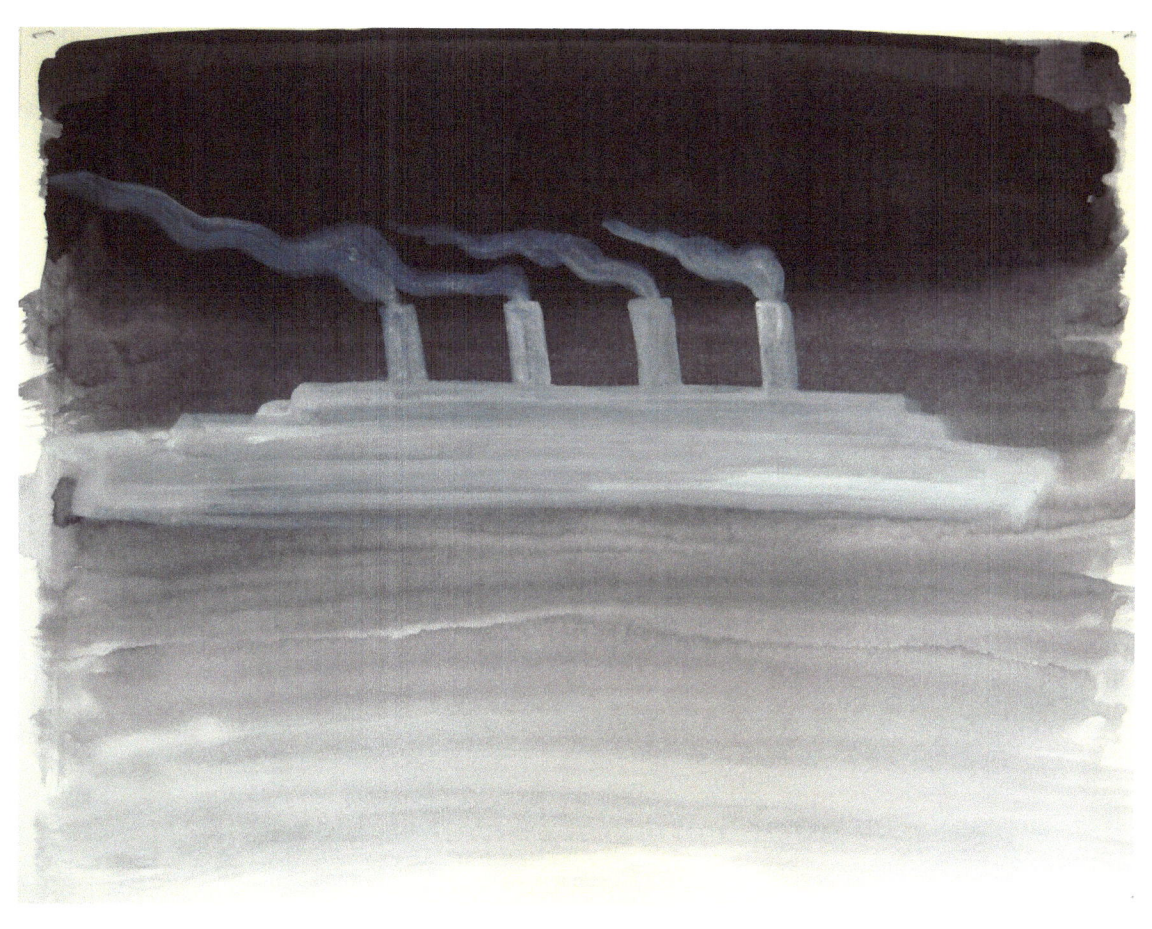

Ghost Ship, 2013
ink on paper, 50 x 65 cm (19 ½" x 25 ½")

GHOSTS

These paintings were inspired by analog video art from the 70s, the green screen chromakey effect, old beige plastic computer monitors, spring air, Hana Zagorová, California and dead technology. When computers die do they leave a ghost? When we pass through a room, do we leave some essence behind, some ectoplasm like the trail of a snail? A still life is made up of objects, usually on a table, and their relationship with the surrounding space. I'm interested in the way objects see the world, how people become phantoms in the world of plants, how the speed of technological change forces us to abandon our old machines. The way the objects around us become dispensable reminds us that we are too. Are computers more important than people? Do we use our tools or do our tools use us? And what about love? Can it find a place among the ruins? Surrounded by old junk, everything becomes ghostly.

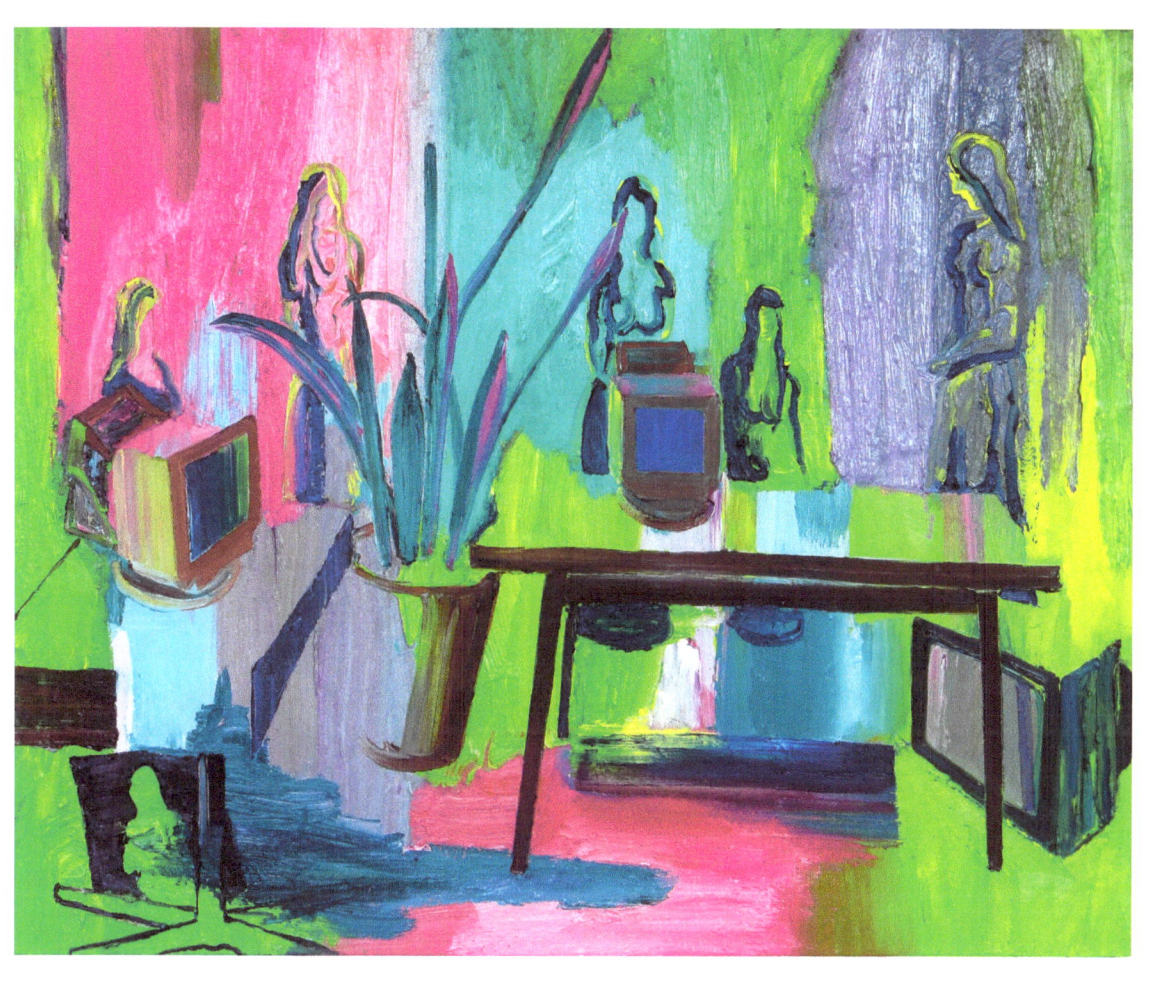

Ghosts, 2014
oil on canvas, 120 x 150 cm (47" x 59")

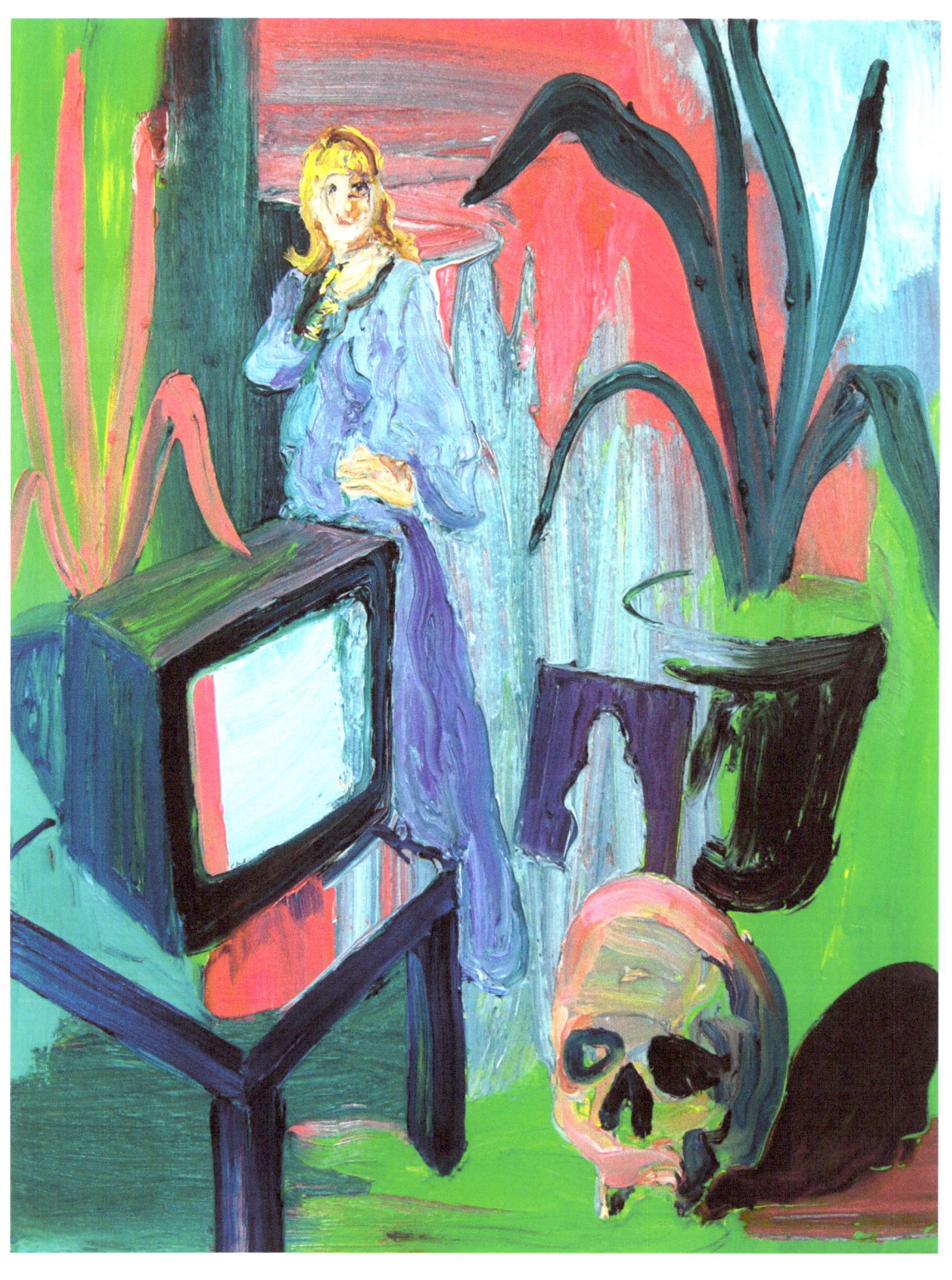

Hana Zagorová, TV and Skull, 2014
oil on canvas, 90 x 70 cm (35 ½" x 27 ½")

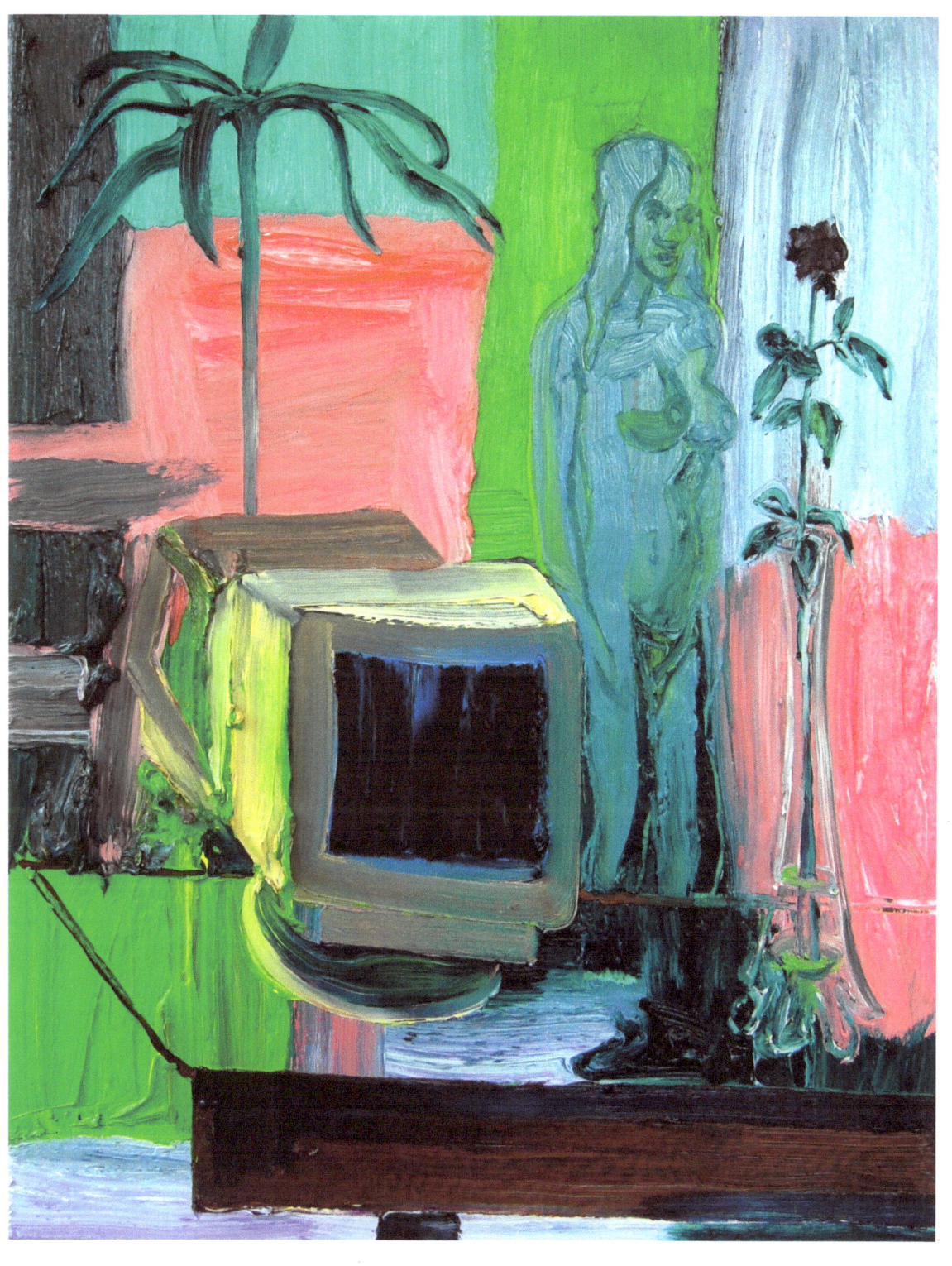

Monitor, Nude and Rose, 2014
oil on canvas, 90 x 70 cm (35 ½" x 27 ½")

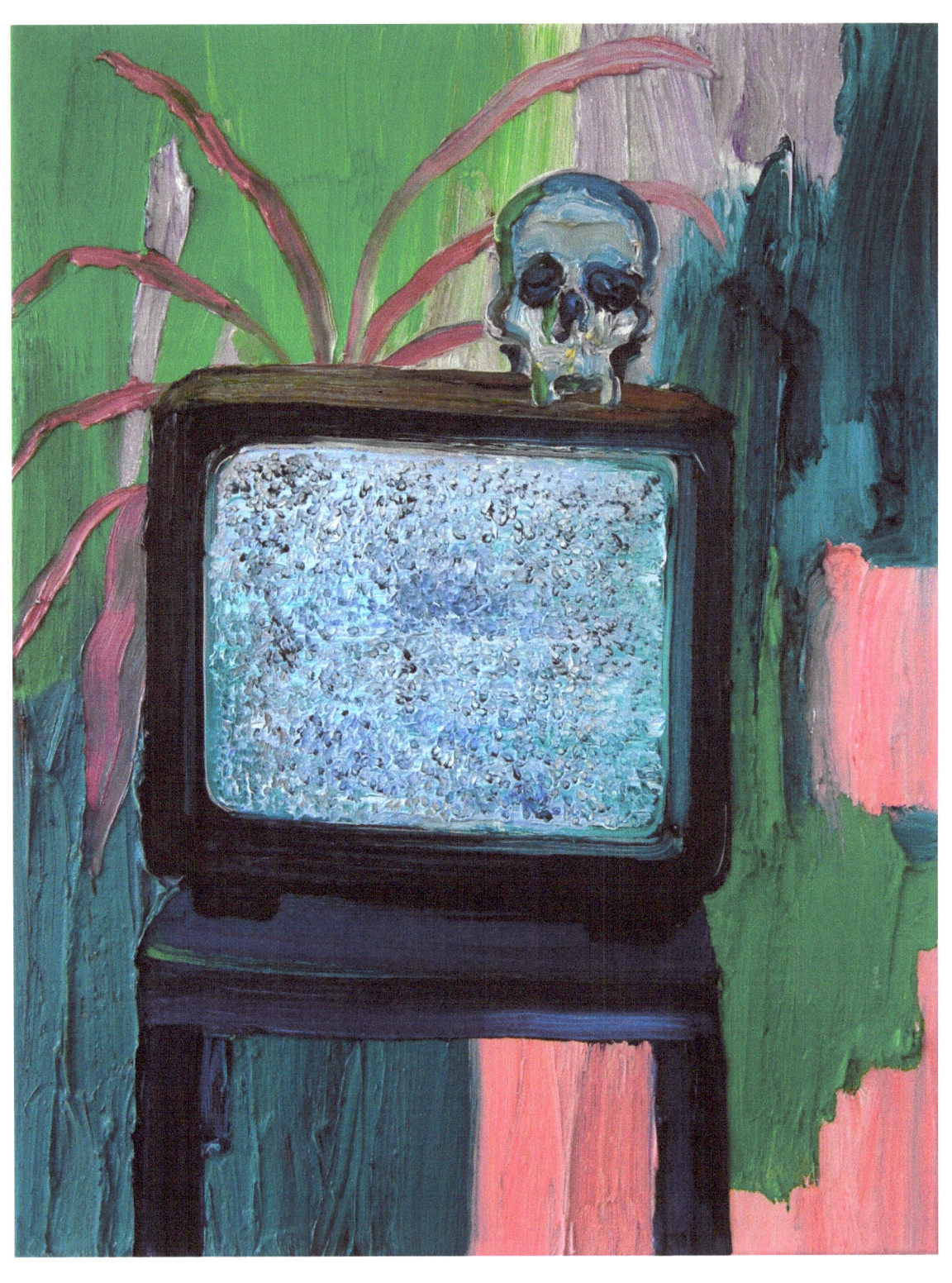

Skull on a TV, 2014
oil on canvas, 90 x 70 cm (35 ½" x 27 ½")

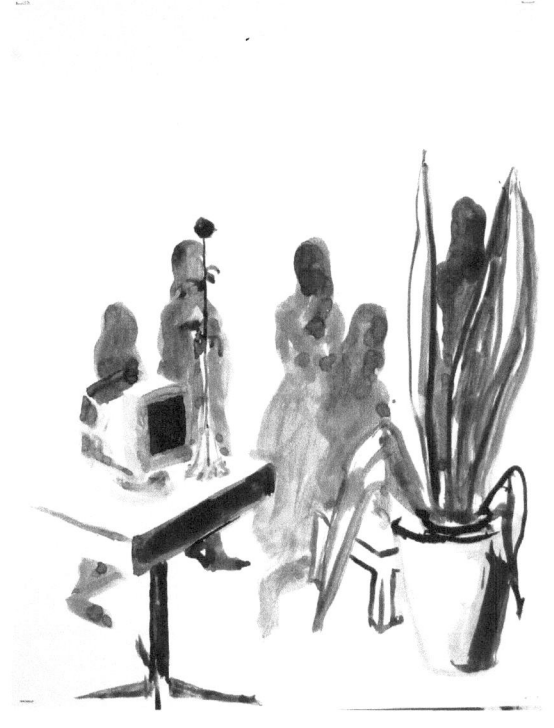
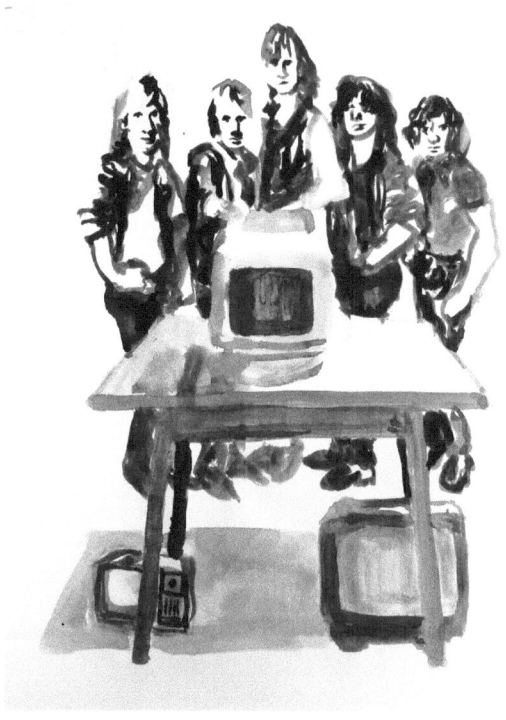
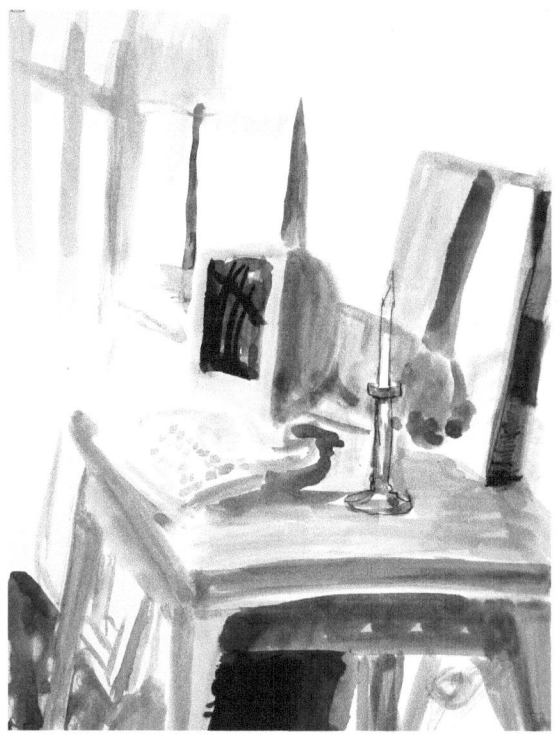
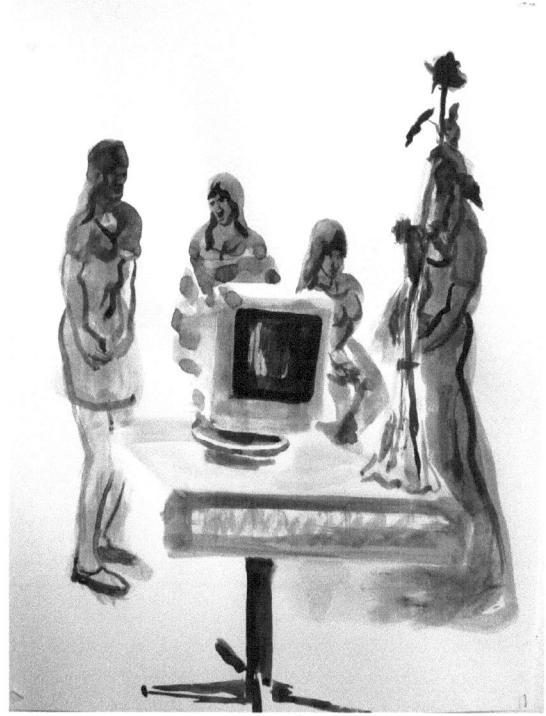

ink drawings
various sizes

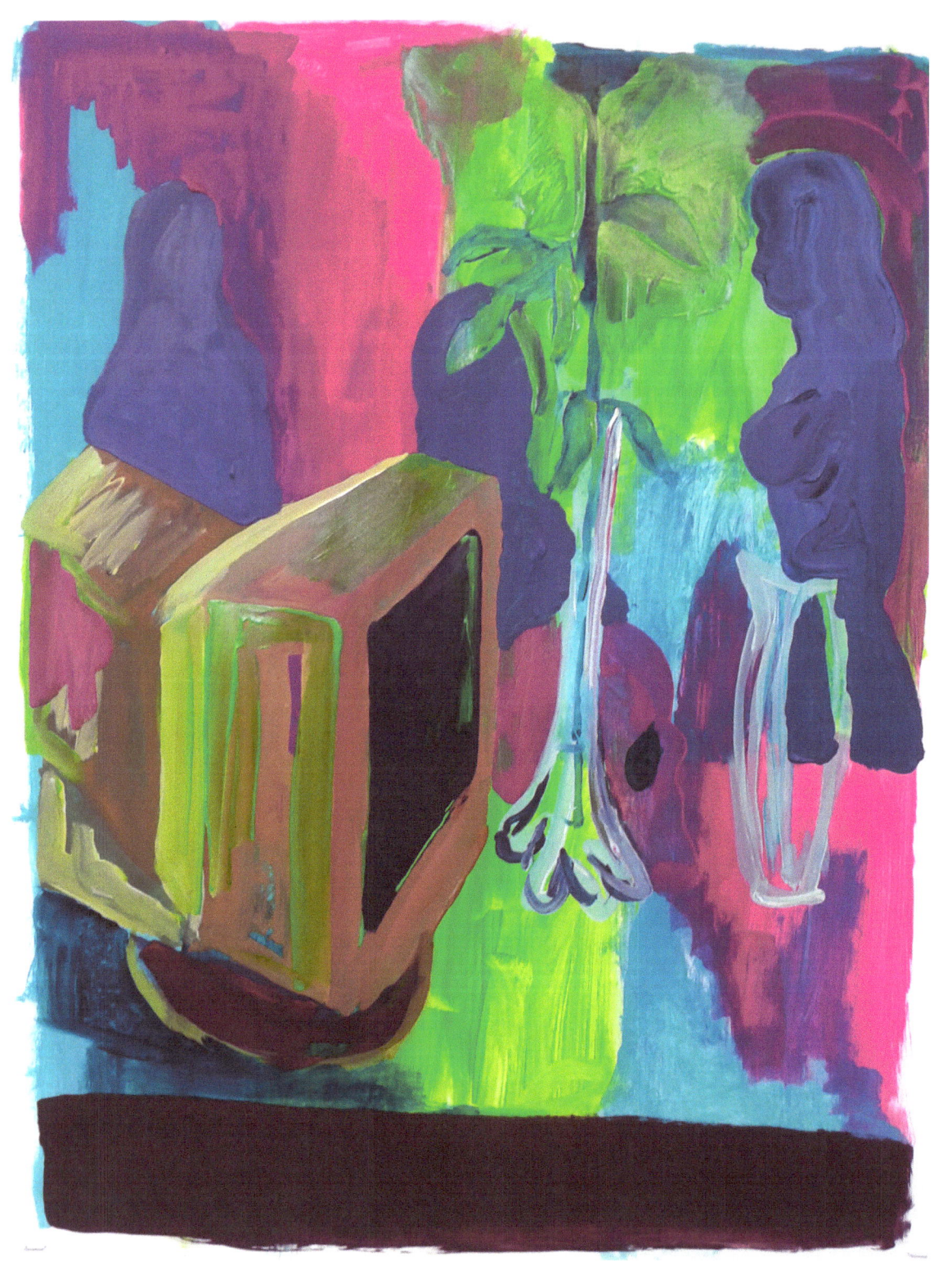

Ghosts (study), 2014
acrylic on paper, 65 x 50 cm (25 ½" x 19 ½")

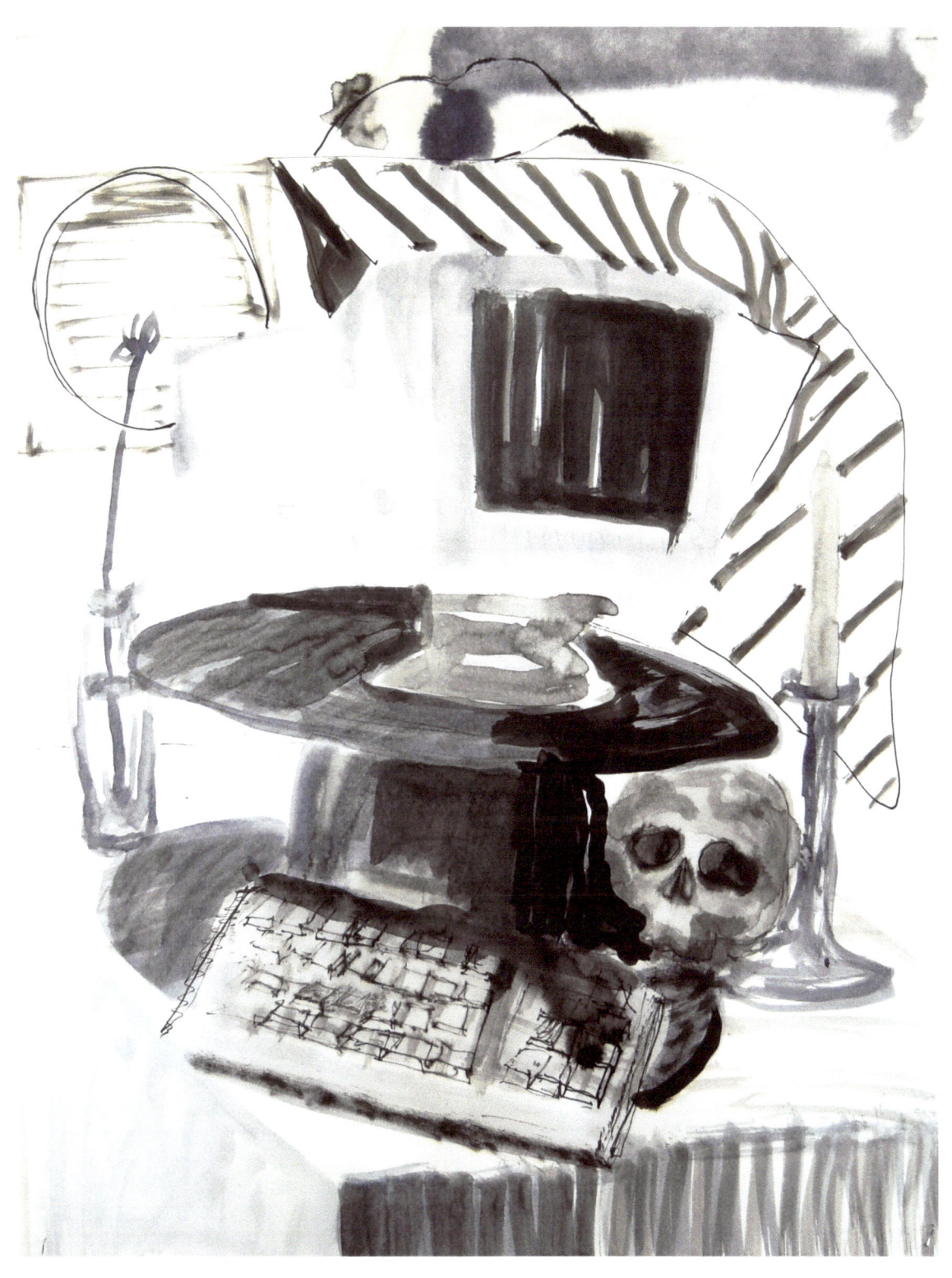

Monitor and Spool, 2014
ink on paper, 65 x 50 cm (25 ½" x 19 ½")

STUPID COMPUTER

These works, developed in the fall of 2014, grew out of themes present in the Ghosts/Green Screen paintings. In these works the common experience of sitting or standing at a computer for many hours is satirized and revealed to be just about as stupid as we all know it is. And yet we keep doing it, fascinated by the internet's steady stream of information and banal clickery. The position of the body in relation to the computer is one that fascinates me, as we generally hunch over in front of the screen as if taking communion at a kind of shrine, the dispenser of the morning email. The memento mori altars I have been constructing, still lifes as symbolic landscapes, find an analogy in the computer desk and within the "desktop" itself. One primary issue in the adoption of new technology is the way we often don't recognize what we are losing in the trade. Are you smarter than your smartphone? And always the underlying question remains, in terms of cybernetics and connectivity in the period of late Capitalism: Who is using who? If computers are replacing people, we have to wonder who is truly stupid? And yet, in an absurdist world, we can only laugh and remember, it's only a machine. At least for now.

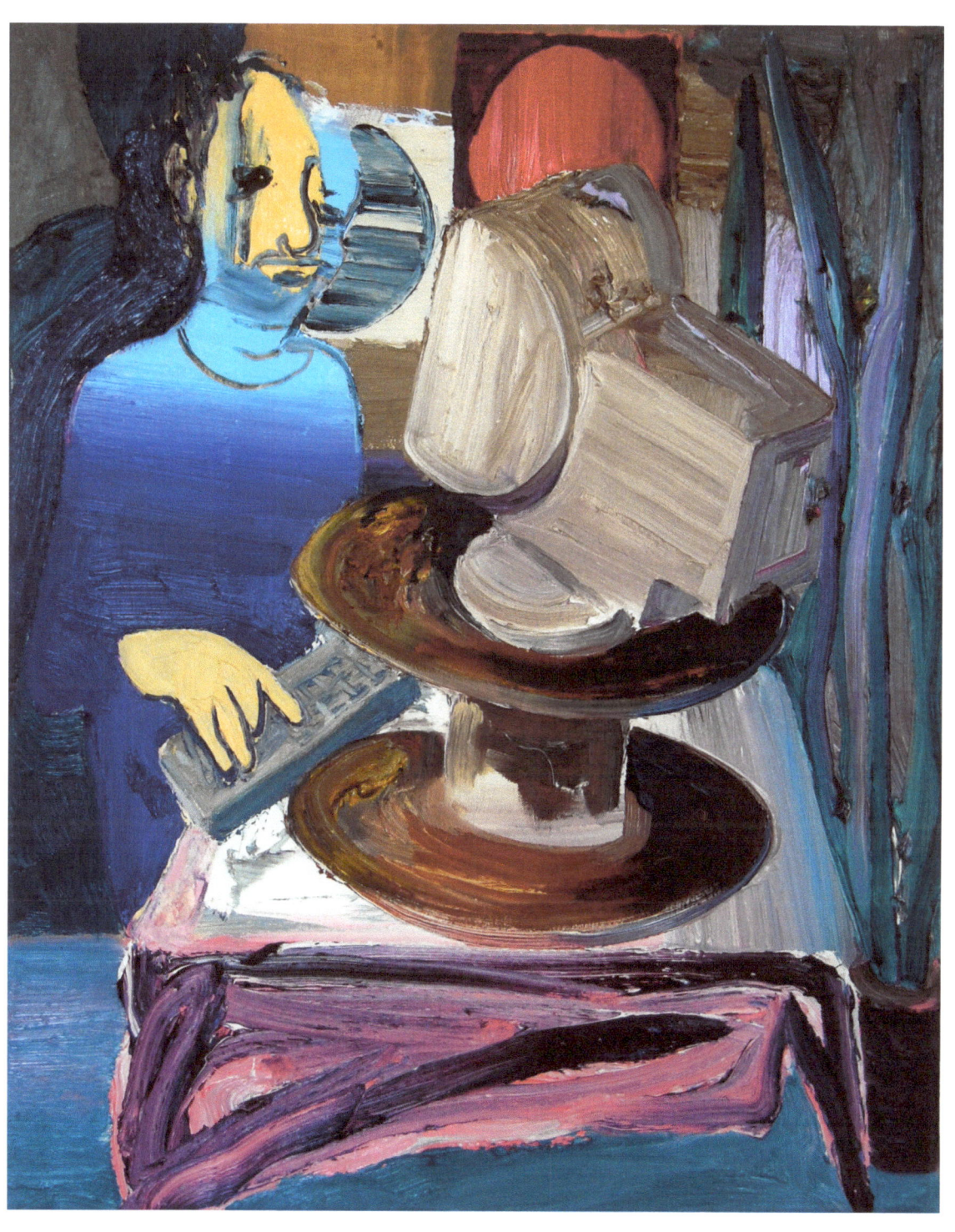

Standing Desk (Early Adopter), 2014
oil on canvas, 80 x 60 cm (31 ½" x 23 ½")

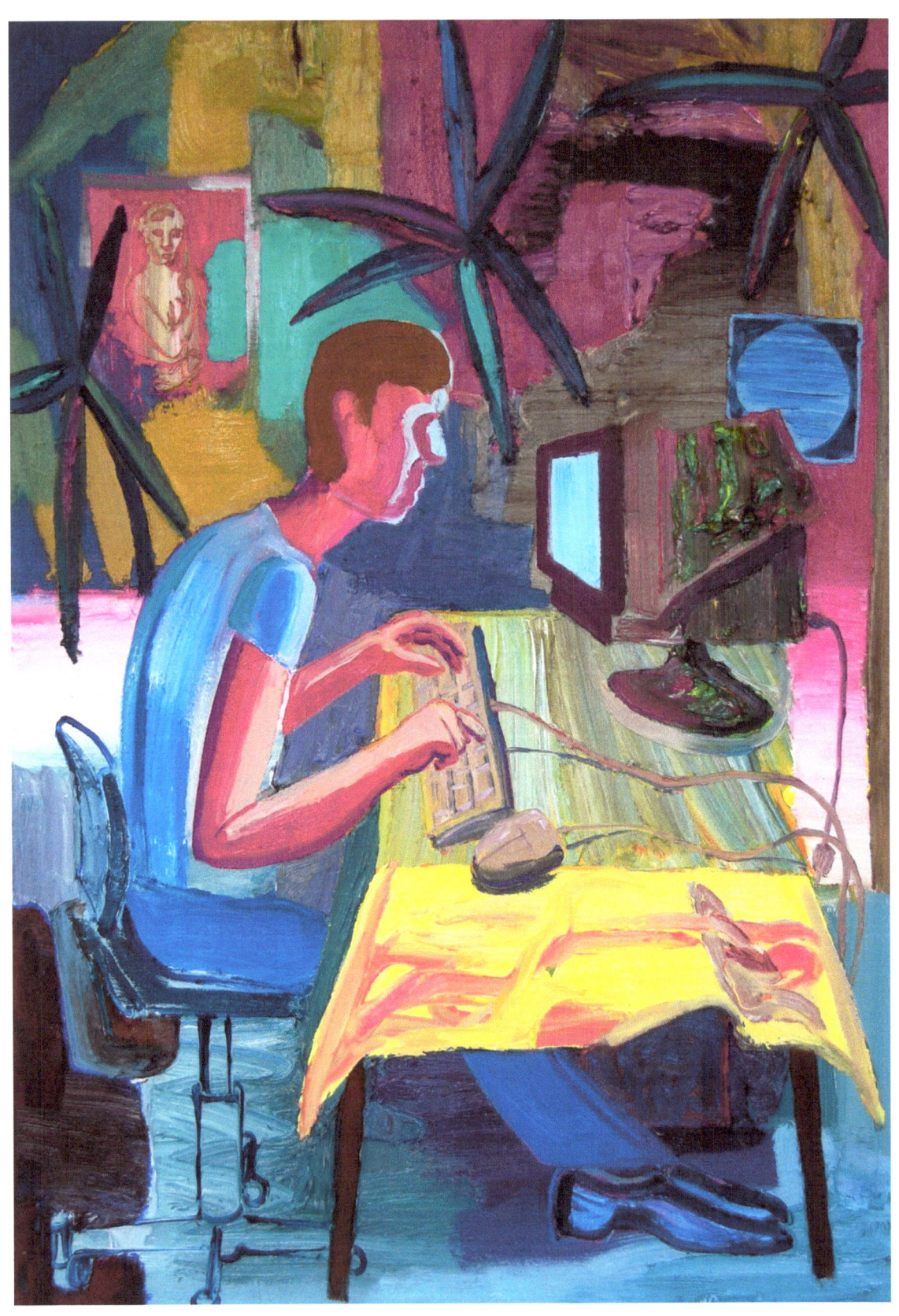

At the Computer, 2014
oil on canvas, 120 x 85 cm (47" x 33 ½")

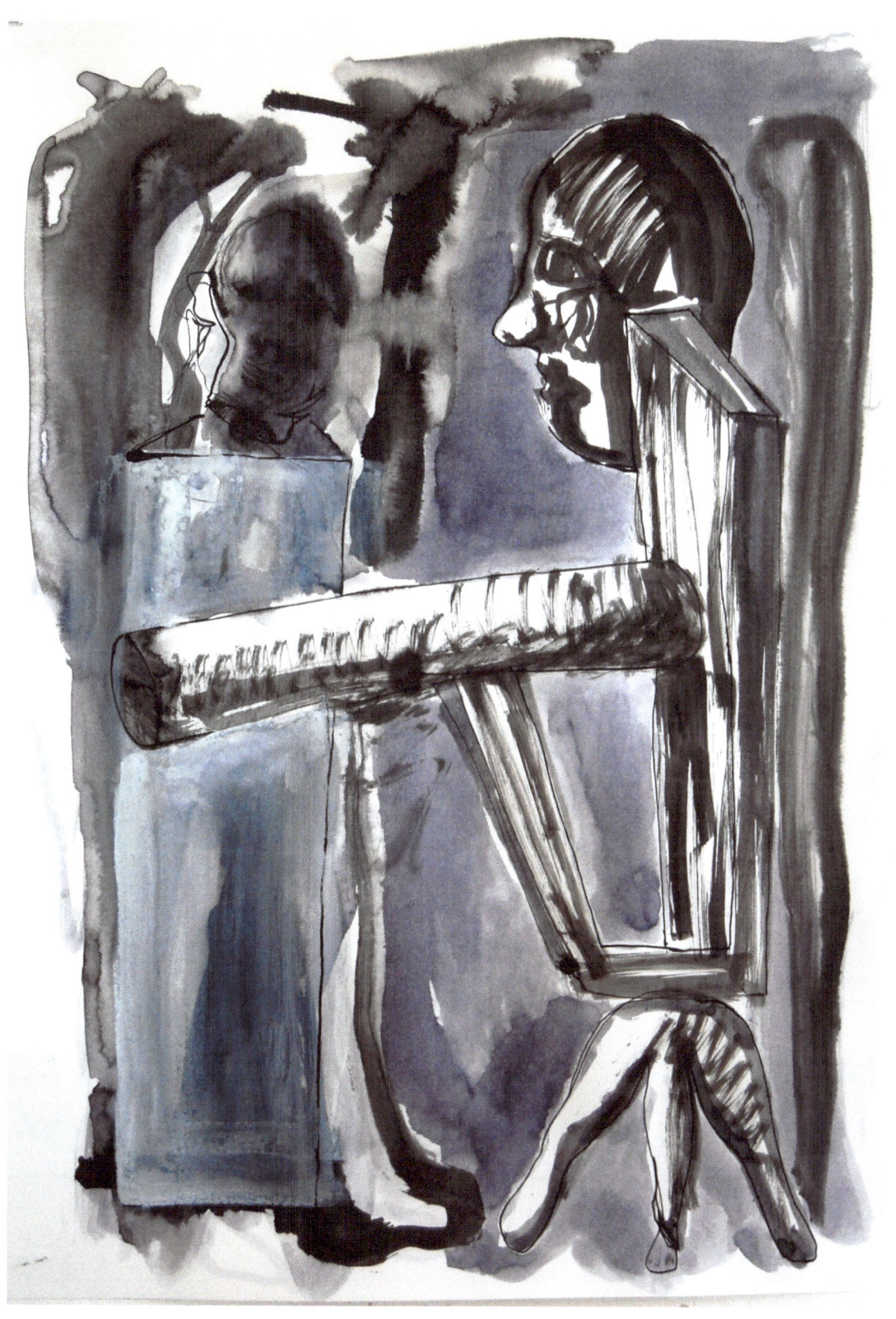

Two Sculptures, 2014
ink on paper, 65 x 50 cm (25 ½" x 19 ½")

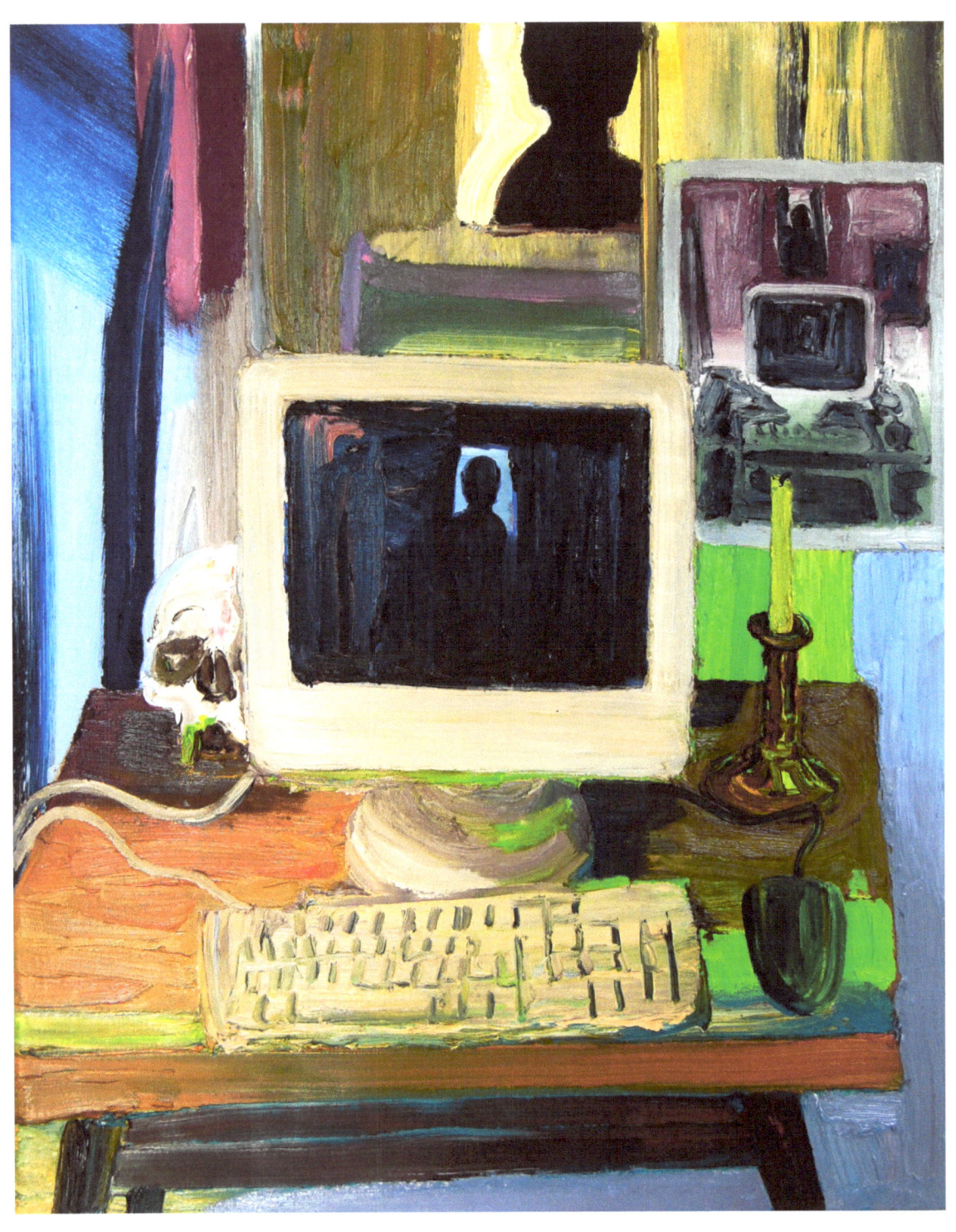

Monitor and Mirror, 2014
oil on canvas, 80 x 60 cm (31 ½" x 23 ½")

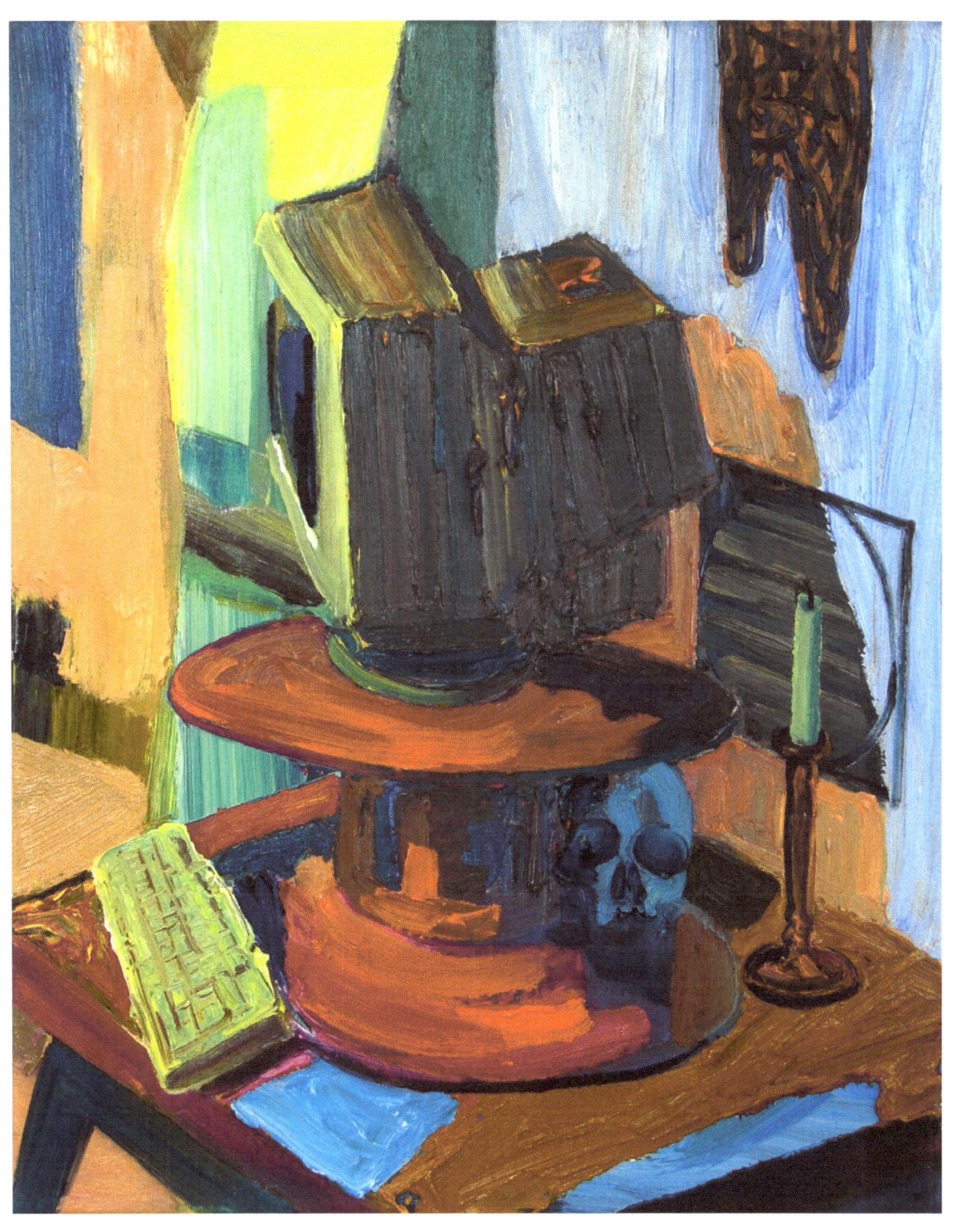

Monitor and Skull, 2014
oil on camvas, 85 x 60 cm (33 ½" x 23 ½")

My studio/atelier is located in the former production plant and offices for the historic Czech automobile producer, Praga. The building dates from the mid-1940s on the site of the old factory for the aircraft manufacturer Aero. It is said that the Nazis produced their mysterious UFO aircraft here during the Occupation.

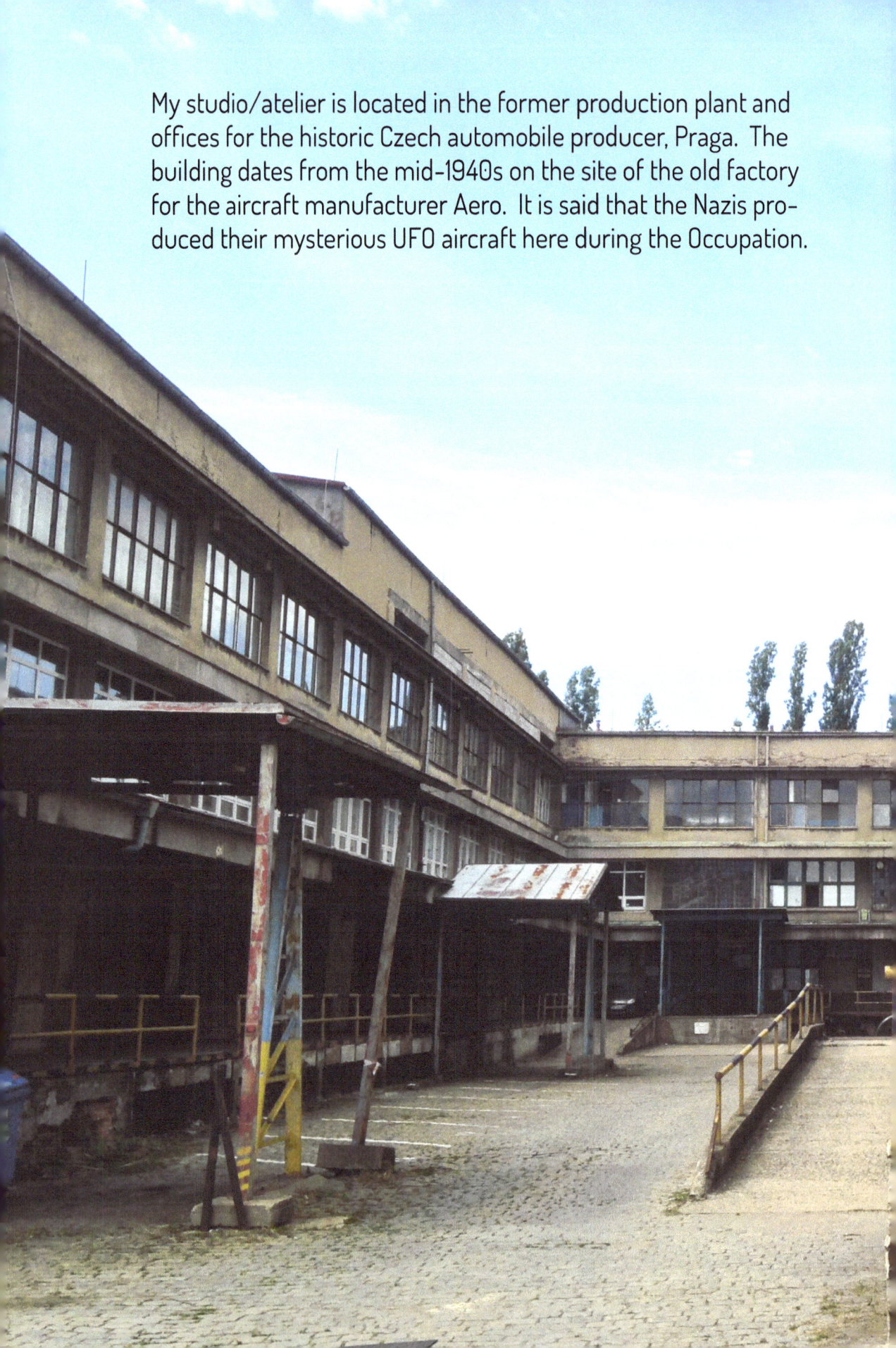

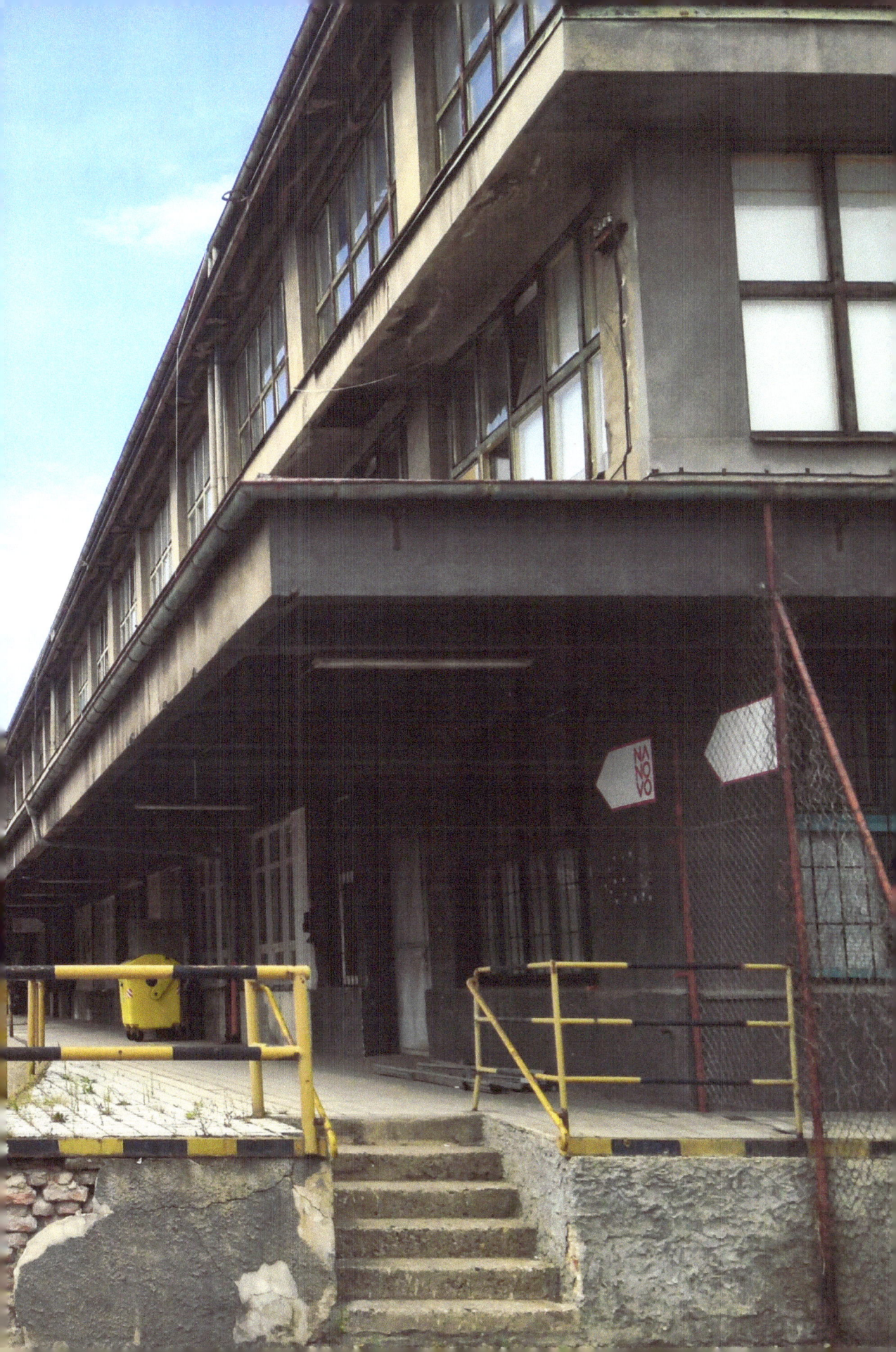

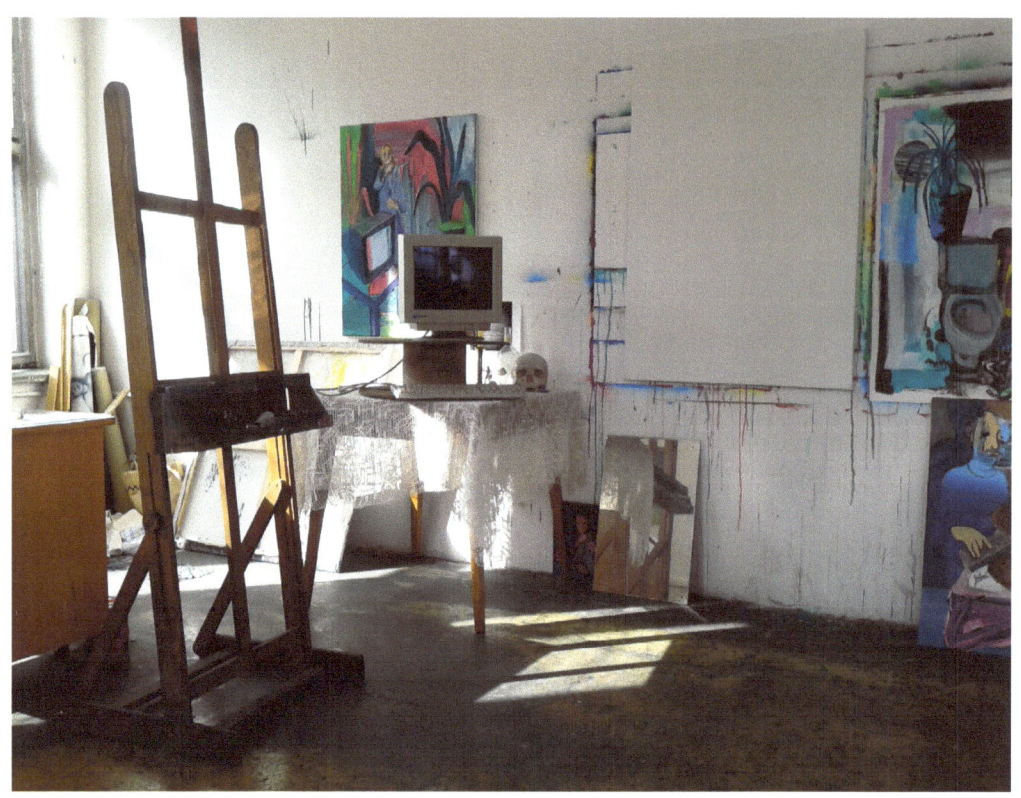

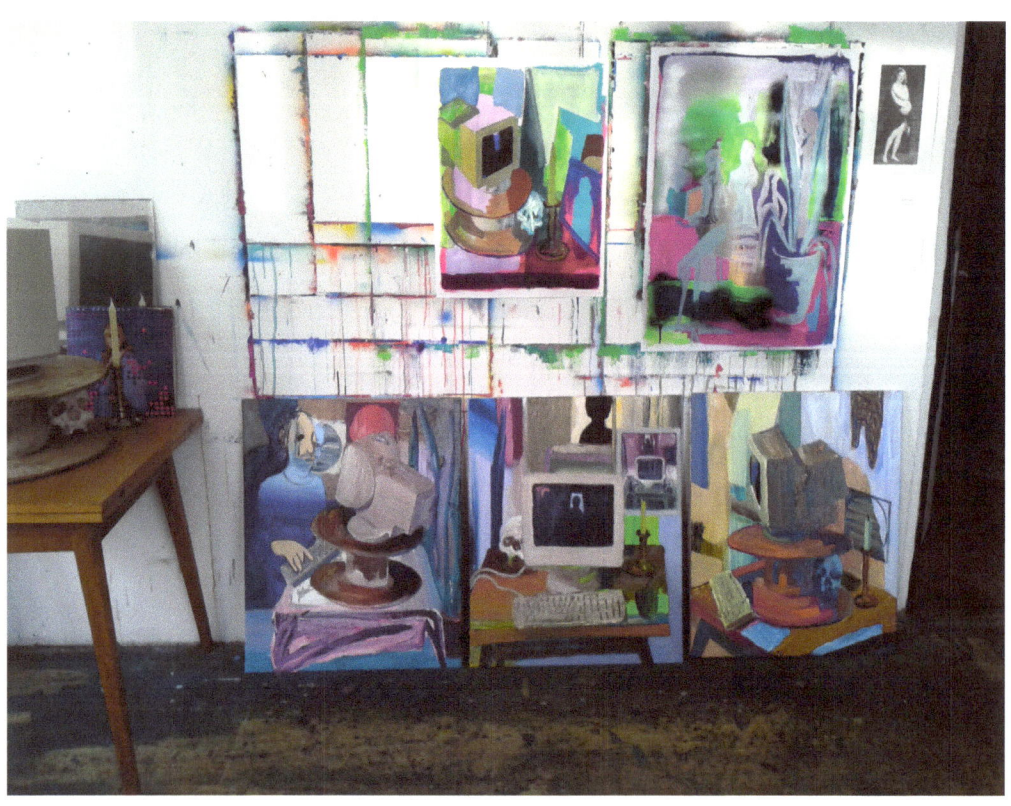

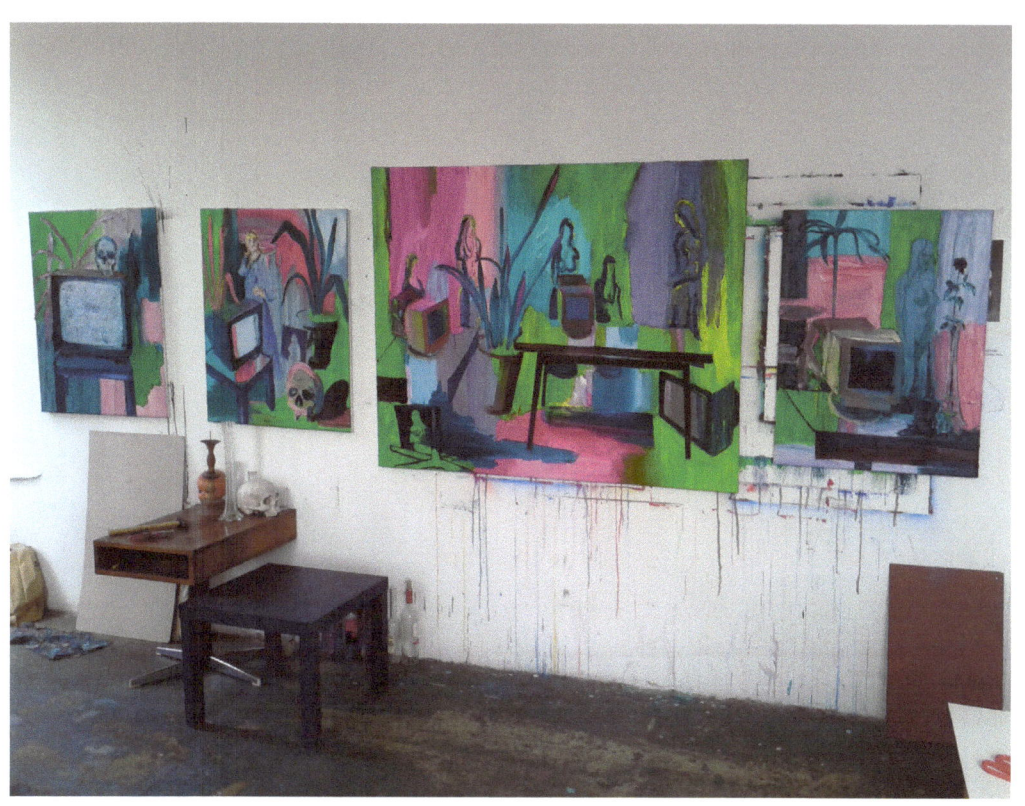

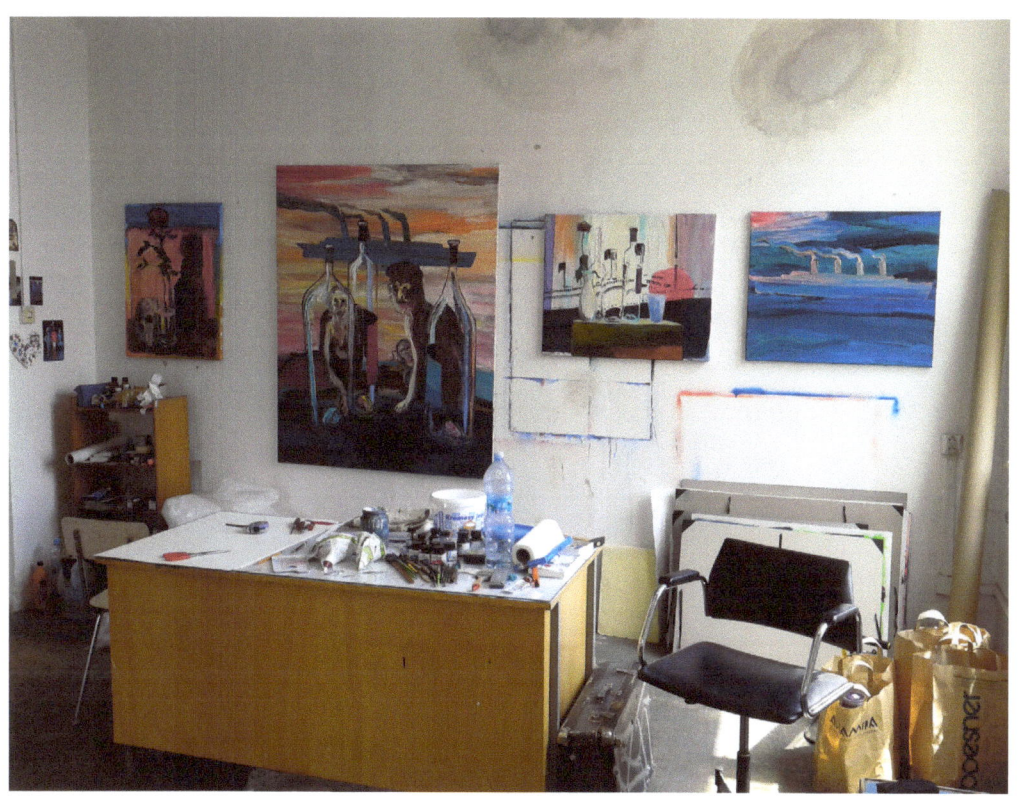

studio interiors

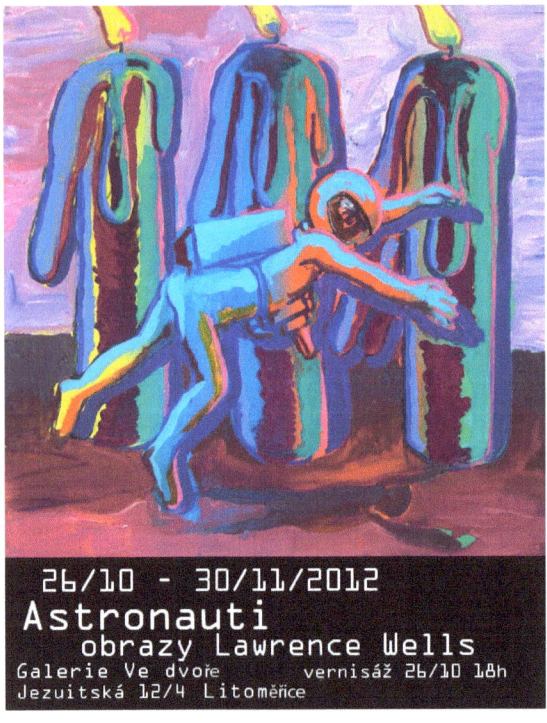

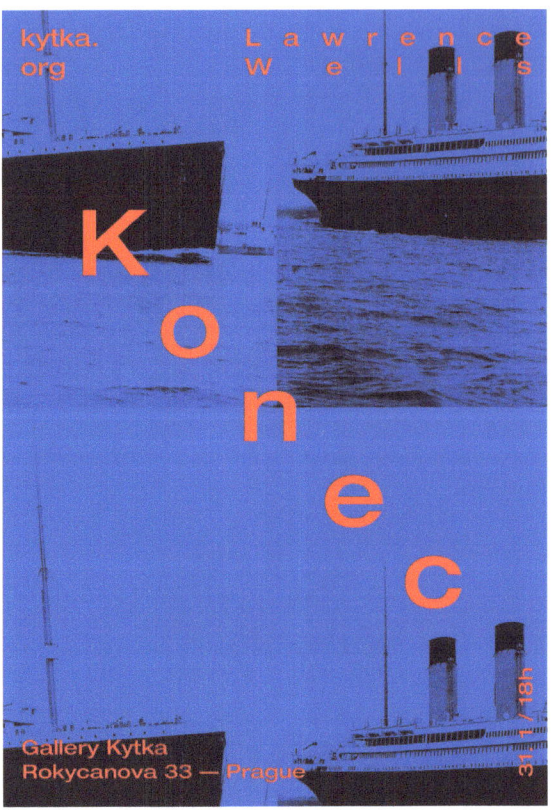

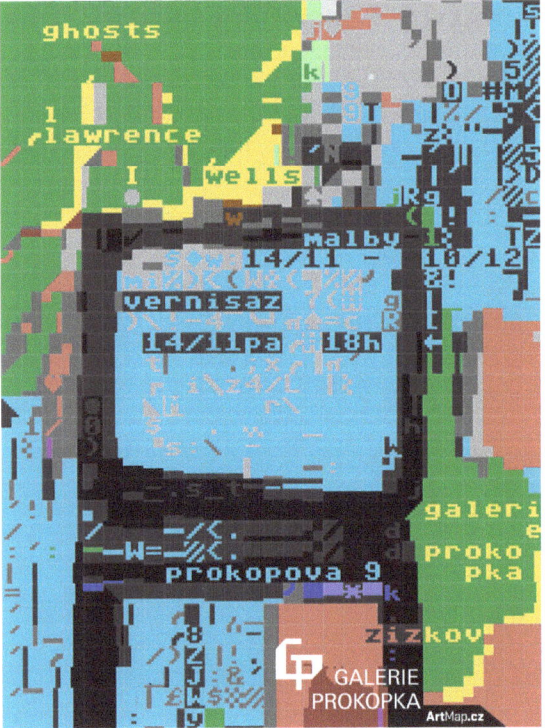

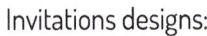

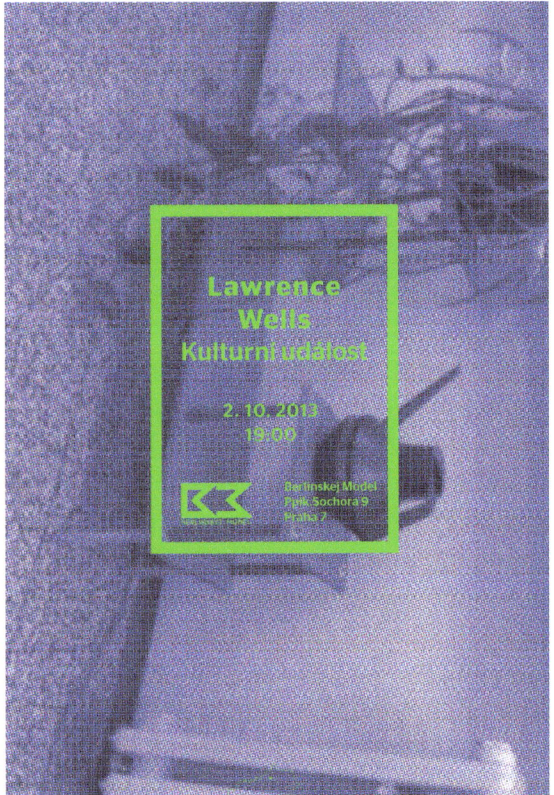

Invitations designs:
Lawrence Wells, Matěj Lacko, Richard Bakeš,
Daniel Vlček
This book documents six solo exhibitions
that Wells had in the Czech Republic from
2011–2014,

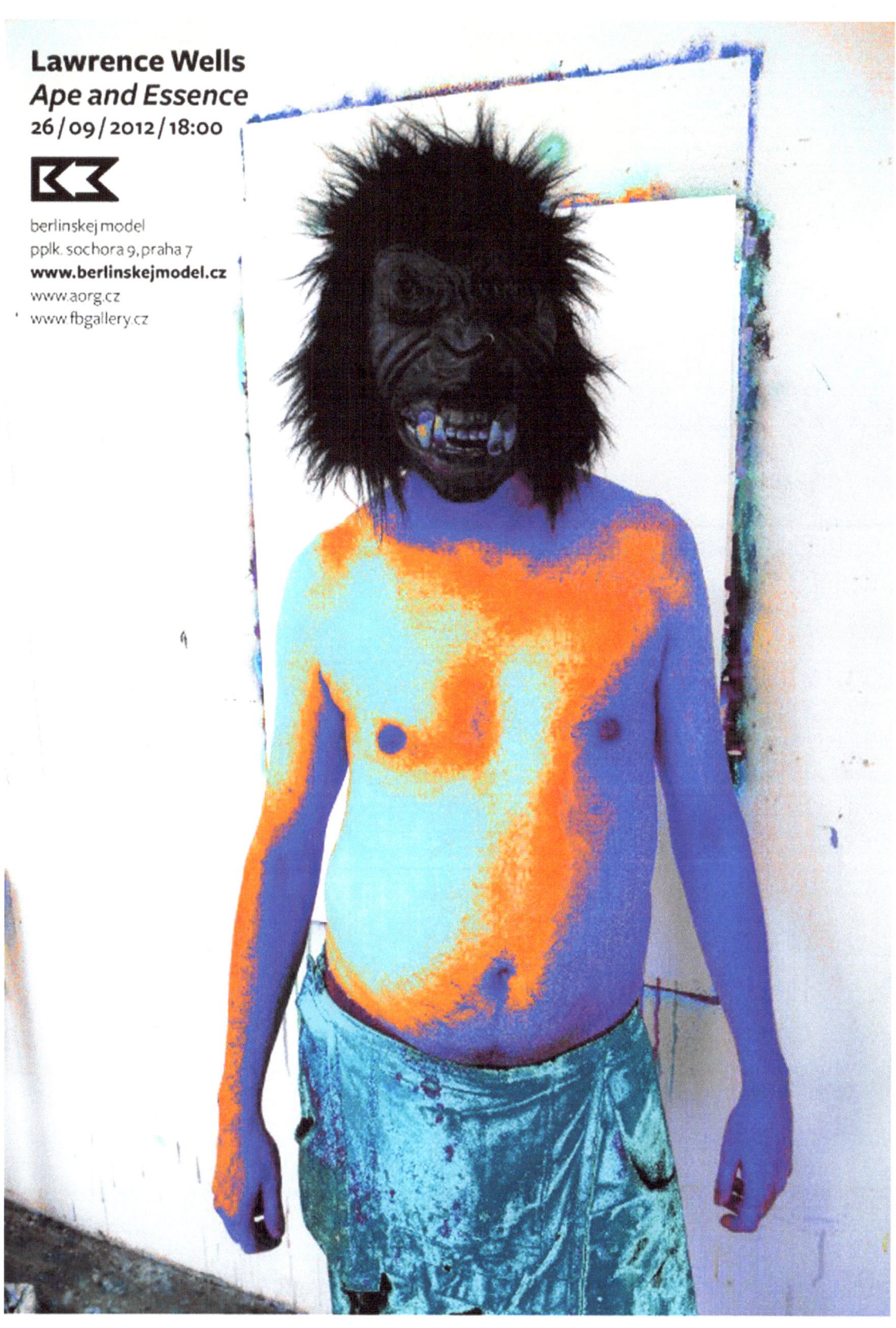

Lawrence Wells
Ape and Essence
26 / 09 / 2012 / 18:00

berlinskej model
pplk. sochora 9, praha 7
www.berlinskejmodel.cz
www.aorg.cz
www.fbgallery.cz

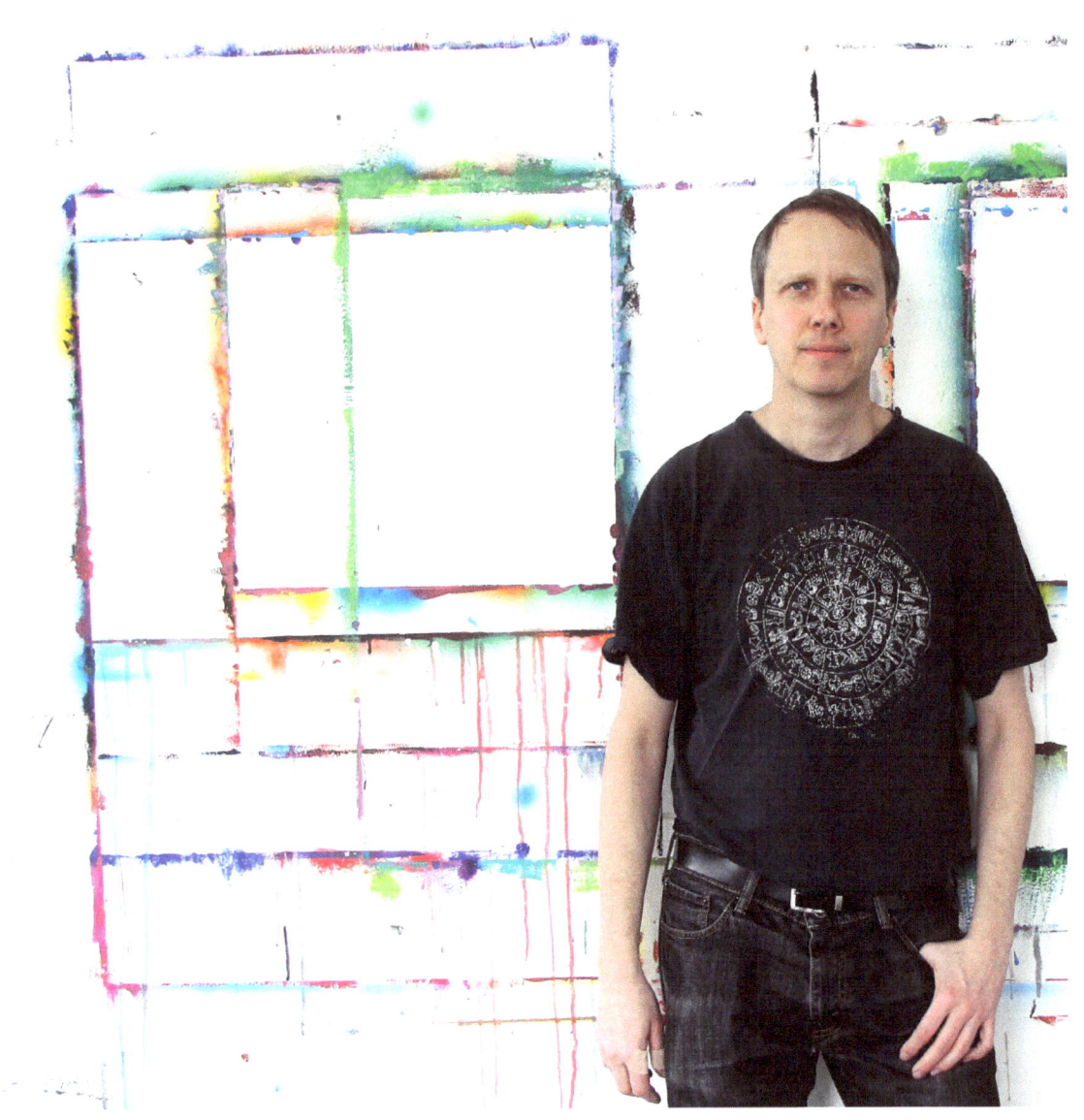

photo: Zdeněk Kovář

EXHIBITIONS

Lawrence Wells (b. 1965) is an American painter and long-term resident of the Czech Republic. He studied painting at Indiana University, and received his MFA from the University of Mississippi (1992). Wells was among the first wave of American expats to Prague in the early 90s. He returned to the USA in '93 and after 8 years, living in New Orleans and New York, he returned to Prague in 2001. In the years 2007–2008 he had a residency at Meet Factory. From his studio in the former industrial Prague district of Vysočany, Wells continues to exhibit in Europe and the USA.

Solo Shows

2014 "Ghosts", Galerie Prokopka, Prague, Czech Republic

2014 "Konec/The End". Galerie Kytka, Prague Czech Republic

2013 "Kulturní událost/Cultural Event", Berlinskej model, Prague, Czech Republic

2013 "Moon Monkey Candle", Galerie AM180, Prague, Czech Republic

2012 "Astronauts", Galerie Ve dvoře, Litoměřice, Czech Republic

2012 "Ape and Essence", Berlinskej model, Prague, Czech Republic

2009 Marathon, Prague, Czech Republic

2008 Marathon, Prague, Czech Republic

2007 Exit Gallery, Prague, Czech Republic

2006 Exit Gallery, Prague, Czech Republic

2004 Alternatiff Gallery, Prague, Czech Republic

2004 Hidden Gallery, Prague, Czech Republic

1997 Mermaid Gallery, New Orleans, LA

Group Shows

2013 "Global Locals", Galerie NTK, Prague, Czech Republic

2013 "45 Výstava", Pragovka, Prague, Czech Republic

2012 "My Wildlife as an Animal", Abrazo Interno Gallery, Clemente Soto Velez Center, New York, NY

2001 "Fuji Fox Freedom", Millennium Film, New York, NY

1998 "Internet List Show", National Institute of Health, Baltimore, MD

1996 Two Painters, Positive Space Gallery, New Orleans, LA

1993 American Exhibition, U Kralovsky Louky Gallery, Prague, Czech Republic

1993 "Tape Show", (Exhibitor/Curator), Asylum Gallery, Prague, Czech Republic

The author would like to thank the following people for their contributions to the book: Larry Wells, Ken Nash, Lisa Howorth, Branislava Kuburović, Matěj Lacko, Richard Bakeš, Daniel Vlček, Milan Mikuláštík, Zdeněk Kovář, Tomáš Roubal, David Adamec, Jere Allen, Bill Dunlap, Ondřej Bartoš, Anežka Hošková, Tomáš Turnovec, and my dear wife Magdalena Wells.